AUSTRALIA

Carl Robinson

Photography by Bill Bachman

Hong Kong

Reprint 1991

Grateful acknowledgement is made to the following authors and publishers
for permissions granted:

Pan Books (Australia) Pty Ltd for
The Bay of Contented Men © Robert Drewe 1989

J B Blackwell and Ruth Lockwood for
Alice on The Line by Doris Blackwell & Douglas Lockwood

Viking Penguin Inc. & Georges Borchardt for
The Songlines © Bruce Chatwin 1987

Collins Ltd, Angus & Robertson for
"Clancy of the Overflow" by A B Paterson © Retusa Pty Limited 1921

The Pub Owner's Wife from The Outback
© Thomas Keneally 1983 reprinted by permission of Tessa Sayle Agency

Distribution in the United Kingdom, Ireland, Europe, and certain Commonwealth
countries by Hodder and Stoughton, Mill Road, Dunton Green,
Sevenoaks, Kent TN13 2YA

Editor: Robyn Flemming
Picture Editor: Carolyn Watts
Map Design: Bai Yiliang
Design: Janice Lee
Cover Concept: Raquel Jaramillo and Aubrey Tse
Production House: Twin Age Limited, Hong Kong

British Library Cataloguing in Publication Data has been applied for.

Printed in Hong Kong

Carl Robinson is an American journalist who has lived in Australia since 1977. Born in the United States in 1943, he has spent most of his life overseas, growing up in the Belgian Congo (now Zaire) and then spending a dozen years in Asia, mostly in South Vietnam. He began his journalistic career in Saigon with the Associated Press (AP) in 1968 and covered the war in Vietnam, Laos and Cambodia until 1975. Posted by the AP to Sydney, he resigned one year later to live permanently in Australia and in 1979 became Special Correspondent for *Newsweek* magazine. In this capacity he travelled widely throughout Australia, New Zealand and the South Pacific. He has since retired to open a restaurant.

Robinson holds a BA (cum laude) in International Relations from the University of Redlands in California. He speaks French, Vietnamese and Swahili.

He and his Vietnamese-born wife, Kim-Dung, have three children—Laura, Alexander and Lincoln.

Contents

Special Topics

Maps

Remains of rural existence, South Australia
(Following pages) Based on a popular cartoon strip, the Ettamogah
Pub near Albury-Wodonga attracts a steady stream of visitors

Excerpts

(Clockwise from top) Roots of a ghost gum, or eucalypt, wind through a sandstone formation in central Australia; the only water for miles—a farmer's water tank on the Nullarbor Plain, South Australia; bracken, or fern, in a temperate forest of southeastern Australia

Introduction

Australians are a laconic people. They love to abbreviate words and to use nicknames; this saves them the trouble of uttering any more words than necessary. The name of their country is no exception, although some like to drawl Aus-tra-li-a out into four long syllables! So, for many Aussies, it is quite fashionable these days to call the place 'Oz'. They use the expression innocently enough. But with its imagery of the popular 1930s' movie *The Wizard of Oz*, the nickname neatly sums up a special quality about Australia. Stuck off in a far corner of the globe, the giant island-continent is literally a world apart. In many ways, to visit Australia is to pass through a time warp into a Land of Fantasy.

Although foreign visitors arriving in Sydney or Melbourne take some initial comfort in the European appearance of these cities, it does not take long to sense that there is something very different—even mysterious—about Australia. The seasons are reversed, the trees shed their bark rather than their leaves, and the native flowers have no smell. And then there are the strange Australian animals—not just the well-known kangaroo, koala and platypus, but wombats, bandicoots and Tasmanian devils as well. Even the light is different. In contrast to the northern hemisphere, the skies are a bright and dazzling blue. And at night, the heavens open up to reveal an incomparable view of the Milky Way galaxy and, below it, Australia's most enduring symbol, the Southern Cross.

Then, there is the land itself. Australia is the oldest continent on earth—and it shows. In Western Australia, the rocks of the Pilbara date back 3.5 billion years. The country has a flat, dry and worn-out appearance which newcomers, used to the dramatic landscapes of more geologically active continents, often find slightly disconcerting. In the deserts of central Australia, for example, all that remains of once-grand mountain ranges are circular-shaped ridges. From the air, they resemble massive skeletons bleached by the sun. Australia's forests of eucalypts, or gums, look scrawny and forlorn until one has had time to appreciate their stark beauty. Between its legendary golden beaches, much of Australia's coastline is craggy and rugged. Even the continent's original inhabitants, the Aborigines, have the appearance of an ancient people.

Australia's beauty is subtle. It comes from the continent's incomparable vastness, its distinct colours and its unique light. Visitors to Australia are soon seduced by its unique form of enchantment.

For a long time, this alien quality flatly discouraged any thoughts of European settlement. The place simply did not fit the early explorers' dreams of a gold-rich continent rumoured to exist in the far South Seas. Historians now agree that Portuguese explorers were the first Europeans to 'discover' Australia in the 16th century, with the Spanish dropping by shortly afterwards. They were followed by the Dutch who, in a burst of exploration in the 1600s, charted all but the east coast of what they called New Holland. They even discovered and named Van Diemen's Land, now the island of Tasmania. But they saw little of value in such a dry and desolate continent, much less in dealing with the continent's inhabitants. In one of the more infamous descriptions of the Aborigines from this era, an English buccaneer named William Dampier labelled them as 'the miserablest people on earth' who 'setting aside their human shape, differ little from brutes.'

It took another 100 years—and the famous English explorer James Cook—to do something about New Holland's lousy reputation. Approaching from a totally different direction, the explorer stumbled on to the continent's previously 'unknown' east coast. (Evidence now points to discovery of this coast by the Portuguese but, fearful of Spanish retribution, they kept it a secret.) The Great Navigator landed at Botany Bay near Sydney in April 1770 and, after sailing up the coast, came away with a radically different attitude from his predecessors. (Interestingly, Cook sailed right past Sydney's spectacular harbour, believing it to be only a small inlet.) 'In this extensive country, it can never be doubted but what sort of grain, fruits, roots etc of every kind would flourish here,' he wrote glowingly. In contrast to Dampier, and reflecting the by-then fashionable philosophy of the 'noble savage', Cook lavishly praised the Aborigines for their lack of materialism, describing them as 'far happier than we Europeans'. The explorer decided this was a place worth holding on to. At the northern tip of today's Queensland, Cook claimed his discovery for King George III and named it New South Wales.

But Cook quickly found that his enthusiasm to colonize the newly claimed and far-away continent was hardly shared by the bureaucracy back home. They sent Cook off on another long voyage and put his discovery on the back-burner. In a fascinating twist of history, it took the American War of Independence in 1776 to change official attitudes towards New South Wales. The revolt resulted in the loss not only of England's valuable American colonies but also its favourite dumping ground for its convicts. By the late 1780s, London had a real prison crisis on its hands. The solution, officials finally decided, was to turn Cook's discovery into a convict colony. It was the perfect island prison. On 26 January 1788, after eight months at sea, the First Fleet and its shipment of 750 convicts anchored in what is now Sydney Harbour, marking the start of European settlement of the continent. It was hardly an auspicious beginning.

Much happened over the next 200 years. As the following chapters will explain in detail, Australia was settled as a collection of separate British colonies. The rivalry between them was often fierce—and sometimes downright counter-productive. For example, they all selected different gauges for their respective rail systems. But, by the 1890s, a wider public sentiment began to prevail, and, after long negotiations and a referendum, the colonies agreed to a federation. On 1 January 1901, these new states became the independent Commonwealth of Australia, with the English monarch as head of state.

Today, Australia is still an adolescent country with a short, but often violent, history. In those early days of European settlement, the native Aborigines were driven nearly to extinction by disease and massacre. Taming the inhospitable land for farming and mining saw another form of violence, as did fighting the Empire's wars far from home. But the process produced a tough breed of people. Although a terrible defeat, the brave stand by the Australians on the shores of Gallipoli in the First World War—known as the ANZAC tradition—bonded Australia into a nation.

These days, that grim arrival of convicts back in 1788 is proudly celebrated every 26 January as Australia Day. For generations, Australians will dine out on personal memories of that grand day-long party in 1988 when an estimated two million people crowded around and on to Sydney Harbour to mark the official start of Australia's Bicentennial celebrations. Moreover, being able to trace one's ancestors back to those early convicts is now a matter of considerable pride.

Contrary to the popular view, however, most of Australia's 16.5 million inhabitants are not of convict origin. Within a generation, Australia—like the United States and Canada—had become a nation of migrants. At first, most of these new settlers came from Britain and Ireland. But, since the Second World War, Australia's ethnic mix has changed significantly, with millions of migrants arriving from eastern and southern European countries, the Middle East and, most recently, from Asia. Today, one in three Australians comes from a non-English-speaking background. As a result of this wave of migration, modern Australia—especially its cities—has a cosmopolitan feel that surprises many visitors. While the majority of Australians remain of Anglo-Celtic origin, modern Australia is a surprisingly multicultural society—and a remarkably successful one.

The Land of Oz qualities are also reflected in its people. Many visitors arrive believing that Australians are merely Down Under versions of Britons and Americans. Although there are some superficial comparisons with these other English-speaking peoples, Aussies are actually quite different and have their own distinctive national character—even a special way of speaking (see box). It is hard not to like the Australians. With the odd exception, they are a friendly, hospitable and fun-loving people who make visitors feel instantly at home, especially outside the country's major cities. Conversation comes easily and is often wildly humorous, especially if the beer is flowing. Australians have a strong egalitarian streak and everyone is a 'mate', from the prime minister on down. Their most scathing remarks are reserved for people caught boasting—or big-noting—themselves. And even if you do not always agree with them, Australians can be brutally honest and will rarely hesitate to speak their minds. They also have a healthy dose of cynicism and, as the nation's politicians know only too well, are a hard people to fool. Their heroes tend to be anti-authoritarian losers, such as the notorious 19th-century bandit Ned Kelly.

While these character traits are easy enough for outsiders to handle and even enjoy, others require a bit of care and understanding. Australians are notorious practitioners in the art of friendly verbal abuse, especially among themselves, and it is easy to get caught in the crossfire. But unless you have done something horribly wrong, when an Aussie calls you a 'bloody Pom' (English), a 'septic tank' (rhyming slang for Yank, or American), or even a 'bastard', he does not mean any offence. It is just his way of showing affection! At the same time, Australians can be scathingly self-deprecating, especially about their own country. After all my years in Australia, I wonder if this is not just their way of soliciting compliments from outsiders. But to be on the safe side, it is best not to agree with them. Instead, flatter them by saying what a great country Australia is!

Behind their frequently cynical and irreverent façade, Australians are extremely sensitive to how they are seen by the outside world. Where else, for example, are visiting entertainers, straight off the plane, constantly asked by serious journalists, 'How do you like Australia?' But Australians are an immensely proud people, even a touch arrogant at times. While not as openly patriotic as others, there is nothing quite like a sporting victory—especially against the English or Americans—to stir up the average Aussie. For example, when the 12-metre yacht *Australia II* dramatically won the America's Cup in 1983, ending the New York Yacht Club's 132-year hold on the coveted trophy, the entire country took the rest of the day off—with the personal permission of the prime minister. And in recent years, the keen interest overseas in all things Australian, following the success of the film *Crocodile Dundee*, has filled many Australians with pride at being 'The Flavour of the Month'.

While Australia and its people are indeed unique, it is worth pointing out that there is also a very serious side to life Down Under. (Many outsiders are surprised to hear, for example, that the country is one of the most heavily urbanized in the world, with 90 percent of its population living in cities.) As visitors quickly discover when they pick up their first Australian newspaper, Australia suffers from serious social and economic problems similar to other Western nations. It is a 'three-dimensional' country, with all the modern ills of drugs, crime and poverty. Even the environment is showing signs of man's abuse.

Compared to the alternatives, however, Australia does live up to its nickname of 'The Lucky Country'. Its people enjoy a casual, out-of-doors lifestyle. The climate is mild, the air and waters unpolluted and the streets relatively safe. There are not the extremes of wealth found in other countries. Most Australians are proudly, and conservatively, middle class, boasting the highest rate of home ownership in the world. With the exception of newly arrived migrants, they much prefer leisure to hard work. The average worker, for example, receives six weeks' vacation a year. And when they are on holidays, Australians pick up a 15 percent bonus on top of their regular pay.

Australia's passion for leisure means there is no shortage of attractions to tempt foreign visitors, who often have the impression that the whole country is on a permanent holiday. At the most sedentary level, there are Australia's colourful pubs (see box). For the price of arguably the best beers in the world, visitors can join one of the country's oldest institutions—the Drinking School—where everyone buys a round of drinks for his or her companions. Especially at weekends, many hotels offer free musical entertainment ranging from jazz and hard rock through to country and western. Bush music—using traditional instruments and tunes from England and Ireland—provides a particularly good insight into the Australian character and history.

Then, even if not always understandable to outsiders, a host of spectator sports—such as cricket and three types of football—are held throughout the year (see box). Australians are keen gamblers, and horse, harness and dog races take place almost daily. In recent years, legalized casinos have opened in many states.

For the more active, Australia's cities boast golf courses, tennis and squash courts, and cycling tracks. With so many parks, joggers always have room to run. Out of town, bushwalking, or hiking, and snow skiing are popular activities. And, not surprisingly for the world's biggest island, the Australians' greatest love is the water. 'Chucking a sickie'—phoning in sick and then disappearing to the beach or the yacht for the rest of the day—is a national affliction, especially on those incomparable bright summer days. For many Australians, Christmas Day is not complete without a barbecue at their favourite beach. (But for some, a big meal in the middle of summer is just not quite right; they have started a tradition of celebrating Christmas in the middle of the southern winter!)

Such choices are challenge enough for any tourist. But an even more challenging feature about the country—and one rarely appreciated before the visitor arrives—is Australia's sheer size and variety of places to see. The continent is as large as the United States or all of Europe—and not nearly as easy to explore. If anything, with few expressways and most people living in the coastal cities, Australia feels even larger.

There is a lot more to Australia than the vast and desolate Outback, and the problem for the visitor is what, or how much, to see in a limited period of time. As this guide will describe, Australia has everything from sophisticated cities to one-pub towns, with the climate ranging from the temperate southeast to the stifling tropics of northern Australia. In the winter months, for example, you can snuggle up next to a log fire in a Tasmanian 'bed-and-breakfast' one day and be snorkelling along the Great Barrier Reef the next. And in summer, you can go just as quickly from lying on a deserted beach to climbing majestic Ayers Rock in the desert centre of Australia. On the other hand, you may simply want to pick one spot and stay there for your entire holiday.

Although Australia's attractions are primarily scenic, the country also has a fascinating history—both before and after European settlement—that is also well worth exploring. Spurred on by the recent Bicentennial, Australians are now examining themselves as never before. You will not see many brass plaques or billboards pointing out items of interest, but there is no shortage of detailed histories and guides to help you. Make a habit of browsing through news agencies and book shops. Information Centres—denoted by the international symbol of a lower-case 'i'—also make good stops. The staff are polite and always ready to help, especially if you are visiting from overseas.

Given Australia's huge size, there are obvious limitations to a book of this kind. Even in an entire lifetime, there is always more to see in Australia, another little corner to explore—and enough to fill volumes. But for the visitor with a sense of adventure and a bit of time, it is hoped that this guide will help to narrow down the formidable choices Australia has to offer.

Australia

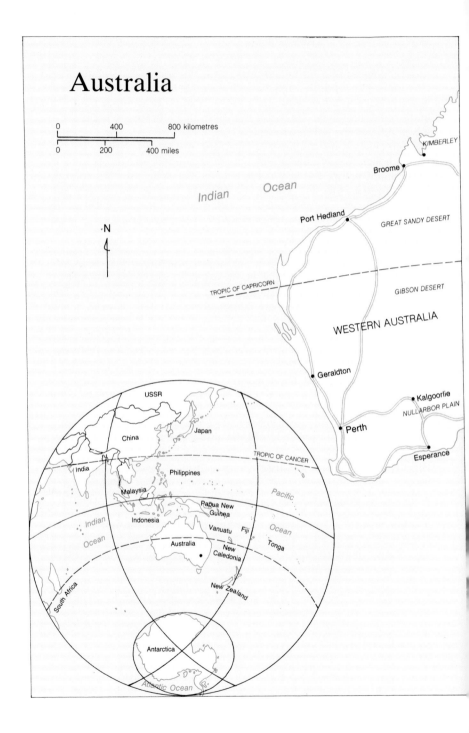

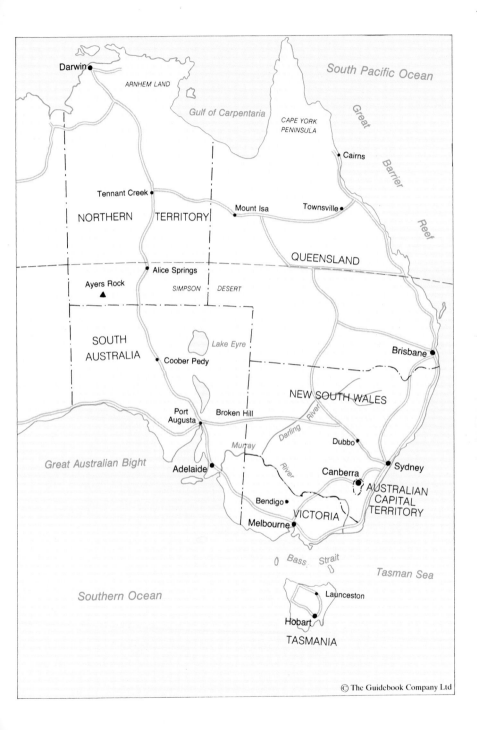

Darwin

ARNHEM LAND

Gulf of Carpentaria

South Pacific Ocean

CAPE YORK
PENINSULA

Cairns

Great

Barrier

Tennant Creek

NORTHERN   TERRITORY

Mount Isa

Townsville

QUEENSLAND

Reef

Alice Springs

Ayers Rock

SIMPSON   DESERT

SOUTH
AUSTRALIA

Lake Eyre

Coober Pedy

Brisbane

NEW SOUTH WALES

Port
Augusta

Broken Hill

Darling   River

Dubbo

Murray

Great Australian Bight

Adelaide

River

Canberra

Sydney

AUSTRALIAN
CAPITAL
TERRITORY

Bendigo

VICTORIA

Melbourne

Bass   Strait

Tasman Sea

Southern Ocean

Launceston

Hobart

TASMANIA

© The Guidebook Company Ltd

Facts for the Traveller

Getting There

As a result of Australia's recent tourist boom, now running at over two million visitors a year, getting there has never been easier. The bad news is that, unless you are flying in by chartered Concorde, no one has yet found a way to make the trip any shorter. So be prepared for a good dose of jet lag after your arrival.

By Air

Qantas, Australia's international carrier, flies into Sydney, Melbourne, Adelaide, Perth, Brisbane, Cairns, Townsville and Darwin from the United States and Canada, plus several European, Asian and South Pacific nations. (The airline also runs a weekly service from Harare, Zimbabwe, to Perth and on to the east coast, and the domestic carrier, Australian Airlines, links Hobart, Tasmania, with Christchurch, New Zealand.) In addition, airlines from those countries have regular flights into Australia. Connections are also provided by Air New Zealand.

For those looking for more exotic approaches, Aerolinas Argentina runs regular flights from Buenos Aires over Antarctica to Auckland, New Zealand. Air Nuigini, Papua New Guinea's national airline, flies into Australia through Port Moresby from Asia and Hawaii. Royal Air Brunei provides a back-door connection into Darwin. At the moment, 33 international airlines fly into Australia and by the 1990s this is expected to rise to over 40. The government has also recently opened the door to charter operators such as Austria's Lauda Air.

Air fares to Australia are comparatively expensive, and travellers should shop around before purchasing their tickets. Because of strong competition between airlines, this can often mean considerable savings. Fares also vary according to the flying season, time of purchase and duration of stay. During the Australian summer—from December to March—flights are heavily booked and reservations should be made well in advance.

Travellers can make other savings by paying for as many features of their trip as possible in advance, such as internal flights, hotels and car rentals.

By Sea

While some 99 percent of tourists arrive in Australia by air, it is still possible to arrive in this old-fashioned way. The easiest way is to catch a liner heading Down Under for the summer cruising season. (From Sydney and other ports, the vessels then take passengers on cruises of the South Pacific and Asia.) The main companies offering passage are the Royal Viking Line, P&O and CTC (the Soviet cruise company). All three offer cruises—beginning in November or December—from England and the United States to Australia. In addition, Royal Viking has an annual cruise from Hong Kong, and you can also board a CTC liner on the return leg of its annual return-cruise from Australia to Asia. Other options include the Italian-owned Achille Lauro's annual cruise around the Cape of Good Hope to Australia and occasional world cruises via Australia by Cunard, including its flagship the *QEII*, and Royal Viking. Freighters calling into Australian ports are another, but more difficult, possibility.

Some tourists also arrive on private yachts, but entry requirements are quite strict. Only a limited number of ports can be used, and prior notification of arrival is required for customs and immigration checks.

The same visa requirements apply as for air travellers.

Visas

Visas are required for all travellers, except for New Zealand citizens, and are available from all Australian diplomatic missions overseas. Maximum stay is six months, extendable under special circumstances. But on-the-spot 72-hour transit visas are available for those with confirmed onward bookings.

As an island-continent, Australia is free of many diseases, such as rabies. To keep it that way, tough quarantine rules apply. For that reason, your aircraft will be sprayed with disinfectant either en route to Australia or immediately after landing. The importation of food, animals and plant products is strictly controlled. Smallpox and yellow fever vaccinations are required for all travellers arriving from infected countries.

There are no import restrictions on currency, but travellers are not permitted to take out more than A$5,000 in Australian currency. Customs allows duty-free importation of one litre of alcohol, 250 cigarettes or 200 grams of tobacco, and goods up to a value of A$400.

Getting Around

To make a trip to Australia truly enjoyable, visitors should schedule the maximum amount of time possible. A one-week holiday hardly allows enough time to recover from jet-lag. But even after longer stays, many visitors—and long-term foreign residents—depart feeling that they have barely scratched the surface of such a large and varied continent. But do not drive yourself too hard; you can always come back later for another look.

There are endless ways to get around the vast continent of

Australia—everything from simple hitch-hiking to luxurious chartered jet. The country boasts a modern transportation system offering efficient air, rail and bus services. There is also an extensive road system that includes some expressways. For those with only a limited amount of time, the best way to see Australia is to fly to a destination and then rent a car.

By Air
Australian Airlines and Ansett are the country's two major domestic air carriers, flying into all major cities. (Qantas also flies domestic passengers but only in conjunction with international travel.) With their extensive networks, the two domestic airlines offer reasonably priced packages that allow travellers to make several stops without backtracking, such as Sydney to Alice Springs and then on to Cairns. They also offer round-Australia tickets for about A$1,000—a real bargain. Also, for those who prefer to work out their itinerary after they have arrived, a 25 percent discount on internal air travel is available upon presentation of your airline ticket and passport.

East-West Airlines and a score of smaller state-based airlines, some

affiliated with Australian Airlines and Ansett, service regional centres.

By overseas standards, internal flights in Australia are relatively expensive. But fares should drop with the deregulation of the airline industry in November 1990 and the introduction of new carriers and competition.

For well-heeled adventurers, several operators run all-inclusive flying tours around Australia, ranging from one to two weeks in duration. Using old DC-3s or other prop-driven aircraft which fly low over the countryside, such tours are an excellent way to visit the more remote parts of Australia. (Melbourne-based Air Adventure Australia, for example, runs tours to over a dozen destinations, from the Great Barrier Reef across the Outback to Broome and the Bungle Bungles of Western Australia, with prices ranging from A$3,000 to $5,000.)

By Rail

Rail services link all of Australia's mainland capital cities, except for Darwin. They provide a comfortable and relaxing way to travel around Australia, although the quality of the trains themselves can vary considerably.

Few would argue, however, that the *Indian-Pacific*, which runs between Perth and Sydney, ranks as one of the great railway journeys of the world. The 4,000-kilometre (2,500-mile) transcontinental voyage from the Indian to the Pacific Ocean takes three days. The *Ghan*, which replaced the romantic narrow-gauge *Old Ghan* in the early 1980s, makes a two-day run from Sydney to Alice Springs in central Australia. Both provide modern first- and economy-class accommodation but are more expensive than flying. The pub car, with its own piano and well-stocked bar, is a popular spot on these trains to socialize and watch the endless countryside roll by.

Other lines connect the major cities of southeastern Australia and, from those, services run out into the country centres. For the more adventurous, Queensland Railways runs a narrow-gauge service from Brisbane all the way up to Cairns, including a six-day 'Daylight Rail Tour' that stops at first-class hotels and resorts along the way. All state-run railways offer special passes of various duration as well as package tours.

By Bus

Bus travel is another alternative, especially for travellers with more time than money. Modern buses, some equipped with their own video systems, travel around virtually the whole country. Because of intense competition, fares are much cheaper than rail travel. Special passes, ranging up to a month, offer considerable savings and allow you to make as many stops as you wish. Be warned, however, that some of those long runs through the flat and desolate Outback can be quite a strain. In early 1988, in far-western Queensland, one desperate German tourist on a bus stripped off his clothing, ordered the bus driver to stop, then ran off into the bush—never to be seen again.

More upmarket, a number of companies—such as Australian Pacific—provide guided bus and four-wheel-drive safari tours through the Australian Outback. By day, the tours take in various sights, stopping frequently for hikes or a swim. In the late afternoon, the vehicles pull into a campsite where travellers pitch their own tents before sitting down to a hearty meal and an evening around the campfire.

By Car

For those who prefer to travel independently, an excellent way to set your own pace and itinerary is to rent a car or campervan. Major car rental companies offer reasonably priced weekly and monthly rates. (In most cases, a valid foreign driving licence is accepted, but it is best to come equipped with an International Driver's Licence as well.) For a small additional charge, the companies allow the vehicle to be dropped off in another city.

Especially in the southeastern corner of Australia, doing your own driving is a great way to see the most of the countryside in a short period of time. Here, as in the rest of Australia, there are always plenty of motels or caravan parks in which to spend the night. Hiring your own vehicle, even just for a weekend, is also a convenient way to explore the area around cities you have reached by air, rail or bus travel. The only serious problem—especially for Americans and Europeans—is learning to drive on the 'wrong', or left, side of the road. (A quick word of warning: if you are driving, do not drink. All the states have tough drink-driving laws that allow police to pull over motorists at any time for breath-testing.)

Getting around Australia's cities is not nearly so tricky. All major cities and holiday spots offer a wide variety of guided bus tours to points of interest. As most are located on rivers or harbours, there are also guided water tours. The cities also provide a wide range of public transport. Some are tourist attractions in their own right, such as the Melbourne trams, Sydney's monorail and the Sydney Harbour ferries. Although Australia's cities sprawl out in all directions, their downtown areas are quite compact and perfect for walking tours.

Captain Cook on his Hosts...

From what I have said of the Natives of New Holland they may appear to some to be the most wretched People upon Earth; but in reality they are far more happier than we Europeans, being wholly unacquainted not only with the Superfluous, but with the necessary Conveniences so much sought after in Europe; they are happy in not knowing the use of them. They live in a Tranquility which is not disturbed by the Inequality of Condition. The earth and Sea of their own accord furnishes them with all things necessary for Life. They covet not Magnificent Houses, Household-stuff, etc; they live in a Warm and fine Climate, and enjoy every wholesome Air, so that they have very little need of Clothing; and this they seem to be fully sencible of, for many to whom we gave Cloth, etc, left it carelessly upon the Sea beach and in the Woods, as a thing they had no manner of use for; in short, they seem'd to set no Value upon any-thing we gave them, nor would they ever part with anything of their own for any one Article we could offer them. This, in my opinion, Argues that they think themselves provided with all the necessarys of Life, and that they have no Superfluities.*

Captain Cook, Captain Cook's Journal During His First Voyage Round The World Made In HM Bark 'Endeavour'

. . . and a Note from the Editor

* The native Australians may be happy in their condition, but they are without doubt among the lowest of mankind. Confirmed cannibals, they lose no opportu-nity of gratifying their love of human flesh. Mothers will kill and eat their own children, and the women again are often mercilessly illtreated by their lords and masters. There are no chiefs, and the land is divided into sections, occupied by families, who consider everything in their district as their own. Internecine war exists between the different tribes, which are very small. Their treachery, which is unsurpassed, is simply an outcome of their savage ideas, and in their eyes is a form of independence which resents any intrusion on their land, their wild animals, and their rights generally. In their untutored state they therefore consider that any method of getting rid of the invader is proper. Both sexes, as Cook observed, are absolutely nude, and lead a wandering life, with no fixed abode, subsisting on roots, fruits, and such living things as they can catch. Nevertheless....

Captain W J L Wharton, RN, FRS (in the 1893 edition)

General Information

Health

Ironically, Australia's biggest health hazard is one of its main attractions—its legendary sunshine. The country has the dubious honour of having the world's highest skin cancer rate. This is perhaps hardly surprising for a nation whose leisure focuses so heavily on sun-baking at the beach. But Australia does have a lot of sunlight and, especially for those arriving from the northern hemisphere, sunburn can strike quickly. When spending prolonged periods out of doors, use a strong sun-block cream. Or, better yet, get into that Aussie invention, zinc cream, now available in five psychedelic colours as well as the standard white. The brilliant sunshine is also a good excuse to pick up an Australian-made hat.

Another serious health hazard comes from the country's unique wildlife. Australia has poisonous spiders, such as the Redback and Trapdoor, whose sting can cause death unless the patient is given immediate treatment. The same applies to the Tai Pan snake, reputedly the most poisonous in the world. At the beach, care must be taken against stinging jellyfish, the blue-ringed octopus and poisonous fish. Sharks are also a hazard, although actual attacks are rare. Many popular city beaches are equipped with shark nets, and boat and aerial patrols keep them away from other beaches. In Australia's northern tropics, marauding crocodiles are a growing menace. While signs warning against swimming in such waters make a nice souvenir picture, they are no joking matter. When walking through the bush, keep an eye out for the wide-leafed 'stinging tree' which causes excruciating pain that lasts for hours.

Finally, while more of a nuisance than a health hazard, Australia is notorious for its flies, especially in summer. (The habit of waving them out of the way is called the 'Australian salute'.) Mosquitoes are also a problem, even in subtropical areas, but are not infectious. The best protection is insect repellent.

Tourists to Australia are not entitled to Medicare, the government-funded national health care scheme, so you should check with your own medical insurance company for coverage during your visit. But excellent medical facilities are available throughout the country. For simple consultations, medical practitioners charge a standard fee of around A\$20.

Jet Lag

Everyone has a pet theory about dealing with this affliction. In a world-first, an Australian scientist has even invented a jet lag pill, now undergoing testing. But until it is widely available, the best advice is to stay awake as late as you can after you arrive. (Most planes from overseas arrive early in the morning.) Then, get a good 14 hours' sleep and you will wake up the next morning in the local time zone. Midday naps help to fill in the blanks. Above all, do not try to sleep if you can't sleep.

Climate and Clothing

Australia has a wide range of climates. In the southeastern corner of the continent and the southwestern corner of Western Australia, there are four distinct seasons. In winter (June – August), temperatures can drop to below freezing in Tasmania and the mountainous regions of the mainland, including the capital city, Canberra. In cities such as Sydney, Melbourne, Adelaide and Perth, winter temperatures rarely drop below 7°C (49°F). In summer (December – March), temperatures in these regions can soar to above 38°C (100°F). In the tropical north, the climate is similar to that of Southeast Asia and is dictated by the rainy (November – April) and dry (May – October) seasons. In the desert country of central Australia, temperatures in summer may rise to above 38°C (100°F), and while the winters are decidedly milder, the nights can be quite chilly.

Consequently, clothing will depend very much on when and where you plan to visit. In the summer months, and all year round in the tropics, pack light clothing and, if you want to blend in with the locals, bring along your favourite T-shirts and shorts. But even in summer, temperatures can drop sharply in the evenings so do include a light jacket or sweater. If you are planning to go out on the water or into monsoon country, a waterproof windbreaker is always useful. For winter visits to the southeast, pack a heavier coat and your favourite sweater. Because homes in Australia are not centrally heated, you often need a sweater even indoors.

Currency

Australia has a metric system and the Australian dollar is the official currency. A floating exchange rate applies. Avoid exchanging currency at hotels or airports, where the rates are generally not as favourable, and use banks instead, all of which are authorized exchange agents. Travellers' cheques receive a higher rate than currency. All major credit cards (Amex, Diners, Visa and MasterCard) are widely accepted throughout Australia. The currency is decimal, and notes are denominated in $100, $50, $20, $10 and $5. Coins run from the fairly useless 1- and 2-cent pieces to 5-, 10-, 20- and 50-cent coins. In recent years, the government has issued $1 and $2 coins. The controversial $2 coin, introduced in 1988, is as small as a 2- and 5-cent piece, although of a different colour and slightly thicker.

Tipping

Tipping is not traditional in Australia, although that is starting to change. The most common explanation for this is that Australia's powerful unions have guaranteed that service industry workers are well paid, with generous penalty rates, or extra pay, for night and weekend work. For a long time, the only exception was the well-established tradition of bar patrons leaving behind small change when buying drinks. Taxi drivers do not expect tips but are thankful for small change. Tipping in restaurants has become more widespread, and is usually 10 percent of the bill. Porters have set fees, but a tip of between 50 cents and one dollar is sufficient for hotel staff. The best advice is to be selective. If you are pleased, by all means tip. Otherwise, even in restaurants, don't feel obliged.

Etiquette

Australians do not stand on ceremony and are very informal. When alone in a taxi, you are expected to sit up front with the driver. Conversation comes easy with Australians, and the use of first names is common. If invited to a home for dinner or a barbecue, bring along a bottle of wine or several cans of beer.

While businessmen still tend to favour conservative dark suits, Australians are generally casual dressers. Few restaurants will refuse you service for not wearing a coat and tie. But you may be tossed out if you are too casual, such as arriving in the standard Aussie summer uniform of shorts, singlet and thongs. The operative expression at many establishments these days is 'neat casual'.

Communications

Australia has a world-class communications system. Most countries can be dialled direct from hotel rooms and many public phone booths. Reverse-charge, or collect, calls are put through quickly. (Local calls cost 30 cents.) Telegrams, telexes and facsimiles can be sent through Australia Post and the Overseas Telecommunications Corporation (OTC). Several private companies also provide such services. In addition to stamps, Australia Post sells a wide variety of padded envelopes, cardboard boxes and mailing tubes that are ideal for shipping souvenirs and gifts home. Airfreight, including the shipment

of documents, is handled by several major forwarding companies, with most offering door-to-door service.

National Holidays

Australians love their leisure time, and there is no shortage of long weekends and holidays throughout the year. In addition, most workers receive an average of six weeks' vacation time a year. Summer—when the children are on school vacation—is their favourite time off. (Also, many factories close down for the entire month of January.) The school year is divided into four terms, or semesters, with two-week breaks whose dates vary according to the state. Summer vacations run from mid-December until early February.

Australians celebrate Christmas, New Year and Easter as holidays, usually with an extra day off. The closest Australia has to a national holiday is Australia Day on 26 January, the date marking the beginning of European settlement in 1788. But until the Australian Bicentennial in 1988, it was rarely celebrated with much enthusiasm. Anzac Day on 25 April, marking the anniversary of the ill-fated landing of Australian and New Zealand, or ANZAC, troops at Gallipoli in 1915, honours the nation's military past. The day begins with solemn services and street parades and ends with joyous reunions of old 'diggers', or soldiers. The Queen's Birthday is marked with a long weekend in June. A ban on firecrackers has lately turned this into a more subdued holiday.

Australia's most widely celebrated informal holiday is the first Tuesday in November when the entire country stops for the running of the Melbourne Cup, the country's leading horse-race. While it is a formal holiday in the Victorian capital, not much work is done anywhere else. People run office 'sweeps', or draws, attend luncheons or head for the pub to watch the famous two-minute race.

The Media

Australia's media provides a comprehensive coverage of the outside world, so you need not worry about losing touch. There is a national newspaper, *The Australian*, and the major city newspapers such as *The Sydney Morning Herald* and *The Age* in Melbourne are worth reading. (The afternoon tabloids are less newsworthy.) The Australian Broadcasting Corporation (ABC) is the local equivalent of the BBC and has a strong reputation for its impartiality and reliability. Its radio and television stations blanket the country. The Special Broadcasting Service (SBS), the government-funded multicultural station, runs quality imported programmes and excellent foreign news and commentary. Commercially-owned radio and television stations provide a steady diet of news, talk-back, sports and entertainment. For the visitor, watching television commercials can be more fun than the programmes, which tend to be American or British. Satellite links keep Australia in instant touch with the world. If you are up late and cannot sleep, the American NBC's 'Today Show' comes on at midnight. Many overseas sporting events, such as grand prix racing, the Super Bowl and the World Series, are broadcast live.

Shopping

For the souvenir-hunting tourist, Australia offers a lot more than just its famous stuffed koalas. Do not worry, there are still plenty of these popular Aussie-style teddy bears around. Made from kangaroo skin, they range all the way up to the giant-size model which will almost need an aircraft seat to itself when you leave. Some even have music boxes inside that play *Waltzing Matilda*. There are also many ordinary stuffed animals for sale, one of the cutest being the chunky marsupial known as the wombat.

There is no shortage of souvenir shops around the country. They are stocked with the usual kitschy stuff, much of it made outside Australia, but they also have quite tasteful locally made souvenirs. For better-quality goods, visit the large department stores, such as Grace Bros, David Jones and Myers, or the wide variety of chic boutiques and speciality shops. Art galleries and antique shops are well worth browsing through. (Shopping hours are generally 9 to 5 on weekdays, with a half-day on Saturday.) Many cities and towns have colourful weekend markets, such as Paddy's Market in Sydney and the Fremantle markets, which offer a wide range of souvenirs. These often provide the only retail outlet for many Australian-made arts and crafts, such as leather work and porcelain. Even if you are not buying anything, these markets are always full of atmosphere.

As elsewhere, there is a wide range of T-shirts and sweatshirts to show friends and relatives back home where you have been. Some are quite artistic and colourful, such as those by Ken Done and aboriginal artists. Others are just plain clever, like printing the words 'Down Under' upside down, or 'Downundaland', a play on the name of the primeval land mass from which Australia originated, Gondwanaland. In central Australia, where flies can be a real nuisance, you can buy a T-shirt painted with the insects. And then, there are those that are utterly tasteless—like the blood-splattered T-shirts that give you the appearance of having been attacked by a shark or a crocodile.

On a more serious level, Australia manufactures excellent outdoor gear which reflects the country's rugged pioneer history. Many items are already exported and gaining wide popularity overseas. But for the visitor, not only are there considerable savings to be had but also a wider choice. For something distinctly Australian, pick up an 'Akubra' hat. Made of rabbit fur, these cowboy-style hats come in a wide range of models, each with its own name. (The company, which can barely keep up with the demand, also makes the famous Australian Army 'digger' hat with the flipped-up brim.)

Equally distinctive is an oilskin raincoat first worn by the horsemen of Australia's mountain country and later popularized by the movie *The Man from Snowy River*. Sold under the label 'Dryzabone' (for 'dry as a bone'), they are guaranteed to keep you dry, even in the heaviest downpour. Then, there are warm wool-lined leather vests and coats, tough coalmen's jackets and durable moleskin trousers. R.M. Williams outlets are good one-stop stores to purchase such gear, although they are also available in other stores.

Australia's early prosperity as a British colony came from its successful breeding of the Merino sheep. This is reflected today in a wide range of woollen products. For keeping your feet warm in winter, pick up a pair of 'Ug boots'. ('Ug' stands for 'ugly'.) Rather crude and functional in appearance, these sheepskin boots come in several models and are extremely comfortable for wearing around the house. Wool seat covers look particularly good in the car back home, and throw-rugs add an extra touch around the house. Australian-made wool sweaters are good bargains. If you are looking for something artistic and very Australian, there are well-known designer Jenny Kee's bright and colourful sweaters illustrated with animals, flowers and other patterns.

The country is famous for the opals that come from wild and rustic Outback settlements like Coober Pedy and Lightning Ridge. Every major city in Australia has several outlets specializing in opals and other precious stones such as emeralds and sapphires. They are sold either unmounted or in jewellery, some quite tastefully designed by local artisans. But these stones can be quite pricey and rip-offs are not unknown. So, do shop around. Australia also mines the world's only 'pink diamonds', in the Kimberley region of Western Australia. They are still quite rare—and expensive.

In recent years, Australia's Aboriginal communities have experienced a cultural renaissance. In the process, they have also learned the value of selling their artifacts to tourists. Galleries specializing in their artwork have sprung up all over Australia, many run by the Aborigines themselves. The most stunning are acrylic paintings from central Australia known as the Papunya School, which

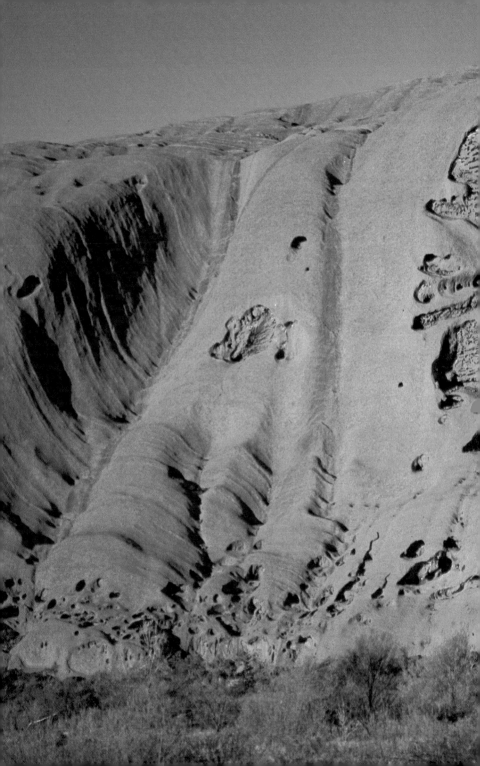

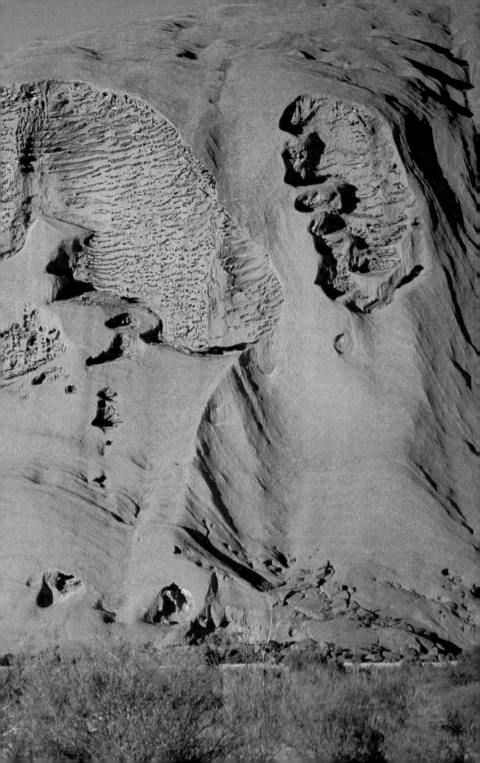

are gaining a wide following overseas. In a style reminiscent of the *pointillisme* style of the French Impressionists, these paintings are derived from ancient sand paintings and depict legends from the Aborigines' legendary 'Dreamtime'. Alice Springs is the best place to purchase these paintings. Other Aboriginal artifacts worth buying are bark paintings from the Northern Territory's Arnhemland and wooden carvings of animals and food bowls. Boomerangs, complete with throwing directions, are available throughout Australia.

Finally, if you want to take advantage of your liquor allowance at customs on arriving home, buy up a few bottles—or a cask—of Australian wine. Port and rum also make good drinkable souvenirs.

Food and Drink

Australia does not really have a national cuisine. But that hardly means it is no fun to dine out, although the level of service does attract frequent criticism. While many old-timers can still recall the days when the best meal out was the Sunday roast over at grandma's place, the restaurant scene has changed dramatically in recent decades. Much of this has come from the successive waves of migrants from Europe, the Middle East and Asia who have arrived in the country since the Second World War. They have applied and refined their recipes to exploit Australia's incredibly rich mixture of fresh ingredients. As a result, Australia today has an astounding variety of restaurants. In addition to the popular international-style cuisine, the choices range from Italian and Greek through to Lebanese and Indian and on to Chinese, Japanese, Thai and Vietnamese.

Australia is justifiably famous for its seafood. Many establishments serve nothing else, while others—including most ethnic restaurants—feature seafood prominently on their menus. The best introduction to Australia's unique selection, and a standard feature of seafood restaurants, is the ubiquitous 'seafood platter'. (These are usually for a minimum of two people and come either cold or hot, although some restaurants offer mixed platters as well.) After what always seems like a long wait, a giant platter arrives at the table to a cheerful round of 'oohs' and 'aahs', usually followed by someone saying, 'How am I going to eat all that?'

The cold seafood platter typically includes a selection of raw Sydney rock oysters, Balmain or Moreton Bay Bugs, local or New Zealand mussels, giant prawns, half a crayfish (lobster), and a whole Mud, Spanner or Blue Swimmer Crab. (With their prehistoric appearance, the 'bugs'—a crustacean roughly ten centimetres, or four inches, long—are especially fascinating.) Sometimes yabbies, a freshwater crustacean now grown commercially, are included. The hot seafood platter includes a selection of deep-fried seafood such as calamari (squid), mussels, scallops, prawns and fish.

Australia also has a wide selection of sea and freshwater fish, served either whole or in fillets and cutlets. At the top of the list are ling, gemfish, ocean perch, John Dory and jewfish. From Australia's tropical north come species such as Coral Trout and Red Emperor, and the giant succulent barramundi. Local trout and salmon also feature on many restaurant menus.

Australia is a major producer of beef and lamb, much of it for export, and these meats feature prominently on restaurant menus. Australians have perfected Rack of Lamb into an art form. Many hotel restaurants offer this traditional dish and it is well worth a try. Pork and chicken are also regular menu items, with game birds, such as quail and pheasant, now a feature of more upmarket and ethnic restaurants.

For more exotic fare, Australia's wild animals have recently started putting in an appearance on restaurant menus. Kangaroo meat, renowned for its gamey flavour and low cholesterol, is well worth a try, either as a steak or part of a stew. But despite their large numbers which sees about two million slaughtered legally every year, kangaroo is presently only available in South Australia and the Northern Territory. Although a protected species, crocodile meat—from animals grown commercially—is becoming popular restaurant fare, especially in northern cities such as Cairns and Darwin. The flavour is like a cross between chicken and fish. Water buffalo, which roam wild in the Northern Territory, are also available up north. With a taste much like beef, buffalo is often served as a steak.

To wrap up your meal, desserts are frequently a showcase for fresh Australian fruit. The variety reflects the country's mixture of climates and ranges from traditional fruits such as apples, citrus fruits and grapes through to a wide selection of tropical fruits including bananas, pineapples and mangoes. (Passionfruit and kiwi fruit, best eaten with a spoon, are a nice treat.) Recently, more exotic Australian-grown tropical fruits such as lychees, custard apples and jackfruit have also become available. (Neighbourhood fruit and vegetable stores are fascinating places to pick up a healthy snack.) If you love sweets, try Australia's famous pavlova—a tasty meringue topped with strawberries, kiwi fruit and whipped cream. Australia also produces an excellent choice of cheeses to top off your meal.

Of course, the real challenge—as anywhere—is finding and selecting a good restaurant. (For liquor, restaurants are either licensed or BYO, meaning 'bring your own'.) In most of Australia's large cities, you can purchase a comprehensive 'Good Food Guide' listing a wide choice of establishments. These guides can be purchased from newsagencies or bookshops for about A$10. Newspapers and free tourist guides, such as *This Week in Sydney* and other similar publications, are another source of information, although they often have a bias in favour of their advertisers. Locals are also an excellent source of information. (A small personal selection of top restaurants in each capital city is listed at the back of this book.)

One interesting feature of Australian restaurants, and frequently commented upon by visitors, is that many allow customers to split the bill on their individual credit cards.

If you are looking for just a quick snack, Australia has hundreds of fast-food outlets. (Yes, they have McDonald's, Kentucky Fried Chicken and Pizza Hut outlets too!) But for something very Australian, try a meat pie, which ranks as something of a national dish. They are widely available in take-away food shops, sports stadiums and pubs. The best ones, however, come from tiny bakeries. Liberally sprinkled with tomato sauce, or ketchup, they really hit the spot when you are feeling famished. (Sausage rolls and pasties are also worth a try.) For something a bit more filling, try ordering a hamburger 'with the lot'—my personal favourite. This monster-size burger, which puts the Big Mac to shame, consists of double meat patties, a fried egg, rashers of bacon and a mixture of lettuce, tomato and onion topped with a large slice of beetroot. (The tricky part is eating it without the beet sliding out and staining your clothing!) Another great snack, and one that reflects the country's English heritage, is fish and chips.

Finally, Australians love a 'barbie'. For many Aussies, there are few greater pleasures on a warm summer's evening than opening a can of beer and tossing a few steaks and 'snags', or sausages, on the backyard barbecue. And do not go using that Paul Hogan line—from his highly popular American television commercials—about 'throwing another shrimp on the barbie'. Here, they are called prawns—or giant shrimps. Visitors do not have to look hard to enjoy this custom, and barbecues are a regular feature of many guided tours.

Australians love a beer. Despite their reputation, however, they are not the world's largest consumers of what they affectionately call 'the amber fluid'. (In fact, they are about sixth or seventh down the list.) But there is little question that for flavour and 'kick', Australian beers rank up there at the top. (The alcohol content for most is 4.9 percent.) In recent years, the growing concentration of brewing into the hands of two large producers has turned off many consumers who swear the beer no longer tastes the same. As a result, there is a growing trend

towards 'boutique beers', or beers brewed the old-fashioned way on a pub's premises (see box).

But there is more to drink than beer. Many visitors are pleasantly surprised to discover that Australia produces an excellent selection of wines. Although a fairly recent development, wine is a source of considerable pride to many Australians, and they are quite ready to share their enthusiasm with visitors. (Their steadily rising consumption has actually led to a drop in beer sales.) Wine is made in virtually every state and territory, and a visit to a wine-growing district, such as South Australia's Barossa Valley, is an excellent way to familiarize yourself with the choices. Licensed restaurants usually offer a wide choice of whites and reds, but if you are selecting wine to take to a BYO establishment, stick to the well-known labels such as Orlando, Penfolds and Wolf Blass if you are unsure about what to choose. For after-dinner drinks, try some Australian port wine—among the world's best.

New South Wales

Where Modern Australia Began

It is hardly the sort of name that rolls easily off the tongue. And you definitely have to think twice before deciding what to call the people who live there. But for Australians, New South Wales is so deeply rooted in their history that no one would even suggest changing its name. It is where modern Australia began. Although the place bears little resemblance to South Wales in Britain, Captain James Cook thought the name suitable when he claimed the continent's east coast in 1770. And when British authorities began to ship convicts to the continent 18 years later, Cook's discovery became the Colony of New South Wales—a vast and largely unexplored region encompassing more than half of present-day Australia.

Over the next century and a half, New South Wales was sharply reduced in size as Victoria, Queensland, South Australia, the Northern Territory and then the Australian Capital Territory were sliced off to form separate entities. It was rather drastic surgery. Today, with Sydney as its capital, New South Wales is Australia's fourth-largest state after Western Australia, Queensland and South Australia. (While not yet a state, the Northern Territory has the third-largest area.) Located in the temperate southeastern part of the continent, the state occupies a still quite sizeable 800,000 square kilometres (310,000 square miles), or roughly the same area as California.

New South Wales has a surprising—and dramatic—diversity of landscapes, and its tourist officials proudly emphasize that it 'offers the Australian Experience in one state'. For starters, it has one of the world's loveliest cities, and also the nation's largest—Sydney. But elsewhere, except for its western region, the state hardly fits the Outback image of Australia. Its most dominant geographical feature is the heavily forested Great Dividing Range, which runs roughly north–south through the state and inland from the coast. While not that high compared to the mountain ranges of other continents, the range is rugged, marked by sharp escarpments and deep gorges. In the south, the range rises to form the Snowy Mountains and Australia's highest peak, Mt Kosciusko (2,228 metres, or 7,370 feet), a popular skiing area in winter. The watershed provided by the range has made the eastern third of the state lush and fertile. To the west lies Australia's richest wheat-growing region, while along the range and in the gentle hills falling away to the coast, large areas are covered in thick eucalypt forests.

Fronting on to the Pacific Ocean, the 1,200-kilometre- (750-mile-) long New South Wales coast provides more spectacular scenery. Here, the many rivers have carved magnificent harbours, such as famous Sydney Harbour, or formed wide and shallow lagoons protected from the pounding sea by sandhills. Between the rugged tree-covered headlands lie sandy beaches, many of them virtually deserted. Adding to the coast's beauty, the vegetation changes dramatically as one travels northwards into the subtropics. Along the North Coast, the dull-coloured eucalypt forests of the south are joined, and eventually overwhelmed, by the lush greenery of the tropics. The state's Outback provides yet another side to New South Wales. This is a land of vast dry plains which only grudgingly offers a living to its handful of inhabitants. Scattered in tiny towns or remote stations, the region's colourful characters are as much of an attraction as the land itself.

With its ideal climate and hospitable landscape, it is hardly surprising that present-day New South Wales was the first part of Australia to be settled by Europeans just over 200 years ago. It has continued to attract a steady stream of newcomers ever since. Today, with more than one-third of the country's population, or 5.6 million people, New South Wales is the most heavily populated state in Australia. (Over half of those, or 3.5 million, live in Sydney.) This steady flow of newcomers—from other states as well as overseas—has strongly influenced its character. New South Wales, and especially Sydney, is where people go to make it 'big' in Australia. And while it might strike visitors as a fairly sedate place, Sydney—by Australian standards—is a hustler's town where, like the rugby league football they play locally, the ambitious put their heads down and charge.

But there is another side to this migrant culture. Like neighbouring Victoria, New South Wales has received most of the millions of non-English-speaking migrants—mostly eastern and southern Europeans and, more recently, Asians—who have moved to Australia since the Second World War. As a result, the state and its capital have lost much of their Anglo-Celtic character and are now heavily cosmopolitan. Although it is most visible in the wide selection of restaurants, this change extends throughout society.

Given this incredible mixture of backgrounds, it is obviously difficult to generalize about the character of New South Welshmen—or Welshpeople, as they might be called these days. But if they have one common trait, it has to be their smug feeling of superiority over other Australians, mixed with a slight touch of arrogance. In their minds, this is confirmed by the state's high population and the importance to the Australian economy of its manufacturing, mining and agricultural industries. Together, these have long given New South Wales tremendous political and economic clout. (No government can win

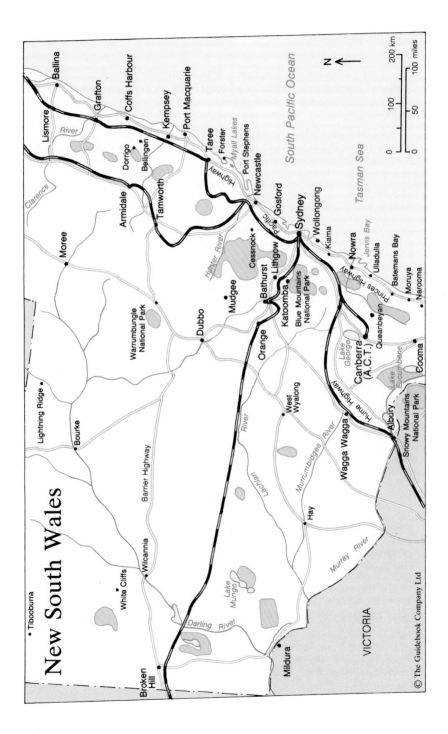

New South Wales

power in Canberra, for example, without taking New South Wales.) And like their trans-Pacific neighbour, California, they see themselves as sophisticated and at the vanguard of modern Australia. Everyone else just has not caught up yet. Of course, these traits hardly go down well in the rest of the country and evoke a sentiment not unlike that felt by many Americans towards New Yorkers, or Britons to Londoners.

History

The early history of Australia is very much the history of Sydney and New South Wales. When the First Fleet arrived in January 1788, its commander, Captain Arthur Phillip, had orders to establish his convict settlement at Botany Bay, where Cook had spent several weeks during his voyage in 1770. But almost immediately, he concluded that the bay's sandy soil and poor water supplies would barely support his fledgeling community. With a few men, Phillip headed 15 kilometres (nine miles) north by boat and discovered what he delightfully described as 'the finest harbour in the world', surrounded by fertile soil and adequate water. He briefly considered naming the place Albion. Instead, he chose Sydney, after the British official behind the venture. The fleet sailed in on 26 January and, after the male convicts were unloaded, a flag-raising ceremony marked the formal beginnings of the colony. When the women convicts were unloaded a week later, a drunken party ensued which is now laughingly referred to as 'The Inaugural Orgy of New South Wales'.

But such diversions were rare in those early days. Life was so harsh that the colony barely survived its first two years. Despite the area's lush appearance, the new settlers found the soil rocky and the trees too tough for their axes. Worse, because most of the convicts had come from cities, they had neither the skill nor the inclination to turn their hand to farming. Discipline was tough, and floggings—even the occasional execution—soon became a regular part of life. Relations with the native Aborigines deteriorated into the grim pattern that was to characterize the white settlement of Australia. Driven off their traditional lands, the Aborigines soon fell victim to disease, alcoholism and massacres at the hands of the newcomers. Meanwhile, what was to become the city of Sydney was slowly taking shape. Parramatta, now a thriving western suburb and the geographical centre of Sydney, was founded early to take advantage of better farming land. Further exploration opened up new areas along the coast and up into the foothills of the Blue Mountains to the west.

In those days, the British worried about the French, who were also shopping around the neighbourhood for new colonies. Moving quickly, other explorers ventured out by sea from Sydney, and their discoveries were soon consolidated by further convict settlements. Because of its strategic location 700 kilometres (435 miles) northeast of Sydney, Norfolk Island was occupied early and quickly earned a reputation as a brutal prison colony. In 1798, George Bass and Matthew Flinders determined that Van Diemen's Land, later Tasmania, was separated from New South Wales by a strait. They charted the island's entire coastline and, five years later, a convict settlement was established there. But, in importance, none of the early explorations matched Flinders' circumnavigation of the continent between 1802 and 1803. For the first time, the voyage demonstrated that New South Wales and New Holland were not separated by sea. Flinders suggested that 'Australia' — after the Latin *terra australis*, or southern continent — would be an appropriate name for this newly proven continent. But it was years before London accepted the idea and the word came into general use.

It was no easy task to administer New South Wales. The colony's early history was marked by bitter quarrels over how convict labour should be used, whether by the government or free settlers, and over the rights of emancipated convicts and their offspring. A succession of military governors often found themselves at odds with an increasingly powerful Establishment of former officers and wealthy settlers such as John Macarthur, who started the merino wool industry. The most notorious case involved Captain William Bligh, best known for the *Bounty* mutiny. When he attempted to crack down on the use of rum as currency after his arrival in 1806, he was deposed within 18 months in a military coup by the corrupt New South Wales Corps.

Relative calm returned when this so-called Rum Corps was recalled to England. Bligh, now remembered in a short downtown street next to the Sheraton Hotel, was replaced in 1810 by the man widely regarded as the Father of Australia, Governor Lachlan Macquarie. He and his convict architect, Francis Greenway, left a mark on Sydney that is still visible today in its historic public buildings and street layout. Although the number of convicts was steadily increasing, Macquarie moved quickly to improve their lot and that of ex-convicts.

The new governor also stimulated the colony's expansion. In a feat which dramatically affected future settlement, the explorers Blaxland, Wentworth and Lawson finally conquered the previously impassable Blue Mountains in 1813, opening up rich grazing land in the interior. Australia's first inland settlement, Bathurst, was founded two years later. By the time Macquarie left in 1821, the foundations had been laid for a strong agrarian economy, a solid transportation system and the beginnings of legislative government.

Sydney soon became a thriving port for the export of wool and wheat. With new lands opening up for settlement, New South Wales was swamped with free settlers who began to agitate for an end to the transportation of convicts to the colony. In 1840, such shipments were finally abolished. A further impetus to the settlement of inland New South Wales came with the discovery of gold near Bathurst in 1851, when thousands of prospectors—including many from the California fields—rushed into the colony. For the rest of the century, the colony developed rapidly through further migration, the expansion of agriculture and industry, and the construction of new roads and railroads. When the push began for federation from Britain in the 1880s, New South Wales led the way.

Since the foundation of the Commonwealth of Australia and independence from Britain in 1901, New South Wales has maintained its pre-eminent position. The state is the most populated, and most developed, in Australia. But increasingly, its residents are finding that there are limits to continued growth. As the earliest settled part of the continent, the state has also experienced some of the worst ravages to the environment, such as widespread soil erosion, salination and, in its cities, growing pollution. In the late 1980s, there is a growing sentiment that enough is enough.

Getting Around

As Australia's leading gateway, Sydney is a regular stop for most tourists visiting the country. But as noted earlier, there is a lot more to see in New South Wales than its capital city. Fortunately, the state is a very easy place to explore.

New South Wales has extensive internal air, rail and bus networks. But the best way to get around—as the following sections assume—is to hire your own car. This allows maximum leeway in planning an itinerary and makes it easy to get off the beaten track. Whether you just want to explore around Sydney or head interstate into Victoria or Queensland, it is an ideal way to travel. (Alternatively, you can fly into any major town outside Sydney, hire a car and then explore from there.) All major car rental agencies operate in New South Wales and there is a host of smaller, and often cheaper, companies. (Normally, an extra charge applies for dropping the car in another city.) For a higher fee, the larger companies also offer self-contained campervans that sleep two or more adults. (Other companies specialize in hiring houseboats, cruisers and yachts.)

Tourism is a highly developed industry in New South Wales, and for those who do not wish to drive and prefer to let someone else do the

Surf lifesavers compete against one another at a surf carnival (above) and pull together in a rescue exercise (right)

planning, there is a tremendous variety of bus, rail, aerial and even water tours operating out of Sydney and other major cities. (Some combine all four means of transport.) For those looking for more excitement, adventure tours operate throughout the state and offer everything from rock climbing, bushwalking and canoeing through to ballooning, gliding and horse-riding.

The Tourism Commission of New South Wales operates Travel Centres throughout the state, and in Brisbane, Melbourne and Adelaide, which provide detailed information and can arrange travel, accommodation and tours. (The Commission also has overseas offices in London, Los Angeles, Tokyo and New Zealand.) Even if you have waited until after your arrival to plan an itinerary, the centres are an excellent starting point and the staff are always helpful. They will suggest places to see, how to get there and the latest bargains. They can also put you in touch with tourist associations throughout the state.

New South Wales is famous for its wide choice of ethnic food, especially in Sydney. There are also many seafood and 'international' restaurants throughout the state. (In small country towns, however, the best restaurants are often in motels, even if you are not a guest.) While you are travelling around, keep an eye out for the quaint little establishments that offer Devonshire Teas—hot scones (or muffins) covered in strawberry jam and whipped cream. Often located in or alongside antique shops, they make a most refreshing stop. The state has a large wine-growing industry, principally in the Hunter Valley north of Sydney, with most vineyards open for tastings. Some even provide meals and accommodation. There is also no shortage of pubs (known as hotels) throughout the state, and those in country towns, many of them quite historic, always make a fascinating stop. (Many provide basic, but filling, 'counter-lunches'.)

Sydney

If you are lucky, and the aircraft is making the right approach, the best introduction to Sydney comes before you even land. As the plane lowers its landing gear and lines up for its final approach, you will catch your first breathtaking view of **Sydney Harbour**. Stretching 20 kilometres (12.5 miles) inland from a rugged narrow entrance, the bright blue harbour is an eyeful of wooded headlands separating numerous bays and coves. Beside one of these coves rises the modern skyline of Sydney's business district, with the city's best-known symbols, the **Sydney Harbour Bridge** and the **Opera House**. From there the city stretches out in all directions, a vast collection of verdant parklands and red-tiled roofs. That glimpse quickly disappears as the plane grinds to a halt at **Kingsford-Smith International Airport** on nearby Botany Bay. From the airport, downtown is a 20-minute bus or taxi ride away.

With a population of 3.5 million, Sydney is Australia's largest and most cosmopolitan city. With its near-perfect climate, the city is also one of the most beautiful in the world. Strictly speaking, the name refers only to the downtown area, which has relatively few residents. In fact, most people live in separately administered suburbs, each with its own name and shopping centre. Strung out over roughly 2,500 square kilometres (965 square miles), Greater Sydney is one of the largest metropolitan areas in the world. Most houses are set on their own block of land, with room out back for a garden, pool and barbecue area. Large areas of the city are set aside for open space, giving much of Sydney the appearance of an endless parkland.

There is a surprising variety of suburbs, but prestige comes from how close one lives to the water, especially Sydney Harbour. Australia's most expensive homes are concentrated along its southern shore in Sydney's posh **Eastern Suburbs**, such as **Point Piper**, **Double Bay** and **Elizabeth Bay**. Other wealthy areas are along the so-called North Shore and in oceanside suburbs such as **Palm Beach** and **Vaucluse**. In recent years, former inner-city working class suburbs, such as **Paddington** and **Balmain**, have turned trendy as young professionals have moved in and extensively renovated colonial-era terrace-houses. Others prefer the 'bush' and have moved to the city's outer fringes where they have built hobby farms on large blocks of land. While there are some run-down areas, they are hardly slums by world standards.

Because of its topography and the way it has grown over the past 200 years, Sydney gives the impression of being an unplanned city. Except for the business district, a legacy of Governor Macquarie, the city has few straight streets. The city's few expressways come to a grinding halt just as you are getting up speed, and all the main roads, mostly undivided four-lane highways, wind their way nonchalantly up, down and around the hills. For the visitor, it can be a bit disorienting. (A street directory is always a worthwhile purchase.)

But much of Sydney's layout has been dictacted by its topography. While the land between the airport at Botany Bay and downtown is flat, for example, most of the city is set on undulating hills or rocky ridges. On Sydney's leafy **North Shore**, some ridges drop off quite sharply into valleys of mature native trees. Sydney's myriad waterways have also affected its layout—to say nothing of its lifestyle. The city is surrounded by water on three sides. Along the coastline on both sides of Sydney Harbour are numerous sandy beaches, separated from each other by rugged sandstone headlands. On the city's northern outskirts,

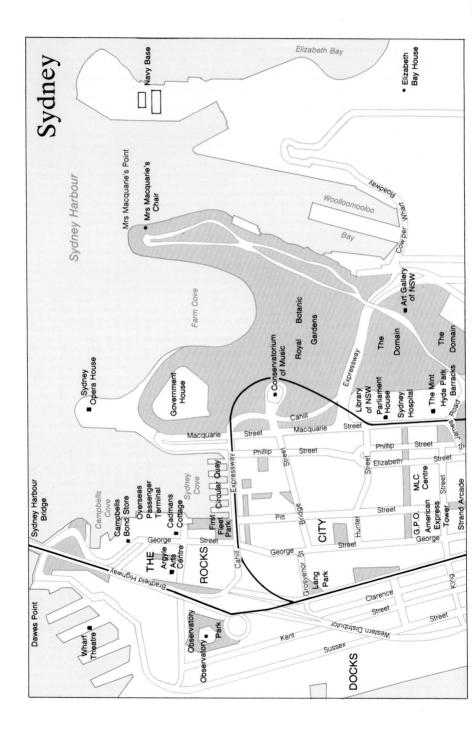

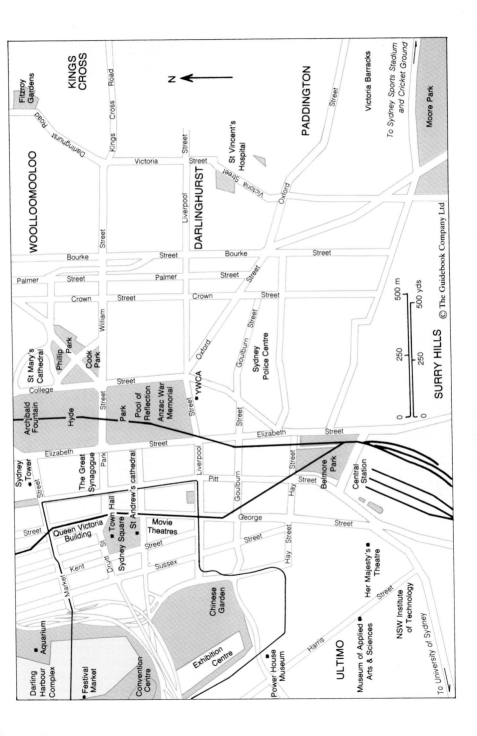

the majestic **Hawkesbury River** flows into **Broken Bay**, a harbour nearly as large as Sydney's, while to the south, the smaller **Georges River** runs into **Port Hacking** at **Cronulla**. All except Botany Bay are drowned river valleys, and the headlands are the favourite, and most prestigious, places to live.

The easiest way of getting around is to use Sydney's extensive public transport system of suburban trains, buses and ferries or one of its many taxis. There is also a wide range of guided tours of the city and its environs. (For the self-driver, parking can be a nuisance in the city unless you are staying at a hotel, but having your own car is quite useful for exploring the suburbs and other nearby sights.)

The best place to begin your sightseeing on foot is at **Circular Quay**, on the edge of Sydney's spectacular harbour and where the European settlement of Australia began in 1788. Governor Phillip's landing place, first known as Sydney Cove, has been in continuous use since then, first as a wharf for visiting ships and then as a ferry terminal. But in the 1950s, short-sighted officials effectively blocked off the area from the rest of the city by erecting an overhead expressway and railway. Despite repeated calls ever since to rip down the monstrosity, no politician is prepared to accept the responsibility and traffic chaos that would doubtless ensue. But leading up to Australia's Bicentennial in 1988, the state government poured millions of dollars into a much-needed renovation of this historic precinct. The result is a pleasantly landscaped and sun-drenched space linking The Rocks and the Sydney Harbour Bridge on one side with the Opera House on the other. But the compact appearance of the area is deceiving—there is enough right here to keep the visitor occupied for several hours.

Circular Quay—pronounced 'key'—is an important bus, train and ferry terminal and, by Australian standards, the area bustles with activity. In one of the world's most pleasant commuter journeys, thousands of people travel to work by ferry or hydrofoil from outlying harbour suburbs. At midday, many workers return to eat their bagged lunches on the grass or to catch a bit of sun. Others make their way to nearby restaurants and pubs, often to emerge much later. The surrounding sights also attract chattering groups of uniformed children on school excursions. 'Buskers', or street musicians, make a lucrative living entertaining the passing crowds. Adding to the nautical atmosphere, visiting cruise ships are often docked at the nearby and recently rebuilt **Overseas Passenger Terminal**.

The Quay is also the main departure point for harbour cruises, a highly recommended and delightful way to see this part of Sydney. Regular ferry services are the cheapest, with the one to the seaside suburb of Manly a particular favourite. (The trip takes about 40 minutes; if you are in a hurry, catch the hydrofoil.) There are also daily tourist ferries; one allows passengers to stop off and rejoin the ferry as they please and two others offer two and a half-hour cruises with full commentary and refreshments. In addition, the long-established privately owned Captain Cook Cruises runs a wide range of daytime tours and a delightful nightly four-hour Candlelight Tour. (There are several other smaller operators, including sailing vessels, departing from other points on the harbour.)

A short walk to the west of the Quay is **The Rocks**, a rocky ridge where much of early Sydney was built. In the late 1960s, the historic area was saved from wholesale demolition by militant union action. Since then, its 19th-century buildings have been faithfully restored into one of the city's most charming tourist attractions. Horse-drawn carriages operate through the area or, without too much energy, everything is within easy walking distance. Dwarfed by the surrounding buildings, tiny **Cadman's Cottage**, near the water's edge, is Sydney's oldest surviving dwelling, designed and built by Francis Greenway in 1815. The **Argyle Centre**, once a group of bond stores and warehouses, has been converted into a tasteful collection of craft, antique and gift shops, galleries and a number of restaurants, coffee shops and bars. A stroll up through the **Argyle Cut**, hewn out of solid sandstone by the convicts, will bring you to a quaint village green bordered on its northern side by a collection of Georgian- and Victorian-era cottages and terraces. On another side is the **Garrison Church**, built in the 1840s and one of Sydney's oldest.

For a panoramic view of the harbour and the Blue Mountains in the distance, head further up the hill to the **Sydney Observatory** which is now a museum. When you have worked up a bit of a thirst, drop into **The Hero of Waterloo** in Lower Fort Street. This former barracks, built of sandstone, is one of Australia's oldest pubs, and the cosy atmosphere will soon have you in conversation with the old-timers. A bit further away are the **Lord Nelson**, which brews its own beer, and the **Palisades**, an old working-man's pub. From here, streets lead down to the harbour and under the bridge, passing **Pier One** and **Campbell's Storehouse**—both offering fine restaurants with spectacular harbour views—and back to where you started. At weekends, many of the hotels in The Rocks offer live entertainment.

When the **Sydney Harbour Bridge** was completed in 1932 after five years of construction, it provided the first road access to the city's northern suburbs. The bridge was soon embraced as Sydney's most enduring symbol and was affectionately dubbed 'The Coathanger'. The walk across the bridge to **Milson's Point** and **North Sydney**, Australia's Madison Avenue, takes about half an hour. From the pedestrian

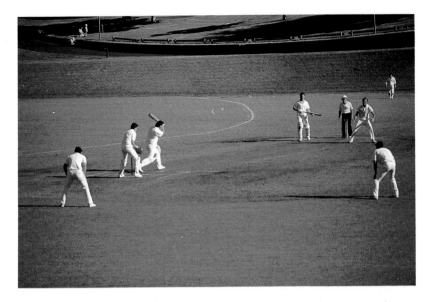

walkway on the eastern side of the bridge, there is a spectacular view all the way out to the harbour's entrance, known as The Heads. Once on the North Shore, the easiest way back to Sydney is to catch a train. For the more energetic, another great view comes after climbing more than 200 steps to the top of the bridge's southeast pylon. Because of growing traffic congestion, a highly controversial tunnel paralleling the bridge is now under construction.

Back at Circular Quay, a walk under a glass-covered walkway in the opposite direction will take you to Sydney's other famous landmark, the **Opera House**. The design was the result of a worldwide competition in the 1950s won by Danish architect Joern Utzon and symbolizes the city's love affair with sailing. But like the present harbour tunnel, the building was surrounded by fierce political controversy. Eventually, Utzon was pushed aside and the complex was completed without him in 1973. Disappointed with his treatment, he has never returned to see his masterpiece. Despite its name, the building is really a centre for the performing arts, with a concert hall, a music room, and opera, drama and movie theatres. To many people's surprise, the two main halls are remarkably small, seating barely 1,500 each. Two restaurants and six bars offer spectacular harbour views. There are daily tours and, with the complex heavily used, there is always something worth seeing. (A programme of events is available at the information counter on the first floor.)

A pleasant walk east from the Opera House leads along a broad walkway skirting **Farm Cove** to **Mrs Macquarie's Chair**. Located at the end of a headland and surrounded by majestic old Moreton Bay fig trees, the chair was carved out of the sandstone rock by convicts for the wife of the governor to rest in during her daily walks. Complete with inscription, the bench-like structure is a fascinating piece of colonial history. With its all-encompassing view of the Harbour Bridge, the Opera House and the Sydney skyline, the point is a favourite place for souvenir snapshots. Out on a small island in the harbour is **Fort Denison**, once a convict prison known as 'Pinchgut', and later fortified against a feared Russian invasion in the mid-19th century. (The Maritime Services Board conducts organized tours of the island.)

Back towards the city from this point, a visit to the **Royal Botanical Gardens**—with its own restaurant and tea rooms—makes a relaxing introduction to Australia's unique flora. (The gardens can also be reached more directly from nearby Macquarie Street.) Further on, **The Domain** is a wide expanse of lawn popular for open-air concerts—such as the summertime Opera in the Park—and weekend soapbox orators. Opposite the park, the recently expanded **Art Gallery of New South Wales** has a fine collection of Australian paintings. (The gallery is open seven days a week and admission is free.) Closer to the city and opposite **St Mary's Cathedral**, Sydney's leading Roman Catholic church, are the semi-formal lawns, flowerbeds and shady trees of **Hyde Park**. Once a horse-racing track, the sprawling park is ideal for a pleasant stroll. Dominated at its northern end by lines of mature Moreton Bay fig trees, one of the park's main features is the ornate **Archibald Fountain**, while at the southern end sits the imposing art-deco **ANZAC Memorial**, built to honour the nation's war dead. (A brief walk into the memorial is a moving experience.) Along College Street, at the eastern edge of the park, the **Australian Museum** is Australia's largest natural history museum and also has an excellent exhibition on Aboriginal culture. (The museum is also open seven days a week, with free admission.)

An excellent alternative way to see these and other parts of downtown Sydney is 'The Sydney Explorer' bus, specially designed to help visitors explore the city at their leisure. Painted a distinctive red, these Mercedes-Benz buses run throughout the day and allow passengers to join or leave at any of 20 stops, including Kings Cross and Elizabeth Bay. For a mere A$10, they are one of the best tourist bargains in town. (Detailed maps of the buses' itineraries are available from hotels and tourist centres and are also on display at each stop.)

For Australia's largest city, the centre of Sydney—running south from Circular Quay—is amazingly small. Built along a rocky headland jutting into the harbour, the city centre is shaped like a long rectangle about ten blocks wide and 20 blocks long. But the advantage is that everything is within easy walking—or bus—distance.

The skyline of downtown Sydney is dominated by modern architecture, such as the soaring **MLC Centre** and the neighbouring **Sydney Tower**, but the city still has a remarkable collection of colonial buildings. Appropriately, the best examples of restored buildings are along **Macquarie Street**, named after the governor who did so much to bring order to the city's early sprawl. For the Bicentennial in 1988, the state government spent millions of dollars on landscaping and widening its footpaths. As a result, a stroll along the street is a pleasant look back into Australia's past, especially along its southern end beginning at the imposing **State Library of New South Wales**. Next door is **Parliament House**, with its distinctive timber verandas and colonnades typical of British military buildings in Macquarie's day. Now home to the state's two houses of parliament, the building was once part of the Rum Hospital, so called because the successful contractors received the rum monopoly for the colony. The main wing of that hospital was replaced by the present **Sydney Hospital**, a large sandstone building dating from the late 19th century.

But Macquarie Street's most impressive building is **Hyde Park Barracks**, next to the **Old Mint**. Designed by Francis Greenway and opened as a convict dormitory in 1817, the two-storey Georgian-style building was fully restored in the early 1980s and now houses a social history museum and a delightful restaurant. Across the street stands another monument to the convict architect, the beautifully proportioned **St James's Church** with its graceful spire and fine wooden ceilings. (After seeing these last two buildings, it is easy to understand why Macquarie soon made Greenway a free man.)

Another pleasant city walk—especially at lunchtime—is down **Martin Place** running from Sydney Hospital on Macquarie Street to the Victorian Renaissance-style **General Post Office** (GPO) and the **Cenotaph** on George Street. Martin Place was one of the first malls to be built in Australia in the 1970s and is the headquarters of Australia's leading banks. Tastefully decorated with trees and benches and dotted with kiosks, the mall features an amphitheatre offering free midday entertainment. (An underground train station provides connections to the eastern and southern suburbs.)

The mall also marks the beginning of the city's main shopping district, starting with a large complex of shops and fast-food outlets on the lower floors of the **MLC Centre**. Just to the south is the **Pitt Street Mall** with several large department stores and shopping arcades. Even

Possum Gully

I was nearly nine summers old when my father conceived the idea that he was wasting his talents by keeping them rolled up in the small napkin on an out-of-the-way place like Bruggabrong and the Bin Bin stations. Therefore he determined to take up his residence in a locality where he would have more scope for his ability.

When giving his reason for moving to my mother, he put the matter before her thus: The price of cattle and horses had fallen so of late years that it was impossible to make much of a living by breeding them. Sheep were the only profitable article to have nowadays, and it would be impossible to run them on Bruggabrong or either of the Bin Bins. The dingoes would work havoc among them in no time, and what they left the duffers would soon dispose of. As for bringing police into the matter, it would be worse than useless. They could not run the offenders to earth, and their efforts to do so would bring down upon their employer the wrath of the duffers. Result, all the fences on the station would be fired for a dead certainty, and the destruction of more than a hundred miles of heavy log fencing on rough country like Bruggabrong was no picnic to contemplate.

This was the feasible light in which father shaded his desire to leave. The fact of the matter was that the heartless harridan, discontent, had laid her claw-like hand upon him. His guests were ever assuring him he was buried and wasted in Timlinbilly's gullies. A man of his intelligence, coupled with his wonderful experience among stock, would, they averred, make a name and fortune for himself dealing or auctioneering if he only liked to try. Richard Melvyn began to think so too, and desired to try. He did try.

He gave up Bruggabrong, Bin Bin East and Bin Bin West, bought Possum Gully, a small farm of one thousand acres, and brought us all to live near Goulburn. Here we arrived one autumn afternoon. Father, mother, and children packed in the buggy, myself, and the one servant-

girl, who had accompanied us, on horseback. The one man father had retained in his service was awaiting our arrival. He had preceded us with a bullock-drayload of furniture and belongings, which was all father had retained of his household property. Just sufficient for us to get along with, until he had time to settle and purchase more, he said. That was ten years ago, and that is the only furniture we possess yet—just enough to get along with.

My first impression of Possum Gully was bitter disappointment—an impression which time has failed to soften or wipe away.

How flat, common, and monotonous the scenery appeared after the rugged peaks of the Timlinbilly Ranges!

Our new house was a ten-roomed wooden structure, built on a barren hillside. Crooked stunted gums and stringybarks, with a thick under-scrub of wild cherry, hop, and hybrid wattle, clothed the spurs which ran up from the back of the detached kitchen. Away from the front of the house were flats, bearing evidence of cultivation, but a drop of water was nowhere to be seen. Later, we discovered a few round, deep, weedy waterholes down on the flat, which in rainy weather swelled to a stream which swept all before it. Possum Gully is one of the best watered spots in the district, and in that respect has stood to its guns in the bitterest drought. Use and knowledge have taught us the full value of its fairly clear and beautifully soft water. Just then, however, coming from the mountains where every gully had its limpid creek, we turned in disgust from the idea of having to drink this water.

I felt cramped on our new run. It was only three miles wide at its broadest point. Was I always, always, always to live here, and never, never, never to go back to Bruggabrong? That was the burden of the grief with which I sobbed myself to sleep on the first night after our arrival.

Miles Franklin, My Brilliant Career, 1901

if you are just browsing, take a stroll through the lovely **Strand Arcade**, the last surviving such structure from the Victorian era. The restored arcade rises three floors to a glass roof, and features wrought-iron railings, cedar panelling and etched glass. (The Harris Tea and Coffee Lounge makes a refreshing stop, and there are also restaurants and cafés upstairs.) At the southern end of the mall is one of the city skyline's most dominant features, **Sydney Tower**. Located above the **Centrepoint** shopping complex, a trip to the top of the 300-metre- (984-foot-) high observation tower provides stunning views of the Sydney region. (Open to 9.30 pm every day and 6.30 pm on Sunday, the tower also features two restaurants.)

Nearby is the **Town Hall**, a wedding cake mixture of Renaissance and Victorian architecture, and the **Queen Victoria Building**, a massive Romanesque-Victorian building that occupies an entire city block. With money from Malaysian-Chinese investors, the building has recently been restored to its former glory and contains a mixture of chic boutiques and restaurants. Just south of this precinct along George Street is Sydney's main movie theatre district. **Chinatown**, sprawling out on both sides of the **Dixon Street Mall**, boasts some of the best cuisine this side of Asia. The **Sydney Entertainment Centre**, with a seating capacity of 12,500 people, is a popular venue for local and foreign entertainers.

Sydneysiders are great 'knockers'. Over the years, every major development in the city has brought out highly vocal detractors—from the Harbour Bridge in the 1930s to the Opera House in the 1950s—only to go silent once the projects were completed and gained wide popular acceptance. The **Darling Harbour Project** on the western side of the city was no exception. When the state government announced plans to redevelop the derelict warehouse district in time for Australia's Bicentennial, the project was widely scorned as a costly extravagance. And while the complex did suffer cost overruns and was not completed on schedule, Darling Harbour has rapidly turned into a popular tourist attraction—for locals and foreigners alike. A visit on a warm summer evening as the setting sun reflects off the nearby city skyline is an enjoyable way to end the day.

So far, no one has missed the world's largest casino that was once planned for the site, but a monorail linking the area to the city, plagued by embarrassing early breakdowns, continues to take much public criticism. With the Sydney skyline as a backdrop, the **Harbourside Festival Marketplace** offers several fine restaurants, most with outdoor seating, fast food outlets and classy boutiques. The complex also includes the **National Maritime Museum**, an aquarium and a convention centre. Through a park of transplanted palms and other trees is the **Chinese Garden**, a fully-imported Bicentennial gift from China. An overhead walkway to the west leads to the **Powerhouse Museum**, open seven days a week and already hailed as one of the world's finest technological museums.

Every city has its nightlife district. Sydney has **Kings Cross**. Located along a ridge east of the city at the top of William Street, the quarter is a colourful, but comparatively tame, collection of bars, restaurants, nightclubs, sex shops and strip joints. Along the crowded sidewalks, 'spruikers' harangue prospective clients into their establishments, while provocatively clad prostitutes openly solicit business. More depressing, however, are the young runaways who are drawn to Kings Cross from all over Australia. Many take up hard drugs and then turn to crime and prostitution to support themselves. Unlike other parts of the city, or Australia for that matter, it is advisable to be extra cautious when strolling about. Despite its seedy veneer, there is another—much classier—side to 'The Cross'. Several of Sydney's leading hotels and restaurants are located here and, because of the district's close proximity to the city, old terrace-houses and apartments are much in demand by young professionals.

No city in Australia has beaches to rival those of Sydney. Besides its harbour beaches, there are 32 surfing beaches within easy distance of the city. (Most can be reached by train and bus service.) All are patrolled against sharks and riptides by capped Surf Lifesavers who personify the legendary 'bronzed Aussie'. On summer weekends, these volunteers keep fit by participating in gruelling surfing carnivals that begin with precision marching and go on to swimming, boat, ski and board races. (The individual champions then go on to compete for the title of 'Iron Man'.)

Bondi Beach, a 15-minute taxi ride from the city, is Australia's most famous beach. (The beach can also be reached by train to **Bondi Junction** and then by bus.) Bondi, pronounced 'bond-eye', lies between two massive sandstone headlands, and its semi-circular shape has frequently been described as the perfect beach. Part of that hyperbole, however, comes from the beach's popularity for topless bathing. For tourists, it is very easy to feel overdressed. But not everything about Bondi is perfect. One of Sydney's major sewage outlet empties into the sea just north of Bondi and, when the currents are blowing inshore, it is time to head for another beach.

The choice of other beaches will literally keep you busy for a month. **Manly**, accessible by ferry or hydrofoil from Circular Quay, is ideally located, with the pounding surf of the Pacific on one side and the calm harbour waters on the other. Further up the northern coast at the far end of a peninsula is lovely **Palm Beach**. About an hour away

from the city by bus, the beach features the crashing surf of the Pacific on one side and the calm waters of Broken Bay on the other. To the south, and accessible by train, is **Cronulla Beach**, one of Sydney's most famous surfing beaches. For those seeking calmer waters, there are also several beaches inside the harbour and around Botany Bay. The city also has three beaches reserved for nudists.

Taronga Park Zoo is the nearest place to the city to see Australia's native animals. (It is open from 9 am to 5 pm seven days a week.) Catch a ferry from Circular Quay and then a bus or the aerial tramway to the zoo's entrance. With a spectacular view of the harbour and city skyline, the animals occupy one of Sydney's prime pieces of real estate. Recently renovated, the zoo is well laid out, and many Australian and 'exotic', or imported, animals are on display. The koala enclosure is one of the most popular, although it is impossible to predict if the animals will be awake. Doped out on the eucalyptus leaves that make up their sole diet, they are fond of ignoring visitors, and not even yelling will wake them up. The kangaroos can also be a bit disappointing. Locked up in zoos far from their hopping grounds, they spend their time lying back in the shade or shuffling around their enclosures. (The kangaroo is best appreciated in its natural habitat, although they do have a fondness for running in front of passing vehicles.)

In addition, there are three commercially-run zoos in Sydney's outer suburbs, but you must either sign up with a tour or have your own transport. These are **Featherdale Wildlife Park** in Doonside, **Koala Park** in West Pennant Hills and **Waratah Park Wildlife Reserve** in Terrey Hills. Their big drawing card is that visitors are allowed to pat and be photographed with kangaroos and koalas, but don't let those koalas' cuddly appearance fool you—they have very sharp claws!

For those seeking a touch of history, head down to **Botany Bay** which, in many ways, is still trying to recover from its rejection by Captain Phillip back in 1788. Heavy industrial development, a large container terminal and the main airport runway have all destroyed much of the bay's pristine charm. Next door to where Captain James Cook landed at **Kurnell** in April 1770, for example, is now an oil refinery. Despite this modern intrusion, Cook's landing place is marked by a park, a beach, a memorial and an attractive museum. (Unfortunately, visitors need their own transport to reach the site.) On the northern side of the bay, and reachable by bus from the city, historic **La Perouse** is named for the famous French explorer who arrived just after the First Fleet. A museum honouring the Frenchman, who later disappeared in the South Pacific, was opened in 1988. Other historic monuments include the **Watchtower**, built by Macquarie to control smugglers and escaped convicts, and **Bare Island**, a 19th-century fort built to deter invasions by the French and Russians.

Around Sydney

One of the nicest things about Sydney is that it is very easy to escape from the hustle and bustle of the city. At weekends and holidays especially, many Sydneysiders do precisely that, heading out on their yachts or to their 'weekenders' along the coast or out into the countryside. Others simply hop in the family sedan or four-wheel drive and join the exodus out of the city. Unfortunately, they always seem to end up at the same place. So, for the visitor looking for the beauty and tranquillity of the Australian countryside, the best advice is to make your escape during the week.

One of the best—and easiest to reach—day-trip destinations out of Sydney is the **Blue Mountains**, about an hour west of Sydney and reachable by road or railway. (Many bus tours also offer trips to the area.) The mountains are part of the **Great Dividing Range** that runs the entire length of Australia's east coast. These mountains are extremely rugged, and it is easy to see why they were such an impenetrable barrier for the first 27 years of the colony. (Their name, incidentally, comes from the bluish vapour released by the eucalyptus trees that dominate the area.) Actually an eroded plateau, the mountains are a maze of thickly forested canyons and gorges flanked by sharp orange-coloured sandstone cliffs. In several places, lovely veil-like waterfalls plunge over the escarpments into the valley floor far below. Early attempts to cross the mountains failed when explorers ran straight into these perpendicular cliffs. Success only came when they pioneered a precipitous track along the ridgeline where the road and railway now stand.

The Blue Mountains are a refreshing change from the hot plains below. The air is fresh and the temperature is always several degrees lower. The quaint little villages and the many deciduous trees introduced by early settlers give a distinctly English feel to the mountains, especially in the winter months. At the height of winter, during the month of July, when snow occasionally falls, the locals even celebrate Christmas! (Just as in the northern hemisphere, springtime brings another type of joy.) To best appreciate the mountains, visitors should plan an overnight stay. There are several hotels and motels, ranging from the top-class **Fairmont Resort** at Leura through to more moderately priced motels. But the best alternative is to stay in one of the area's cosy guesthouses. Very reasonably priced, the cost of a room frequently includes a hearty breakfast. (The best contact, through the NSW Travel Centre, is the Blue Mountains Tourist Authority.)

Much of the Blue Mountains is protected as a national park, and the area abounds with bushwalking tracks, shady picnic spots and camping grounds. And while it has not detracted from the mountains' unique atmosphere, the crisp mountain air and lower real estate prices have also attracted thousands of newcomers in recent years who commute daily to jobs in Sydney.

Katoomba, the area's largest community, lies at the heart of the Blue Mountains and is the first destination of most visitors. From **Echo Point Lookout**, there is a spectacular view of the **Jamison Valley** and a famous rock formation called **The Three Sisters**. (Another lovely attraction is at the nearby information centre where colourful native birds feed right outside its windows overlooking the valley.) For those who want to explore for a couple of hours, a giant stairway called **The Thousand Steps** leads down to the valley floor and a vast network of hiking trails. Another faster—but more hair-raising—way of reaching the floor is provided by the scenic railway, reputedly the steepest in the world, and which once serviced a coal mine.

But while most visitors, especially those on day tours, see little but these highlights, there is plenty more to see in the Blue Mountains— especially if you have your own transport. (For those wishing to spend more time, 'Out and About Bush Experiences' offer overnight and

Aussie Pubs

Known more commonly as hotels, pubs are a long-entrenched Australian institution. Although women are no longer excluded, pubs remain very much the preserve of the Aussie male, a favourite place in which to drink beer and swap yarns with one's 'mates'. For many males, their entire social life revolves around a daily visit to the pub.

There are hundreds of pubs in Australia. In many Outback settlements, the local pub is often the only substantial building! While their architecture, atmosphere and clientele vary widely, dropping into a pub is a great way to soak up the local atmosphere and meet the people.

However, if you plan to visit an Aussie pub, you will need to be aware of a few rules and traditions. While it may not be immediately obvious, pubs do have a dress code, though it may consist of no more than singlet, shorts and a pair of thongs! Secondly, unlike American-style bars, drinks must be ordered at the bar and paid for immediately. (Tips are not expected, but it is customary to leave behind the small change.)

Choosing your drink can be a challenge, especially for newcomers unfamiliar with Australian brands and glass sizes. Typically, pubs have two or more beers on tap, plus a selection of canned or bottled beers. (They also serve mixed drinks, though rarely anything very 'complicated', such as a New York-style martini or a manhattan.) Most pubs offer beer in two sizes—such as the 'middie' or 'schooner' in New South Wales—and service is remarkably quick. After the first order, the refills come easily. In many Outback pubs, however, the only beer available comes in cans or small bottles known as 'stubbies'. Here, customers are provided with styrofoam 'stubbie holders' to keep their drink cool in the sweltering heat.

Many Aussies have a favourite pub, and most are filled with regulars who have known each other for years. As a result, newcomers often feel like they have intruded on a private party. It is not easy to crack the ice, but the publican or bartender usually make a good start and, especially on a quiet day, may introduce you to a few regulars. Alternatively, if you are especially gregarious, or brave, you can make your own approaches around the pub. Once you have entered into friendly conversation and your glass is nearly empty, offer to 'shout a round'—a move that often enlists you into a 'school' with reciprocal drinking rights. But do keep track of who is 'shouting'. In a pub, there is nothing quite as embarrassing as being brusquely reminded, 'It's your shout, mate.'

three-night bushwalks and bicycle tours.) At several locations, short walks lead to lookouts with breathtaking views of the sandstone escarpment and plunging waterfalls. There are also several fine restaurants and lovely tea rooms scattered around the mountains. The **Hydro Majestic Hotel** at **Medlow Bath**, a grand pink-coloured Edwardian structure once a favourite for weekending Sydneysiders, offers spectacular views over the **Megalong Valley** and is worth a stop—or even an overnight stay. A personal favourite is the area around **Blackheath**, another ten kilometres (six miles) west of Katoomba. The town is famous for its Rhododendron Festival every November and has several lookouts offering magnificent views over the **Grose Valley** on the northern side of the mountains. From the town, a road winds down into the nearby Megalong Valley which offers horse-riding and hiking through temperate rain forests. Also worth seeing, but open Fridays to Sundays only, is the **Norman Lindsay Gallery and Museum** east of Katoomba at **Faulconbridge**, the former home of the famous artist whose nude paintings scandalized Australian society 50 years ago.

(As a word of warning, visitors should take extreme care in walking around the mountains. Even the experienced hiker can become lost, sometimes for days, after wandering off the trail. There are also occasional deaths of hikers who have slipped and fallen off precipitous trails.)

Another 45 kilometres (28 miles) to the west, the **Jenolan Caves** are the state's best-known and most spectacular underground limestone caves. Reached by a steep and winding road, the tiny valley floor is dominated by the historic **Caves House**, a large turn-of-the-century hotel. (The caves are a regular stop for day tours from Sydney.)

For self-drivers, an alternative (but more circuitous) way of returning to Sydney is through the coal-mining town of **Lithgow**, further to the west. (There are some nice apple orchards along the way, complete with roadside stalls.) Nearby is the historic **Zig Zag Railway**, a series of ingeniously designed ramps that allowed the first trains to cross the Blue Mountains in 1869. It was later replaced by a series of railway tunnels. On weekends, a steam train relives those early days of clever Down Under engineering. From these two locations, the scenic **Bell's Line of Road** runs through a picturesque fruit-growing area and on back to Sydney. At the foot of the mountains, historic **Windsor** makes a pleasant stop. Founded by Governor Macquarie in 1811, the town has a strong English flavour, with a large village green and a fine collection of sandstone and Georgian buildings. The **Windsor Court House** and **St Matthew's Anglican Church** were both designed and built by Francis Greenway.

Another pleasant day trip is to the vineyards of the **Hunter Valley**, about two hours' drive north of Sydney around the town of **Cessnock**. Surrounded by gentle hills, the region was Australia's first wine-growing district and, with over 40 vineyards, today produces some of its finest wines. Two operators (Australian-Pacific and Newmans) run regular one-day tours of the valley on Tuesdays, Thursdays and Saturdays and, for the well-heeled, Capricorn Air offers a one-day trip out of Sydney airport and another with overnight accommodation. But a more pleasant and relaxing alternative is to drive yourself and then stay overnight at a guesthouse, a bed-and-breakfast pub or a motel. There are also several quality restaurants in the valley, such as Pokolbin Cellars, the Casuarina Inn and Blacklands Restaurant. The Hunter Valley is extremely popular with Sydneysiders, who book out the place for months ahead, so it is best to visit during the week. One of the best ways to see the valley is by hot-air balloon—with a delicious champagne breakfast once you are back on the ground.

Closer to Sydney, a visit to one of its bordering national parks also makes a pleasant outing. For many years, my personal favourite has been the **Royal National Park**, on Sydney's southern outskirts. But unless you are a keen hiker, you will need to have your own transport. When the 7,300-hectare (18,000-acre) site was opened in 1879, it was Australia's first national park and the world's second after Yellowstone Park in the United States. Especially during the week, the park is a paradise of unspoiled bushland, wildlife and picnic spots. Several streams run through the park and, following a rainy spell, cascade gently over waterfalls. Winding paved roads lead to several beaches, including **Wattamolla** which has its own waterfall, lagoon and beach. Along the coast, walking trails pass through shrubland along the tops of sandstone cliffs and then descend to tiny isolated beaches. Further inland, trails pass through tall eucalyptus forests to hidden waterfalls. Birds put out a constant chatter and occasionally kangaroos or wild deer can be spotted. The park, only 35 kilometres (22 miles) from downtown Sydney, is an excellent introduction to the wonders of the Australian bush. Badly devastated by bushfires in 1988, the park is also a fascinating study of how the bush naturally rejuvenates itself after such calamities.

On the northern outskirts of Sydney is the **Ku-ring-gai Chase National Park**, overlooking the beautiful **Hawkesbury River**. (Again, your own transport is essential.) This park lies inland from the sea and is a collection of forest-covered headlands separating inlets and coves. The feel of this sunken river valley is like returning to a prehistoric time. Comfortable cabin cruisers and houseboats are available for rent. The luxurious 70-cabin *Lady Hawkesbury* offers two- and four-night cruises up the Hawkesbury, a river frequently compared to the Rhine.

The South Coast

The South Coast region of New South Wales runs from Sydney to the border of Victoria, a distance of 550 kilometres (342 miles) along the Princes Highway. For those driving from Sydney to Canberra or Melbourne, the route is slightly longer but much more pleasant than the inland run along the hectic Hume Highway. (Alternatively, you can drive down one way and return the other.)

The South Coast was settled relatively early when much land was cleared for dairy farming. These rolling green pastures provide a lovely contrast to the gum forests that remain, many of which are now national parks. To the west rises a line of stark forest-clad sandstone escarpments blocking off easy access to the interior. The rugged coast is marked by a series of lagoons and harbours created by short but swift-flowing rivers and streams. There are several large bays and countless small inlets featuring unspoiled beaches. A warm current right off the coast guarantees not just good swimming but also some of the best fishing in Australia. In summer, the South Coast is a favourite vacation spot for Sydney and Canberra residents.

Wollongong, 82 kilometres (50 miles) south of Sydney, is the state's third-largest city (population 206,000) and a major steel and coal-producing centre. But despite its reputation as the Pittsburgh or Birmingham of Australia, the 'Gong' is hardly an industrial slum. The city's physical setting at the foot of the spectacular **Illawarra Escarpment** more than overwhelms those intrusions. Civic pride is high, best illustrated by its large modern mall and refurbished historic buildings. Lovely beaches and a fishing port adjoin the downtown area. South of the city, the country opens up to a vast panorama with **Lake Illawarra**, a large lagoon, on one side and more of the stark escarpment on the other.

At **Albion Park**, the steep and winding Illawarra Highway leads inland up the escarpment through primitive rain forest and then **Macquarie Pass** on to the **Southern Highlands**, which have a distinct English feel. Giant pine and deciduous trees introduced by the early settlers have nearly overwhelmed the natural forests and surround the spacious old farmhouses. There are several comfortable guesthouses in the area. Just east of **Robertson**, and on the edge of the highlands, be sure to stop at **Ranelagh House**, a four-storey grand hotel built in 1924 which serves perhaps the finest Devonshire Tea in Australia. Further to the west, en route to the busy Hume Highway, the road passes through historic **Moss Vale**, with its fine collection of colonial-era buildings, while **Bowral**, a favourite retreat for Sydney's 'nouveaux riches', is just to the north.

To the south of the Illawarra Highway, a road leads past spectacular **Fitzroy Falls**, its waters tumbling off the escarpment into the rugged valley floor far below, and then winds its way into one of the most beautiful spots in the state, **Kangaroo Valley**, with its distinctive turreted bridge. Virtually surrounded by sheer-sided escarpments, the old farming town has been tastefully restored in recent years and its old hotel and shops make a pleasant stop. (Heading further south, the road winds up and over an escarpment and then rejoins the Princes Highway just north of Nowra.)

Nowra, a dairy and fishing town located on the banks of the wide **Shoalhaven River** south of Wollongong, is the gateway to spectacular **Jervis Bay**, one of the largest natural harbours on the east coast. Still largely undeveloped, the bay is part of the Australian Capital Territory, and its 50 kilometres (32 miles) of untouched beaches boast the world's whitest sand.

One drawback to the Princes Highway—and most other 'coastal' roads in Australia—is that for much of its length the road actually runs inland. So, while frequently passing through picturesque coastal river valleys full of lagoons, sand spits and beaches, the road also runs through forests and farm land. But travellers should not dismiss the numerous beaches and tiny settlements that are usually only accessible by roads running off the main highway.

Further south, the tiny coastal town of **Bateman's Bay** at the mouth of the **Clyde River** makes a pleasant stop for a bite to eat or an overnight stay. Just a couple of hours east of Canberra, the town is a popular weekend and holiday spot for the city's residents. Situated next to the clock tower along the waterfront is one of Australia's best fish-and-chip shops, which should not be missed.

As the Princes Highway continues south to the Victorian border, it passes through several sizeable towns, each with its own atmosphere and attractions and largely untouched by modern development. The temptation for visitors is to stop and explore each one. The best advice is to trust your instincts—and keep an eye on the clock.

At **Moruya**, whose claim to fame is having provided the granite for the Sydney Harbour Bridge, there are numerous historic buildings, while nearby **Tuross Head** boasts twin lakes and stately Norfolk Pines. At **Narooma**, one of the coast's most famous ports, the highlight is a visit to the penguin and seal colonies on **Montague Island**. **Bermagui**, off the Princes Highway, is where game fishing began in Australia, and locals boast that black marlin can be caught only five minutes off the coast. But around here, it is hardly a rich man's sport. Big Game boat parties can be joined for as little as $50, and at nearby **Merimbula**, marlin can be caught right off the pier.

The inland town of **Bega** is the centre of the South Coast's dairy industry and is famous for its cheddar cheese. Cheese factories here and at other spots along the coast are good opportunities to stock up the picnic basket. From Bega, another highway leads inland to the Snowy Mountains and on to Canberra. Dolphins abound along the coast and can frequently be spotted frolicking in the surf or escorting boats in and out of harbours.

Near the Victorian border, **Eden** is one of the loveliest ports along the east coast and has a colourful history. Whaling was once a thriving industry on **Two Fold Bay**, and those boom days are recalled in a **Whaling Museum** and the town's magnificent old buildings. Today, the whales, which are reappearing in growing numbers off shore on their migrations to and from Antarctica, provide a new tourist attraction.

The Snowy Mountains

By world standards, the Snowy Mountains in southern New South Wales are mere molehills. But this does not mean they should automatically be struck from the visitor's itinerary. (Access to the region is through Canberra or up from the South Coast.) 'The Roof of Australia' has long played a special role in the country's folklore. The tough Mountain Men, or cowboys, of the region were immortalized in 'Banjo' Paterson's well-known 1889 ballad, *The Man from Snowy River*. (In the early 1980s, the tale was turned into a popular feature film.) After the Second World War, the ambitious **Snowy Mountains Scheme** — a vast hydro-electric and irrigation scheme — produced a crop of modern heroes when they literally turned the rivers around to feed Australia's parched interior. A monument at **Cooma**, the gateway to the mountains, honours migrant workers from 27 nations who worked on the engineering feat.

The Snowy Mountains, which next door become the **Victorian Alps**, are a continuation of the Great Dividing Range. Much of the land is 900 metres (3,000 feet) or more above sea level and rises to Australia's highest peak, the 2,228-metre- (7,370-foot-) high **Mt Kosciusko**, named after the famous Polish patriot by the mountain's discoverer and compatriot Paul Strzelecki. The **Mt Kosciusko National Park**, with an area of 6,200 square kilometres (2,400 square miles) is the state's largest. Its harsh but beautiful terrain features unique alpine vegetation, such as the Snow Gum, and a wide variety of wildflowers.

In winter, snowfields as large as Switzerland's draw thousands of skiers to the region. While the length of the downhill runs is limited by the elevation, the 'Snowies' offer some of the finest cross-country skiing in the world. There are several resort areas — such as **Thredbo**, **Perisher Valley** and **Smiggin Holes** — and, with nothing snobbish about

skiing Down Under, the *après-ski* can be as much of a scream as
hurtling down the slopes.

In the summer months, the region blooms with wildflowers and
offers a refreshing break from the searing heat and crowded beaches
below. For those who cannot look at a mountain without climbing it,
Mt Kosciusko is a relatively easy climb. A chairlift from Thredbo helps
hikers over the hardest part, and then the 13-kilometre (eight-mile)
walk takes between four and six hours. Another approach is along a
dirt road, now blocked to protect the fragile vegetation, from
Charlotte's Pass. For the more adventurous, there are raft tours down
turbulent rivers and extended treks on horseback. Dams and lakes
formed by the Snowy Mountains Scheme offer the best trout fishing in
Australia.

The North Coast

Unlike in the northern hemisphere, when Australians want to get
warm they head north—especially in the cold winter months. And in
New South Wales that means heading up the Pacific Highway towards
the Queensland border, a full 900 kilometres (580 miles) away. The
first part of the journey passes through what, strictly speaking, is still
called the **Central Coast**, between Sydney and Newcastle.

Only an hour from Sydney by road or train, the **Gosford** district has
enough attractions for a pleasant one-day trip, or a stop en route to the

north. **Old Sydney Town**, just off the highway at **Somersby**, is a re-creation of what the city was like 200 years ago, complete with a magistrate meting out harsh punishment to the convicts. (Open Wednesday to Sunday, it is well worth seeing.) Nearby, there are many lovely beaches, especially along the old coastal road between **Terrigal** and **The Entrance**. Fishing is a popular pastime on **Tuggerah Lake** and **Lake Macquarie**, two large shallow lagoons west of the sandy coastal strip.

With a population of 250,000, **Newcastle** is the state's second-largest city and, like Wollongong south of Sydney, is a heavily industrialized centre. Founded as a settlement for incorrigible convicts from Sydney, 174 kilometres (106 miles) to the south, the city today is a major rail and port centre, and its industries include steelworks, shipbuilding yards and coal-mining. The downtown area, at the foot of some hills and alongside the wide mouth of the Hunter River, contains many old buildings from the colonial era. Imposing **Fort Scratchley**, built in the late 19th century, is now a maritime museum and gives a good insight into the city's fascinating history.

From Newcastle, the New England Highway, an inland alternative to the Pacific Highway, heads westward to the vineyards of the **Hunter Valley** (see page 69) and then all the way to Brisbane. For the traveller in a hurry, the highway is much better than the coast.

As with the Princes Highway, the best sights are off the main road, such as **Port Stephens**, just northeast of Newcastle, with its long

narrow inlet popular for fishing and sailing. The **Myall Lakes National Park** is a tranquil series of waterways stretching north from Port Stephens and located between windswept coastal sand dunes and dense inland forest. Many visitors hire houseboats to explore the lakes, catching their own fish by day and then anchoring for the night as the sun sets. Once torn apart by heavy sand-mining activity, 'The Murmuring Myalls' are an excellent example of how nature, given a chance, can rejuvenate itself. Just to the north, another turn off the highway leads to a long sandspit to **Forster**, one of the loveliest towns along the coast.

After a long run inland through forest and farming country, the highway finally emerges near the coast at **Port Macquarie**, a convict settlement established in 1821. Located off the highway at the mouth of the **Hastings River**, the city is a booming, but slightly overcrowded, retirement and holiday community. (There are plenty of motels, however, making this and Coffs Harbour, another 150 kilometres, or 90 miles, to the north, convenient overnight stopping points.) From here, the Oxley Highway heads inland to **New England** over the Great Dividing Range.

At **Wauchope**, there is a working re-creation of an 1880s sawmiller's village, including a steam train. North of **Kempsey**, a prosperous inland farming community that provides access to several beach resorts, the landscape begins to change. The climate becomes noticeably warmer and this is reflected in the widescale production of bananas and other tropical fruit. Entire hillsides are devoted to banana production. At **Coffs Harbour**, the leading attraction is **The Big Banana**, a tourist complex dominated by a huge walk-through replica of the fruit. It is a banana freak's paradise, with plantation tours and a shop selling an incredible variety of banana-shaped souvenirs. The region includes dozens of isolated beaches to sample, such as **Scotts Head**, **Valla Beach** and **Sawtell**. If the weather is fine, it is well worth lingering in the region for a few days. Inland, quaint **Bellingen** is a historic timber town that has become popular with those seeking an alternative lifestyle.

The tropical flavour of the Far North Coast intensifies in **Grafton** on the banks of the **Clarence River**. The town, one of the loveliest in Australia, is renowned for its shady avenues of jacaranda trees, parks and gardens, islands and historic buildings. The best time to see Grafton is during the annual **Jacaranda Festival** at the end of October when the huge trees burst into purple blossoms. Adding to its charm, the town also features many Queensland-style houses. With corrugated tin roofs, these elegant-looking homes are built of wood and sit high above the ground for better ventilation and protection against floods.

(From here, the Gwydir Highway heads inland to **Glenn Innes** where it joins the New England Highway.)

From Grafton north to the Queensland border is one of the most beautiful parts of Australia. The **Clarence River Valley** was the first sugar-producing region in the country, and the fields of ripening cane along the fertile banks support a string of prosperous little towns, their streets lined with mango, flame and jacaranda trees. At the mouth of the river lies tiny **Yamba**, its beaches still relatively undiscovered by tourists and well worth a visit. A lighthouse offers superb views of the coastline. The Ecuadorian raft 'La Balsa', which completed a trans-Pacific voyage in 1973, is on exhibit at **Ballina**, a sizeable commercial fishing town at the mouth of the **Richmond River**. (Heading west from Ballina, another road that passes through **Lismore** and **Casino** leads to New England.)

Byron Bay, 45 kilometres (28 miles) to the north, is the most beautiful spot on the North Coast and makes a pleasant overnight stop. Its crescent-shaped beach is dominated by soaring **Cape Byron**, the easternmost point of Australia. A road leads to a lighthouse on its peak which provides breathtaking views of the magnificent coastline and the inland mountain ranges. The town itself is a former whaling station and today offers a relaxing old-fashioned atmosphere. One of its most popular pubs is located right in the train station.

North from here to the Queensland border at **Tweed Heads**, the countryside is dominated by the looming presence of **Mt Warning**, a 1,200-metre (3,940-foot) extinct volcano named by Captain Cook. The climb to the summit takes four hours and provides stunning views of the **McPherson Range** along the border and up the coast to the high-rise condominiums of the Gold Coast.

Country New South Wales

Away from the coastline, there is enough to keep the visitor busy for several more weeks. The problem is that, with so much space, one always has to travel a long way to see something worthwhile. For the traveller seeking a taste—but not an overdose—of 'country' New South Wales, the best method is a circuitous route combining a coastal trip with one through the inland, along any of the turnoffs mentioned above.

The country areas of New South Wales—and other states, for that matter—are always well worth a visit. Although most Australians live in cities, 'The Bush'—much as with the American West—has provided them with a national mythology long celebrated by its greatest poets and singers. Forging a life out of such a tough and unforgiving land created the Australian characteristics of egalitarianism, a wry sense of

humour and 'mateship', the easy willingness to help a mate or a neighbour. These values remain strong, giving the bush a comfortable old-fashioned charm. Compared to the hustle and impersonality of the cities, the pace in the country is relaxed and friendly. People always have time for a chat, and visitors in a hurry are considered extremely rude.

Country towns each have their own flavour and history, and range in size from towns such as Wagga Wagga, Dubbo and Tamworth to tiny settlements offering little more than a pub, general store and gas (or petrol) station. But a feature common to all is their prominent memorials to local volunteers who went off to fight, and die, in the wars of the British Empire.

Many visitors, especially Americans, are at first surprised to hear that these Australians' favourite music is 'Country and Western', an eclectic mixture of local and American tunes. But the music soon becomes as natural as the landscape and its people. **Tamworth**, on the New England Highway, bills itself as Australia's Country Music Capital and celebrates with a month-long festival every January. Even those who normally have a low tolerance for country music cannot help but be enchanted by the friendly atmosphere.

The further one travels on the western side of the Range, the more flat and desolate the land becomes. The state's interior is actually one vast flood plain draining into the Murray and Darling River system, and whose waters eventually flow into the Southern Ocean near Adelaide.

Immediately west of the Range, comparatively lush and fertile lands make this one of Australia's richest agricultural areas. The rolling plains, punctuated by wooded hills, produce much of the country's exports of wheat, beef and wool. Settled early, the region is comparatively highly populated. There are literally dozens of towns and country roads to explore. But the most dominant feature of this region is the stark **Warrumbungle Mountains**, which first appear as a low jagged silhouette across the flat wheatlands northeast of **Dubbo**. Closer to **Coonabarabran**, the spires and domes of this unusual volcanic region make an impressive sight. Now a national park, the Warrumbungles provide refuge for a variety of animals as well as hiking and camping. Taking advantage of the area's isolation, the mountains are also home to one of the world's most powerful optical telescopes at **Siding Springs**. (A museum is open daily.) To the northwest is the opal-mining town of **Lightning Ridge**, home of the rare black opal and other precious stones.

Further west, the land flattens out into dry and tough 'marginal lands' where crops rarely succeed and the cattle and sheep are counted in acres-per-head, rather than heads-per-acre. When droughts strike Australia, these areas are the first to feel the pain. **Bourke**, once a thriving port on the **Darling River**, is the largest town in the northwest. From here on, it is 'Back of Bourke', a popular expression for the Outback. Northwest of **Wilcannia**, founded in 1864 and once Australia's third-largest port, is **White Cliffs**, the world's largest opal field. Here, most of the local residents actually live underground in luxuriously carved homes, some even with their own swimming pool.

In the south near the Victorian border is archaeologically-important **Lake Mungo**, part of an ancient lake system that dried up after the last Ice Age, some 15,000 years ago. Evidence of Aboriginal activity in the area has been traced back 40,000 years.

Broken Hill, in the far west of the state near the South Australian border, is the unofficial capital of the Outback, and an oasis in the middle of dry, harsh country. Known as 'Silver City', the city of 29,000 was built over the richest silver, lead and zinc deposits in the world. Those mineral deposits are now running out, and local officials are hoping to keep the city alive as a tourist attraction. The city is home to the world-renowned 'Brushmen of the Bush', such as Pro Hart, Eric Minchin and Jack Absolom, who welcome visitors to their galleries. Outside of the city, tourists can visit the ghost town of **Silverton**, best known as the location for the popular *Mad Max* films.

Australian Capital Territory

The Bush Capital

When the Federal Parliament decided to create a brand-new national capital in the countryside of New South Wales in 1908, many Australians doubted the project would ever get off the ground. It took several decades to prove the sceptics wrong. Today, Canberra—known affectionately as 'The Bush Capital'—is widely regarded as the most successful planned city in the world. Of course, the capital still has its 'knockers', or detractors, but that is mostly because of what Canberra symbolizes to many Australians; it is where all those 'bloody politicians' hang out.

But it is hard to knock the politicians of a much earlier generation for choosing the city's magnificent location. Set against the spectacular backdrop of the Brindabella Range, part of the Great Dividing Range, Canberra spreads out like a vast amphitheatre between a collection of low hills. In contrast to the grass-covered plains around it, Canberra is a great expanse of greenery dissected by broad boulevards lined with native and exotic trees. Off these main thoroughfares are leafy residential areas, their winding streets blending in with the local topography. The capital's monumental buildings, dominated by its hilltop New Parliament House, are set amidst ornamental lawns and gardens around a large artificial lake at the city's centre.

Canberra is a clean and modern city. And while there is a downtown district, known as Civic, most of the city's population live in eight surrounding satellite communities separated by green belts of native eucalypt forests and pine plantations, and linked by landscaped high-speed expressways. A strict building code means there are no unsightly billboards, flashing lights or power poles to spoil the view. Combined with all the greenery, it is not surprising that Australia's capital is often described as a city scattered through a park.

Located 300 kilometres (185 miles) southwest of Sydney and 600 kilometres (370 miles) northeast of Melbourne, Canberra is part of the Australian Capital Territory. Surrounded by New South Wales, the ACT occupies roughly 2,400 square kilometres (926 square miles) and is directly administered and funded by the federal government. (When elections were held for a local representative assembly in early 1989, many residents voted for candidates who were flatly opposed to self-government!) Canberra itself is located at the northern end of the territory, with the remainder a mixture of open grasslands used for farming and pasture and, on its western side, rugged forested mountains protected as national parks. The Murrumbidgee River, one of the country's most famous, originates in the ACT and is joined by

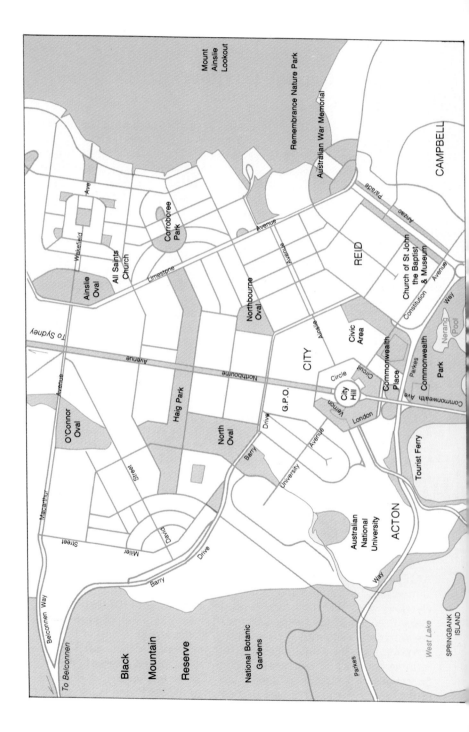

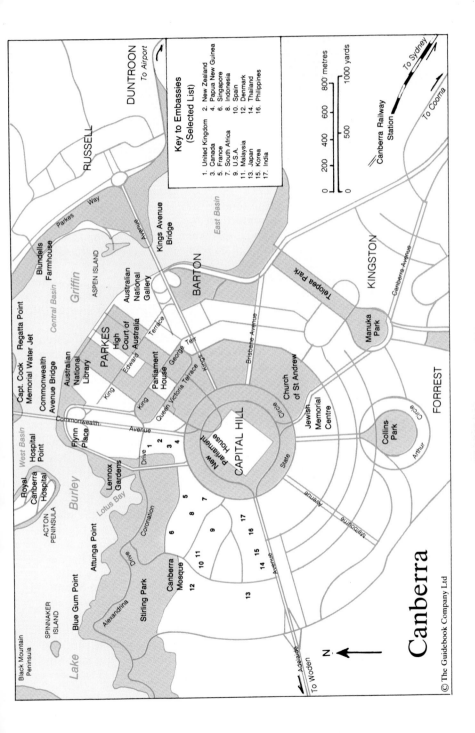

Canberra

© The Guidebook Company Ltd

Key to Embassies
(Selected List)

1. United Kingdom
2. New Zealand
3. Canada
4. Papua New Guinea
5. France
6. Singapore
7. South Africa
8. Indonesia
9. U.S.A.
10. Spain
11. Malaysia
12. Denmark
13. Japan
14. Thailand
15. Korea
16. Philippines
17. India

0   200   400   600   800 metres
0   500   1000 yards

Canberra Railway Station

To Sydney
To Cooma

DUNTROON
To Airport

RUSSELL

Parkes Way

Blundells Farmhouse

Capt. Cook Memorial Water Jet

Regatta Point

Commonwealth Avenue Bridge

Kings Avenue Bridge

Central Basin

Griffin

East Basin

ASPEN ISLAND

BARTON

KINGSTON

Manuka Park

Telopea Park

Canberra Avenue

Brisbane Avenue

Australian National Gallery

PARKES

High Court of Australia

Australian National Library

Parliament House

Edward Terrace

George Terr.

Kings

Queen Victoria Terrace

King

King

Commonwealth Avenue

Flynn Place

Hospital Point

West Basin

Royal Canberra Hospital

ACTON PENINSULA

Burley

Lotus Bay

Lennox Gardens

Attunga Point

Coronation

Drive

Drive

Alexandrina

Stirling Park

Canberra Mosque

Blue Gum Point

Black Mountain Peninsula

SPINNAKER ISLAND

Lake

CAPITAL HILL

New Parliament House

Circle

State

Church of St Andrew

Jewish Memorial Centre

Melbourne Avenue

Collins Park

Arthur Circle

FORREST

Adelaide Avenue

To Woden

N

1
2
3
4
5
7
8
6
9
10 11
12
13
14
15
16
17

several other streams before heading westward into New South Wales. The territory's inland position and higher elevation accentuate its temperate climate, and its four seasons are more extreme than, for example, in Sydney. In winter, when many residents settle in front of their fireplaces, night temperatures can drop to below freezing, and the peaks of the Brindabellas are covered in snow. There are also occasional snowfalls in the city, but they are quickly melted by the morning sun. By contrast, the large number of introduced exotic trees, including many flowering varieties, make spring and autumn in the city particularly beautiful. But in the summer months (December–March), Canberra is often hot and uncomfortable, and the flies and gnats can be a nuisance. For many residents, this is their favourite time to pack up and head to the NSW South Coast, particularly around Bateman's Bay (see page 72).

The territory has a population of about 260,000, mostly in Canberra. Government is, of course, the capital's main 'industry', although with its large number of visitors, particularly other Australians, tourism is also important to the local economy. As a percentage of the population, Canberra residents are the best educated in the country and, especially for its size, the city has developed a rich cultural life of theatres, concerts and exhibitions. And like every national capital, there are plenty of places where you can gather to talk politics.

If you prefer to be distracted from that preoccupation, Canberra boasts more than 250 restaurants and a lively nightlife of discos and clubs, with plans now afoot for a casino. (Because of its more relaxed censorship laws, Canberra has another, more seedy, distinction: it is the national capital of x-rated videos.)

But most of Canberra's residents live a more sedate lifestyle. And even though the vast majority have moved to the capital from elsewhere in Australia, many soon develop a fierce love for the place. The houses are all nicely oversized, and nearly everyone has a fireplace for those cold winter nights. The environment is also conducive to a healthy outdoor lifestyle of hiking, cycling and horse-riding. There is even a local yacht club, and local radio stations regularly broadcast sailing conditions on Lake Burley Griffin. The beaches of the South Coast and the snowfields or hiking trails of the Snowy Mountains are only two hours away.

Visitors may initially find the clean and neat atmosphere of Canberra a bit alienating, especially after more conventional—and less sanitized—cities like Sydney and Melbourne. But it does not take long to adjust to its slower pace and appreciate its successful blending of city and bush.

History

From the moment Australia's separate colonies began to discuss federation towards the end of the 19th century, one of their livelier 'blues', or arguments, was over where to place the nation's future capital. Both Sydney and Melbourne, intense rivals even then, wanted the privilege. After much haggling, they reached a compromise. When the Commonwealth of Australia was established on 1 January 1901, the constitution called for a separate national capital somewhere in New South Wales and 'not less than 100 miles [160 kilometres] from Sydney'. In return, Melbourne would act as the temporary capital of Australia.

But the search for a site soon proved to be a major headache for the nation's early federal governments, leading to two royal commissions and intense public debate. At first, no less than 40 districts in southern New South Wales were proposed. After 23 of these were physically inspected, often with considerable difficulty on horseback and by foot, the list was whittled down to seven. Finally in 1908, Parliament decided that an area around the townships of Canberra and Yass would become the Australian Capital Territory. The land, along with access to the sea at Jervis Bay on the South Coast, was ceded by the state government at no cost. Looking back, it is fun to speculate how things would have turned out if the parliamentarians had chosen Bombala, Tumut or Dalgety instead. Somehow, they just do not sound like national capitals!

Interestingly and somewhat prophetically, the name of Australia's modern capital comes from an Aboriginal word for 'meeting place', or *kamberra*. For thousands of years before the arrival of Europeans, tribes would meet and hunt together through the game-rich valleys and foothills. (Kangaroos can still be spotted occasionally inside the city limits.) But that lifestyle changed dramatically when the first English settlers arrived in the 1820s in the early push out of the Sydney region. They followed earlier explorers who sized up the rich meadows of the Limestone Plains as ideal sheep-grazing country.

Over the years, a small but wealthy 'bush aristocracy' grew up along the banks of the Molonglo River and the headwaters of the Murrumbidgee. The settlers lived on relatively small acreages and, seeking to emulate the English aristocracy, built large manor houses surrounded by gardens and vineyards. They were also the first to import and plant exotic trees to remind them of home. (Now fully grown, these trees—especially pines—are visible throughout the region and are a living reminder of those early days.) The settlers' comfortable lifestyle was typical of the Southern Highlands of New South Wales, with wealthy families adding to their holdings by further

Talkin' Aussie

Australians have their own way of speaking English which does require a bit of adjustment. The accent itself is not that difficult, although many Aussies have a habit of mumbling or running their words together. But their heavy use of home-grown words, slang and abbreviations does result in a unique language.

Aussie English, known as 'Strine', certainly ranks as one of the most colourful and humorous languages in the world. And like the people who speak it, the language reflects the typical Australian's irreverence about almost everything. Nothing is out of bounds. Strine is direct, earthy and proudly profane.

While it has become part of the overseas stereotype of Australians, **G'day** (good day) is indeed a widely used greeting similar to the American 'Hi'. **Ta** means thank you and **ta-ta** is goodbye. In a restaurant, you will find that the **entrée** is actually the appetizer, not the main course, and the meal ends with **sweets** and not dessert. Never ask for a napkin, but rather a **serviette**. And while the menu might call it chicken, everyone else calls it a **chook**. Outside, you wear **sandshoes** (not sneakers) and walk on the **footpath**, never a sidewalk. If it gets a bit cool, you put on a **jumper**, not a sweater, and for swimming you wear a **cozzie**, an abbreviation of 'swimming costume'. The **brolly** comes out when it rains. And like the English, cars come with **boots** and **bonnets**.

When you get into a bit of a **yarn**, or conversation, with your Aussie **mates**, or friends, the language really comes alive. If you sound a bit too critical, they will label you a **whinger** who is **bludging**, or taking advantage of their hospitality. If tempers rise you could get into a real **blue**, or argument. But **no worries, shouting a round** often calms things down, even if the pub is not **posh** (elegant) and only has **tinnies**, or cans.

The Aussies have no time for those they perceive as fools and have a rich, funny and earthy collection of insults to match, such as **boofhead, chucklehead, dickhead, drongo, galah, mutton-head, nong, pinhead** and **wanker**. Colloquialisms can be even more devastating, such as the classic **not the full quid** or **as thick as two short planks**. But Australians do have a soft spot for the **larrikin**, or an independent and slightly wild person.

Drinking and related activities are also rich in slang. An **esky** is a portable icebox for carrying **tinnies, tubes** or **stubbies** to a **barbie**. No one ever gets drunk in Australia; they prefer to get **pissed, sloshed** or **blotto**. And when they have had too much, Aussies speak openly of having a **chunder** or, even more amusingly, of **barking at the lawn** or having a **technicolor yawn**. It is enough to make you a bit **crook**, or sick. At the most polite level, the rest room is called the toilet, but **dunny** is also a common expression.

Fair dinkum (honestly), Strine is a language of its own, and you are bound to take a few new words home at journey's end.

purchases and intermarriage. Wool was the main industry, supplemented by dairy farming and crops. Sydney was a full two days away by coach and rail. Had it not been chosen as Australia's new capital, Canberra would very likely have remained a quaint backwater similar to its present country surroundings.

After surveyors chose the most suitable site for a city in 1909, the hard slog began. Two years later, an international competition was held for the capital's actual design. Out of 137 entries, the winner was a Chicago landscape architect by the name of Walter Burley Griffin. His plan was for a city with a population of 25,000, which he expected to grow to 75,000—or a bit short of today's nearly 300,000. Although Griffin had not actually visited Canberra, the beauty of his plan was in blending the site's natural setting with the proposed city. Dominating the plan was an artificial lake and a 'parliamentary triangle' in which the most important government buildings would be placed. Residential areas would spread out geometrically from there. In October 1913, to much public acclaim, Griffin arrived to build Australia's new capital.

For the next four decades, Canberra's development was very much a touch-and-go affair. At first, progress was slowed by changes of government, a shortage of funds and the outbreak of the First World War. The 'knocker syndrome' also played a role. Early on, many Australians openly questioned if the capital would ever appear. Then came Griffin's turn. Much like Danish architect Joern Utzon's hassles with the Sydney Opera House in the 1960s, the American was soon embroiled in strife with officials over their proposed changes to his grand design. In 1920, he quit. But at least he had won the war on the ground: his plan of the city was a reality. (Griffin moved to Sydney where he became a noted modernist architect.)

Construction continued slowly, but in 1927 a temporary Parliament House was opened, and the parliamentarians finally moved in from Melbourne. (The politicians had to wait another 61 years for a permanent home, today's massive New Parliament House.) The Depression, World War II and post-war shortages caused further delays. It was not until the late 1950s that wide-scale construction began. New satellite cities, not part of the original design, were built to handle the increasing number of departments and civil servants moving to the capital. The plan's centrepiece, appropriately named Lake Burley Griffin, was formed in 1963. Other major national buildings in Griffin's parliamentary triangle, such as the High Court and National Gallery, took longer still. With the opening of the new Parliament House in 1988, the planned city of Canberra was finally more or less complete.

Getting Around

International flights do not service Canberra, but there are regular air,
rail and bus connections from Sydney and Melbourne. (There are
regular day tours by bus from Sydney, but they make for a fairly
exhausting day; for those in a hurry, a better option is to fly up and
then take a day tour.) The city is also a convenient stop for self-drivers
exploring the southeastern corner of Australia and, depending on your
itinerary, can be reached from four different directions. (By the most
direct route, the Hume Highway, Canberra is about four hours' drive
from Sydney and eight hours from Melbourne.) For most visitors, an
overnight stop, or a couple of days, should be enough to sample the
city's attractions.

With a well-developed tourist industry, there are several ways of
getting around Canberra and the ACT. The city has an extensive
public bus network, ACTION, and special sightseeing tickets are
available, including one offering unlimited travel on the day of
purchase. (Timetables and tickets are available from most
newsagencies, bus interchange offices and the Canberra Tourist
Bureau.) In addition, the Murrays bus company runs a Canberra
Explorer service which takes visitors over a 25-kilometre (16-mile) 21-
stop route, complete with commentary, and allows passengers to leave
the bus and rejoin it throughout the day. But while these two are
certainly the best value, visitors may feel more comfortable signing up
with one of several companies who offer half-day, day and evening
tours of the city and its environs. There are also taxis and chauffeur-
driven hire-cars. For those with their own cars, however, it pays to
pick up maps and information as soon as you arrive. But do study
them well. The city might appear an easy place to manoeuvre around,
but with its many roundabouts and flyovers it is easy to get confused—
even when you can see exactly where you want to go. Everyone has a
'how-I-got-lost-in-Canberra' story.

For the more energetic, Canberra is a cyclist's paradise, and bicycles
can be rented at several locations. The city has the best system of
cycleways in Australia, and on a nice day, the ride around **Lake Burley
Griffin** is particularly pleasant. A cruise—one including lunch—around
the lake provides a fascinating perspective on the city. (Rowboats and
paddleboats can also be hired.) Early morning hot-air balloons operate
year-round over Canberra and provide another unusual perspective.

The Canberra Tourist Bureau offices in Sydney and Melbourne are
a useful source of detailed information and can also arrange transport
to the capital as well as tours and accommodation before departure.
For self-drivers coming from Sydney, there is also a Visitor
Information Centre on the main highway into Canberra. And for those

who prefer to arrange their itineraries once they have arrived, the best stop is the Bureau's Jolimont Tourist Centre in the heart of the city. Open daily, the centre is also the main departure point for many tours.

Canberra and its environs offer many attractions. There is even something for wine-lovers, with some 13 wineries located in the Canberra district. While not as well established as in other parts of Australia, they are small, friendly operations and the cool climate, similar to that of Bordeaux in France, is beginning to produce some fine wines. But because of the city's short history, there are relatively few pubs in Canberra, though its many licensed clubs—most of which also feature poker machines—welcome visitors.

Canberra

The best place to begin a tour of Canberra is from one of the capital's three main hilltop lookouts—**Mt Ainslie**, **Red Hill** or **Black Mountain**. Any of these gives visitors an early appreciation of the genius of Walter Burley Griffin's geometric design for the capital. The most spectacular—and highest—view comes from the futuristic **Telecom Tower** atop Black Mountain just west of **Civic**, Canberra's downtown district. Built to provide communications links to and from the capital, the tower rises 195 metres (640 feet) above the summit and has enclosed and open public viewing galleries with breathtaking panoramic views of the entire Canberra region. The tower also has a souvenir kiosk, coffee shop and revolving restaurant. (It costs only A\$2 and is open from 9 am to 10 pm. If you have time, return later for sunset and after-dark views.)

The most prominent feature of Griffin's design—and now the site of most of Canberra's monumental public buildings—is the parliamentary triangle. With the **New Parliament House** at its apex, it stretches across **Lake Burley Griffin** to the northern shore (see map, pages 82–3). Opened by Queen Elizabeth II in May 1988, the unusual building, dominated by an 81-metre (266-foot) stainless steel flag-pole, was designed to fit into the natural shape of **Capital Hill**. In an eight-year billion-dollar project, most of the hill was carted away and stored. Then, after the new parliament was constructed, the dirt was replaced and the slopes covered in grass, giving the building a bunker-like appearance. Australians joke that it is the only parliament building in the world where people can actually walk on top of their politicians!

As usual, the New Parliament House attracted plenty of criticism during its construction, particularly concerning cost-overruns, union disputes and whether the country's poorly regarded politicians were worth such an indulgence. Some of that criticism lingers on today. (Journalists in the parliamentary press gallery, for example, complain that it is now much more difficult to rub shoulders with politicians.) But as an illustration of modern monumental architecture, the building—heavily laden with marble and wood—is definitely worth seeing. In contrast to the cosy old Parliament House located between the hill and the lake, there are vast public viewing areas which exhibit some fine examples of Australian artistic talent, including tapestries, paintings and woodwork. (Set amid fountains outside the main entrance is a large, particularly stunning, Aboriginal mosaic, made in the Papunya style.)

The building is open from 9 am to 5 pm and has a souvenir kiosk and reasonably priced cafeteria. Guided tours are available, and if the House of Representatives is in session, a visit to the public gallery provides an interesting insight into Australian political life. Question Time, when ministers are quizzed on the government's policies by other MPs, often turns into fiery exchanges of verbal abuse spiced with plenty of the Australian vernacular. Widespread hopes that parliamentary decorum would improve with the move to the more elegant new building have yet to be fulfilled.

Located nearby on the southern shore of the lake and at the heart of the parliamentary triangle, the **Australian National Gallery** is the home of the country's art collection. Opened in 1982, the vast building houses a few foreign masterpieces by Picasso, Pollock and Warhol, but foreign visitors may be more interested in the gallery's Australian works, particularly the way early European artists painted their new surroundings. A large collection of Aboriginal artifacts, paintings, sculptures, prints and textiles are also on show, as well as rotating exhibitions on Australian photography, prints and decorative arts. (The gallery is open from 10 am to 5 pm daily and admission is A$3.) The gallery's sculpted gardens are also worth a look.

Next door, and built on the same massive scale as the gallery, is the **High Court** building, the Australian equivalent of the US Supreme Court. Opened as recently as 1980, the building provided the first permanent home for the nation's highest court. Further to the west is the modern Grecian-style **National Library**, home for the country's largest collection of books and documents.

On the northern side of the lake, and on a direct axis between the New Parliament House and Mt Ainslie, is the capital's most popular tourist attraction, the **Australian War Memorial**. With its distinctive copper dome, the memorial is the closest thing Australia has to a national museum and depicts its involvement in nine wars. Since colonial troops were sent to New Zealand in the 1850s to put down the Maori Wars, Australians have given their lives in far-away wars. Mostly in the defence of the British Empire, the campaigns saw

Australia's legendary 'diggers' in the Sudan, the Boer War, the Middle East and French trenches of World War I, and European, North African and Pacific campaigns in World War II. More recently, Australian troops were in Korea, Malaya and South Vietnam. Opened in 1941, the memorial is a shrine, museum, art gallery and national repository for war records. Military hardware is exhibited in the aircraft hall and in the grounds outside. The most moving sections are the Hall of Memory, the Pool of Reflection and a Roll of Honour listing all of Australia's war dead. The Australian War Memorial Shop has an excellent stock of military books, models, prints and posters. The memorial is open from 9 am to 4.45 pm daily, with a visit taking at least two hours.

Lake Burley Griffin, the capital's centrepiece, offers several attractions. Created in 1963 after the damming of the Molonglo River, the lake has 35 kilometres (22 miles) of shoreline, all of it parklands. (There is even a Canberra Yacht Club.) The **Canberra Planning Exhibition** at **Regatta Point**, just off the Commonwealth Bridge, makes an interesting stop. Through a variety of media, the exhibition explains the history and development of this unique city. Nearby is the city's famous **Captain Cook Memorial Water Jet**. Built in 1970 to mark the bicentennial of the explorer's discovery of Australia's east coast, it sends a water column more than 140 metres (460 feet) into the air several times a day. (When a strong easterly wind is blowing, it is also a good way to wash your windscreen as you drive over the nearby bridge.) Further to the east, and a pleasant bicycle ride away, is the **Carillon**, widely regarded as one of the finest bell towers in the world and a gift from the British government for Canberra's 50th anniversary. Elsewhere around the lake, the **Black Mountain Peninsula**—just below the mountain and its distinctive tower—offers a pleasant stop for a stroll, swim or picnic.

Another worthwhile stop is the nearby **Australian National Botanic Gardens**, at the foot of Black Mountain. Devoted totally to native plants, the gardens have over 6,000 species on display, including a rain forest and banksia display. For those interested in Australian animals, Canberra offers the **Mugga Lane Zoo** in Red Hill and, just north of the city, **Rehwinkel's Animal Park**.

If you have a car, exploring Canberra's park-like suburbs is also an agreeable experience. Areas of particular interest are the inner suburbs of **Yarralumla**, **Forrest** and **Red Hill**, where most of the capital's 70 embassies are located. With encouragement from the government, many are built in the national styles of their home countries.

Outside Canberra

Canberra is ideally located to offer a taste of the Australian bush. A visit to the **Burbong** sheep station, or ranch, outside the city is a regular stop for tour groups as well as visiting dignitaries. The visit includes displays of sheep shearing, sheep dogs at work, and boomerang-throwing competitions, followed by a typical Aussie barbecue. The famous **Gundaroo Pub**, which dates back to 1865, is another favourite stop, offering traditional colonial food, bush music and lots of beer. (Tours leave from the Jolimont Centre.)

But for the still largely unspoiled out-of-doors, the best place to visit is the **Tidbindilla Nature Reserve**, about half an hour's drive from the city in the foothills of the Brindabella Range. The reserve is criss-crossed with walking trails and it is easy to spot kangaroos, koalas, emus and other native animals in their natural surroundings. There are also several wildlife enclosures, and rangers are on hand to provide commentaries. Nearby, the huge dishes of the NASA-run **Tinbinddilla Deep Space Tracking Station** provide an important link for American space missions. (The station has a small visitor's centre, but most of the complex is off-limits.)

Further to the south along the banks of the Murrumbidgee River, the tiny village of **Tharwa** dates back to the early days of European settlement and is the centre of a thriving arts and crafts industry. A visit to the **Cuppacumbalong Crafts Centre**, with its hearty lunches and rural views, is well worthwhile. Just north of the township is the **Lanyon Homestead**; built in 1859, it is one of the oldest and most beautiful buildings in the region. Now restored, the homestead is a museum of the early settler period. Nearby is the **Sir Sidney Nolan Gallery**, which features several works by one of Australia's most popular modern artists.

About half an hour northeast of Canberra and across the border of New South Wales, historic **Bungendore** is worth a stop, particularly for those en route to the South Coast. Now a thriving centre for woodcraft, the village also has two colonial-era homes now converted into bed-and-breakfast establishments. Further down the road to the coast, **Braidwood** is a historic gold town classified by The National Trust. Many of its 19th-century buildings have been restored and house craft, antique and coffee shops. If you want to stay overnight, the best place is **Torpy's**, where the A$50 bill includes bed and three square meals.

Finally, visitors flying or driving into Canberra are sometimes confused by the sizeable NSW border town of **Queanbeyan** just east of the capital. In existence long before Canberra was created, the historic town of 24,000 is the principal commercial centre for the surrounding pastoral country. (When accommodation in the capital is fully booked, Queanbeyan is a good alternative.)

*(Following pages) Pounded by the stormy waters of Bass Strait,
the Twelve Apostles sit precariously off the Victorian coast
southwest of Melbourne*   97

Victoria

A Taste of Old England

The popular image of Australia is of a land of wide open spaces. But next to neighbouring Tasmania, it is hard to find a greater contrast to that image than Victoria. Instead of the reddish-browns and vast blue horizons of the Outback, Victoria is temperate in climate, dazzling green in colour, and hemmed in by cloud-covered mountains. It is the sort of place where you have to remind yourself that you are in Australia.

Occupying 227,000 square kilometres (87,876 square miles) in the southeastern corner of the continent, Victoria is Australia's second-smallest state after Tasmania. But like its giant neighbour to the north, New South Wales, the state was one of the first regions of Australia to be settled by Europeans. Drawn by the familiar temperate climate and rich soils, and later by gold, Victoria's population has grown rapidly ever since. Today, with 4.2 million inhabitants—nearly three million of whom live in the capital, Melbourne—it has Australia's second-highest population after New South Wales. (With nearly ten million residents, the two states account for over half of Australia's population of 16 million.)

Despite its small size, Victoria offers an enormous variety of scenery. The state's most dominant feature is the southern extension of the Great Dividing Range, marked in the northeast by the high peaks and plateaus of the Victorian Alps which are covered with snow in winter. To the west are the lower but spectacularly beautiful Grampians. Scattered around the state are more than 50 national parks, covering more than one million hectares (2.4 million acres). Further inland towards the Murray River, the land is flat, and in a tiny pocket in the northwestern corner of the state there is even a taste of the Australian Outback.

But it is along Victoria's long coastline that one finds the most engrossing scenery. Running for 1,600 kilometres (1,000 miles) between the borders of South Australia and New South Wales, the coast is a fascinating mixture of rugged headlands, steep cliffs, long golden beaches and vast bays and lagoons. But as the early settlers soon discovered, the coast's staggering beauty can be deceiving. Along the state's southern edge, Bass Strait—at the eastern end of the Roaring Forties—is one of the most treacherous bodies of water in the world. The Victorian coastline is littered with over 400 shipwrecks, mostly sailing ships from the colonial era.

Blessed by consistent rainfall and its temperate climate, much of Victoria is lush and green, and it is easy to see why the state is

affectionately nicknamed 'The Garden State'. Especially in the country regions, the large number of deciduous trees and pines introduced by the early settlers, the extensive farming and grazing lands, and its old world-style homes combine to give the state a distinctly English atmosphere.

There are other attractions, many of them man-made. The gold-rush days left Victoria with Australia's best collection of 19th-century colonial architecture, not only in Melbourne but also in other once-thriving mining towns such as Ballarat, Bendigo and Beechworth. Intensive settlement has also given the state literally dozens of quaint country and coastal towns, each with its own character and history. For the wine buff, Victoria boasts more wineries—85 at the time of writing—than any other state in Australia. They are scattered throughout the state in the most surprising places, with some barely half an hour outside Melbourne. For the short-term visitor, Victoria's biggest attraction is that nothing in the state is more than half a day's drive away.

Victoria may be a small state, but that has not stopped its residents from developing giant egos. Victorians love to remind visitors that their state was founded by free settlers—and not by convicts as were New South Wales and Tasmania. The rivalry with their northern neighbour is particulary intense, especially when it comes to arguments over who brews the best beer or plays a more exciting brand of football. As a result of their background, Victorians also see themselves as more sophisticated and cultured than New South Welshmen, whom they consider to be brash and hedonistic. There is an element of truth behind those rather broad generalizations. But as one Melbourne friend commented, 'The sun isn't as hot down here either.'

History

After circumnavigating and charting New Zealand in early 1770, Captain Cook was heading west—and towards home—when he stumbled on to the previously unknown east coast of the Australian continent. The English explorer's landfall was at Point Hicks on the rugged eastern coastline of present-day Victoria, 400 kilometres (250 miles) east of Melbourne. Sighting off 371-metre- (1,218-foot-) high Mt Everard behind the point, Cook turned his ships towards Botany Bay and other points north. When the convict colony of New South Wales was established in Sydney 18 years later, explorers soon set out by sea to explore the southern coastline. In 1797, Royal Navy surgeon George Bass sailed past Point Hicks to Wilson's Promontory, the most southeasterly point of the continent and on to Western Port Bay before dwindling supplies forced him to turn back. The following year, joined by Matthew Flinders, Bass determined that Van Diemen's Land (Tasmania) was separated from the mainland by the strait that now bears his name—Bass Strait. Further exploration of the coastline of present-day Victoria took place during Flinders' epic circumnavigation of the continent beginning in 1801.

Early attempts to settle the region proved dismal failures. Fearful of growing French interest in and possible settlement of the continent, a small expedition of soldiers, settlers and convicts under Colonel David Collins put ashore at Sorrento at the mouth of Port Phillip Bay in 1803. But within months, a shortage of fresh water forced the settlement's closure and its residents moved across Bass Strait to Van Diemen's Land. Another settlement on the swampy eastern shore of Western Port Bay in 1826 lasted only a few months before it, too, was abandoned.

There was much more encouraging news from overland expeditions into the Port Phillip district during the 1820s and 1830s. Explorers such as Hamilton Hume, whose trail is now the main highway linking Sydney and Melbourne, returned with tales of rich grazing and farming lands in the south in a temperate climate similar to that of England. In their enthusiasm, they labelled the region 'Australia Felix'. Despite a government ban, hundreds of squatters—or illegal settlers—soon moved in to stake out runs for their sheep. The region's first permanent settlement was established at Portland in 1834 by Edward Henty and his family who slipped across from Tasmania.

With financial backing from land speculators in Van Diemen's Land, John Batman arrived on the shores of Port Phillip Bay the following year. In a bargain with the native inhabitants very similar to that which gave New York's Manhattan Island to the Dutch in the 17th century, Batman purchased 243,000 hectares (600,500 acres) along the bay's northern reaches from the local Aborigines for an odd collection of blankets, knives, tomahawks, clothing and other trinkets. Along the banks of the Yarra River at the northeastern corner of the bay, site of today's Customs House in downtown Melbourne, he formally declared, 'This will be the site for a village.'

Although Batman's treaty with the Aborigines was quickly voided by the New South Wales' governor, the incident finally forced the government in 1836 to open up the district to legal settlement. Orders were also given for surveyors to draw up a grid-iron plan for the town of Melbourne, named in honour of the British prime minister of the day. With the arrival of free settlers directly from England, the population of Melbourne and the district grew rapidly as more regions were explored and then opened up to agriculture. (As elsewhere, the

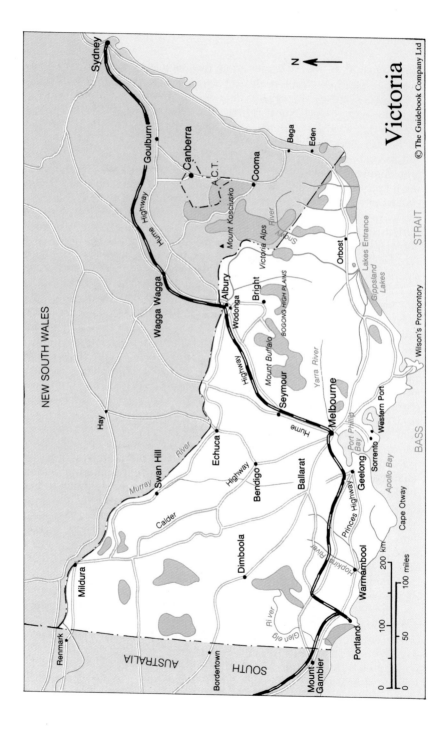

Victoria

© The Guidebook Company Ltd

Aborigines were the main victims of this expansion and by 1856 their numbers had dwindled to only 800, compared to 15,000 when white colonization began.) Soon, the district's residents were agitating for separation from New South Wales. In 1850, the Colony of Victoria was formally created.

The colony's prosperity and viability were quickly assured. The following year, massive finds of gold were discovered around Ballarat and Bendigo, northwest of Melbourne. As word spread, a massive gold-rush was soon underway. Thousands abandoned cities and farms to try their luck, while many thousands more flowed into the colony from around the world. (The rush also attracted many Americans who had failed to find their fortunes as 'forty-niners' on the California gold-fields.) And while not everyone became rich, the gold-rush had profound social, economic and political effects on Australia's development. With gold now attracting so many able-bodied men quite voluntarily, the British government finally terminated the transportation of convicts to eastern Australia once and for all. (Although abolished in 1840, transportation was briefly resumed in the late 1840s.)

Economically, the discovery of gold turned Melbourne, previously only a service centre for farmers and graziers, into Australia's financial capital, a position that continues to this day. Much of the colony's new-found wealth went into beautiful parks and boulevards and in building the many extravagant buildings, ornate churches and impressive monuments that give the city its special charm today. By 1860, nearly half of Australia's population was living in Victoria.

The gold-rush also had serious political consequences. When the government imposed an onerous licence fee on the miners, many charged that this amounted to 'taxation without representation' and an undue hardship at a time when many gold-fields were beginning to lose their productivity. They were further angered by a tough, and frequently humiliating, police crack-down on unlicensed miners. In late 1854, thousands of 'diggers' at Ballarat openly rebelled by burning their licences. The more militant took up arms and built a stockade at nearby Eureka over which they raised the flag of the Southern Cross. On 3 December, after the rebels refused to surrender, troops charged the stockade and, in a pitched battle, 29 men were killed and another 41 wounded, most of them miners. Now remembered as the Eureka Rebellion, the incident was the only armed insurrection ever to take place on Australian soil. But the incident, which raised fears of a repeat of the American War of Independence, so shocked the colony's government that they quickly agreed to many of the miners' demands, including the right to vote and other political concessions. Some years later, the miners' leader, Peter Lalor, was even elected—as a political conservative—to the colony's legislative assembly.

On the land, the squatters' rights were finally recognized by a special Act of Parliament in 1860. Their permanent titles allowed these prosperous graziers—known as the 'squattocracy'—to improve their lands, especially the construction of grand homesteads that are now popular tourist attractions. But not everyone was so fortunate, especially among those trying to make a living off small plots of land. When an Irish-born settler named Ned Kelly killed three policemen in 1878, he was hailed by many of the colony's poor as a Robin Hood. For two years, the Kelly gang roamed around northeastern Victoria, supported by sympathetic farmers and a string of bank robberies. Finally, in a pub at Glenrowan, Kelly draped himself in homemade armour and, in a dramatic shoot-out with police, was wounded and captured. When he was hanged at the Old Melbourne Gaol later in 1880, Kelly's last words were, 'Such is life.' Despite his excesses at the time, Kelly is immortalized as one of Australia's leading folk heroes.

By the turn of the century, Victoria was Australia's most intensely developed colony, producing much of its wheat, wool and prime lambs. Like the Mississippi River in the United States, the Murray River along the northern border with New South Wales became a thriving inland waterway, while irrigation opened up the colony's northern region to crops, especially fruit and grapes. The colony's wealth saw the early construction of an extensive rail and road system. Today, the state's prosperity comes from a mixture of agriculture, light and heavy industry, and oil and natural gas. (Rich deposits in Bass Strait make Australia 70 percent self-sufficient in petroleum.)

Getting Around

Although it does not receive as many international flights as Sydney, Melbourne is a major entry point into Australia for many tourists. (One advantage of this is that the city's international airport is not as overloaded.) There are also regular air, rail and bus services with other parts of Australia. For the self-driver, the trip from Sydney to Melbourne takes about ten hours, but with so much to see in between, including Canberra, it would be foolish to hurry.

In Melbourne, the extensive public transport system includes its famous trams, and there is a wide range of day tours that include sightseeing cruises of Port Phillip Bay. Outside the capital, visitors have the option of travelling by air, rail or bus, or of joining an escorted bus or rail tour. (V/Line, the state-run rail network, offers several reasonably priced tours to several locations, including the

Bendigo gold-fields and the Victorian Alps; there are also several private companies, such as AAT Kings, Newmans and Trans Otway, who offer packaged tours.)

Because of its compact size, Victoria is perfect touring country for self-drivers. All the major highways radiate out from Melbourne, and the road system is the best in Australia. The best strategy is simply to throw your luggage in the 'boot' of the car and explore the state by means of the many peaceful country roads. Eventually, all roads lead back to Melbourne.

The Victorian Tourism Commission, known as Victour, operates in all of Australia's capital cities and has overseas offices in Britain, the United States, Canada, Japan, Singapore and New Zealand. Within Victoria, the commission has an office in Melbourne and connections with regional information offices throughout the state. As elsewhere, Victour provides a wide range of services, including accommodation and transport to and around the state.

Melbourne is famous for its restaurants, which many people consider the best in Australia. Because of its tough licensing laws, the city was the first in the country to popularize BYO—or Bring Your Own liquor—restaurants, and even though the laws are now more relaxed, the tradition is well entrenched. Like Sydney, Melbourne's rich ethnic diversity has contributed much to the range of cuisines available. (Lygon Street in the suburb of Carlton easily offers the best Italian food this side of Rome.) While not as diverse, restaurants outside Melbourne—often in little country towns—offer hearty traditional cooking and seafood. And a stop for Devonshire Tea, lunch at a country pub, or a visit to one of the state's many wineries, is always a pleasant experience.

Melbourne

Much is made of the traditional rivalry between Sydney and Melbourne, Australia's two largest cities. Both are located in the same southeastern region of the continent—an hour apart by plane or ten hours by road. The rivalry, real or not, is the sort of passionate issue that editors in both cities use to excite their readers on an otherwise slow news day. The argument is rarely resolved one way or the other. Comparisons between Sydney and Melbourne are, of course, inevitable. But after years of dispassionate observation, the best conclusion I can make is they are—quite simply—two very different cities. Each has its own unique physical setting and redeeming qualities. (Melbourne's notorious climate, which often features all four seasons in one day, is one of its less redeeming ones.)

With a population of 2.9 million, Melbourne is Australia's second-

Encounter with a Machete

At eight this morning there was a machete lying on the lawn, flat in the middle of my front yard. It gave me a jolt. It's hard to describe the feeling of seeing a machete lying on your lawn when you're picking up the morning paper. I don't own a machete. It's not a common garden tool around here. In my mind a machete is a weapon of foreign guerillas. Rural terrorists. I associate machetes with the random slaughter of innocent villagers, the massacre of peasant farmers who backed the wrong party.

Well, I picked it up—my heart beating faster—and hefted it in my hand. The blade was heavy and sharp; it was in good order. All the while I couldn't believe it was there in my yard, in my hand. I was peering around to see if the machete's owner was about to appear but there were only the usual sleepy-looking suburban houses coming to life. People were backing cars out of their driveways and leaving for work; children were setting off for school; a woman down the street watered her garden. In a moment I began to feel self-conscious standing there in my suit and tie, all set for work, with the rolled newspaper in one hand and a machete in the other.

Belleview is a new suburb: Gillian and I moved here six months ago but we don't know anyone yet. These sandy, gravelly plains on the outskirts of the city were never thickly vegetated, and the developers bulldozed those trees and bushes, mainly spindly acacias, which had perservered. The residents are just starting to establish their lawns and gardens, but it's a battle in the sand. Everything blows away, and when it rains your topsoil washes half a kilometre down the road. What I'm saying is that it's not tropical rainforest or anything. A rake, a spade and a pair of secateurs will see you through. There is no need for slashing and hacking.

So I was standing in the front yard holding the machete and thinking all sorts of imaginative things. How the machete came to get there in the middle of the night, and so forth. It's a long drive to work, to the bank, and I knew the highway would be jammed already, but now I'd found the machete I couldn't just leave.

My mind was whirling. Gillian left work three weeks ago, in her seventh month of pregnancy, and she would be at home, alone, all day. It was our first baby and she was in a state just being pregnant without me mentioning the machete.

So whose machete was it? I didn't know the neighbours, only that the other young couple on the right worked long hours and that the fellow on the left kept Rottweilers. His wife was Filipino and stayed indoors all the time. Her face peeping through the curtains looked wistful. We'd heard him shouting at night. My guess was that a Rottweiler owner was more likely to own a machete, and to care for it so well.

From where I was standing with the machete I lined up the front door of the Rottweiler residence. There was only the low paling fence separating us. Someone could have thrown the machete from the front door to where I stood if they wanted, if they were impelled to do that. But it was hard to think of a reason why.

I couldn't see myself going next door past all the Rottweilers and asking, 'Excuse me, did you leave your machete in my yard? When you were trespassing last night?' By then it was well after eight and my one clear thought was not to frighten Gillian with any quirkiness. Things were making her weepy and anxious lately: all those children on TV with rare diseases, the hole in the ozone layer, fluoride in the water. I wanted to keep her serene. I took the machete around to the back of the house. I pushed it hard into the sandy flowerbed by the corner of the garage until only the handle stuck up, and that was hidden by shadow. Then I got into the car, drove to work and forgot about it.

But tonight as I was driving home past the Hardware Barn I remembered it. The strange feeling came back and I speeded up. These nights the sun sets well before five and our end of the street was in darkness when I pulled up. The Rottweiler house was dark, and our house too. I left the headlights on and ran to the back of the garage.

There is something more alarming than the presence of a machete. The absence of a machete.

Robert Drewe, The Bay of Contented Men, *1989*

largest city. But what the city lacks by not having spectacular Sydney Harbour on its doorstep is compensated for in many other ways. From the moment Melbourne was created in 1837, colonial administrators insisted on carefully planning the city's growth, starting with Assistant-Surveyor Robert Hoddle's classic grid plan for what is now the downtown district. Helped along by the wealth of the gold-rush in the 1850s, Melbourne grew into Australia's most European city, with broad tree-lined boulevards, beautiful parklands and monumental buildings. Adding to the city's charming appearance are its famous trams, some brightly decorated. (One is even a restaurant, the ultimate Moveable Feast!)

The city itself is built on a slight ridge on the northern bank of the **Yarra River**. Nearby is one of the world's largest and most spectacular bays, **Port Phillip Bay**, which empties through treacherous headlands into stormy **Bass Strait**. Melbourne's suburbs stretch out into flatlands and rising hills around the city. Running down the boot-shaped **Mornington Peninsula** on the bay's eastern shore are some of the city's more exclusive suburbs and miles of calm-water beaches. For the visitor arriving by air, Melbourne's **Tullamarine International Airport** is located on a plain 22 kilometres (14 miles) to the northwest.

Because of the flat terrain, the skyline of Melbourne stands out sharply on the horizon. A building boom in the late 1970s and early 1980s has given the city an assortment of modern high-rise buildings, the tallest being those occupied by hotels. At street-level, there is a mini-Manhattan feel about downtown Melbourne but with a much more relaxed pace. Colonial-era buildings maintain their dignity next to their mirror-sided modern counterparts. Some have retained their old façades and built modern high-rise extensions behind them, most notably the Gothic Revival-style Menzies at Rialto completed in 1981. Reflecting Melbourne's role as an important financial centre, many of the buildings are occupied by banking and corporate headquarters. Mixed in with Victorian-era public buildings and ornate churches are retail shops, boutiques and hotels. Melbourne pubs have a more English character, differing markedly in appearance from those in other states. Adding to the city's European feel, many restaurants and coffee shops set up tables and chairs on the wide sidewalks. As the trams clang past, a cup of cappuccino and a croissant, or a fine meal, is the perfect way for the visitor to soak up the atmosphere and plan the day's itinerary.

Without the physical beauty—and distractions—of Sydney, Melbourne puts its energy into more intellectual pursuits and practising an old-world style of sophistication. It has long been said, for example, that Melbourne women dress much more smartly than those in Sydney. That is hardly surprising considering Melbourne is the nation's fashion capital. (A more logical reason is that the city's more temperate climate simply requires more clothing.) Australia's most successful designers, many of whom are now breaking into markets overseas, live and work in the city. Their fashions, definitely worth a look, are on sale at boutiques in the city and exclusive suburbs such as **Toorak** and **Prahran**. The daily **Queen Victoria Market**, one of the city's original buildings, and the Sunday market along the **Esplanade** at **St Kilda** offer less pricey creative clothing and a wide range of arts and crafts, antiques and bric-à-brac of interest to visitors.

At a more profound level, Melbourne clearly leads Australia in the performing arts, producing many of the country's leading entertainers, film-makers and playwrights. The world-renowned Australian Ballet is based in Melbourne, and the Victorian State Opera ranks second only to the Australian Opera. (The latter comes to town for an annual winter season of performances.) The **Victorian Arts Centre**, across the Yarra River from **Flinders Street Station** and marked by its distinctive white spire, is a vast and impressive multi-million dollar complex that ranks among the best in the world. To avoid marring its physical setting, most of the centre is built underground and includes an acoustically excellent concert hall, three theatres and a performing arts museum. The neighbouring **National Gallery of Victoria**, opened in 1968, is Australia's best, featuring works by many of the country's leading artists. (The complex offers daily tours and entertainment events well worth attending.) International pop stars such as Olivia Newton-John, Men at Work and John Farnham all hail from Melbourne. A high proportion of Australia's most successful films, such as *Mad Max*, *Picnic at Hanging Rock* and *The Man from Snowy River*, were made by local directors. The Victorian capital also has a rich theatre-going tradition. Plays or musicals that flop here simply die. The city's lively cabaret scene is the home of Australian satire and wit, even if it is not always comprehensible to outsiders. The colourful **Moomba Festival**, held every March, is a week-long celebration of the city's pre-eminence in theatre, music and the arts. The city's premier cultural event, the two-week **Spoleto Festival of the Arts**, is held every September and attracts leading overseas and local performing and visual artists. The **Summer Music Festival**, held in January, features a wide mixture of music, including outdoor concerts at the **Sidney Myer Music Bowl** in the **King's Domain**.

As a result of heavy post-war migration from around the world, Melbourne is also heavily cosmopolitan. (Visitors are frequently told, for example, that the city has the largest population of Greeks outside that country.) Without any exaggeration, the city offers the finest

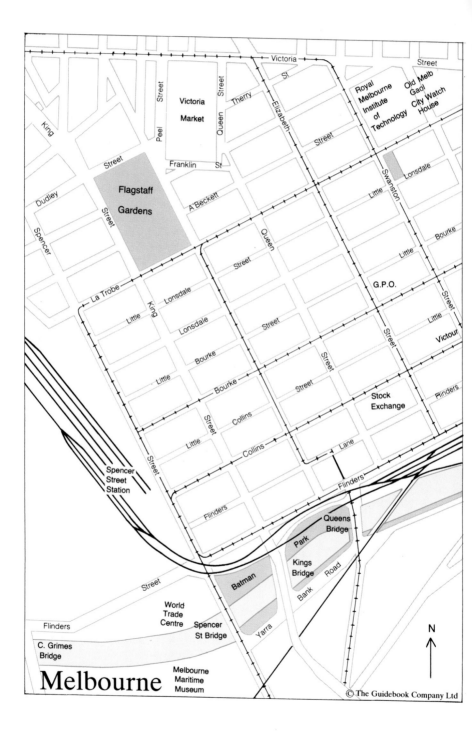

Melbourne

Melbourne Maritime Museum

© The Guidebook Company Ltd

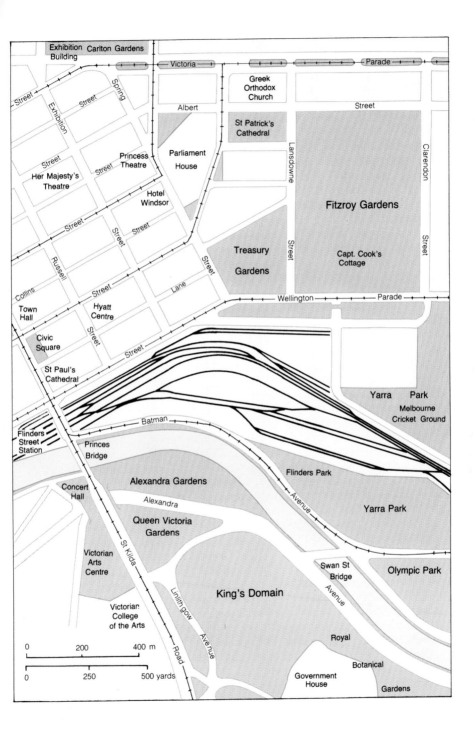

collection of restaurants in Australia, ranging across the ethnic palate from Greek and Italian to Turkish and Vietnamese. Many of the 300 or so restaurants are licensed BYO, or 'bring your own', providing visitors with the added challenge of selecting and buying their own wines.

At the same time, Melbournians treat sport as a religion. Not even the intelligentsia is immune and, for the visitor, it is hard to avoid getting caught up in the evangelical spirit of this pastime. The city is home to Australian Rules Football, a unique brand of football invented on the Victorian gold-fields (see page 118). During the autumn and winter months, passionate supporters pack the city's ovals every weekend, even in the most miserable weather. They then spend days rehashing the games and preparing for the next round. By the time the Grand Final is held in September, the city is gripped by 'footy fever' and up to 100,000 spectators pack into the Melbourne Cricket Ground (MCG).

The Melbournians' passion for cricket is only slightly less restrained. The sport's reputation for sheer boredom did nothing to stop locals from setting the world spectator record for the cricket several years ago. The newly opened **National Tennis Centre**, ranked as one of the best in the world, stages the Australian Open, a grand-slam event held every January. (Visitors are welcome to play tennis on all but the centre court.) On the first Tuesday in November, the entire city takes the day off for another sporting event—the **Melbourne Cup**. Run over 3,200 metres (10,502 feet), the Cup dates back to 1874 and is Australia's leading horse race. (With so many entries, the race is actually more like a stampede.) Like a Down Under version of the Kentucky Derby or Epsom, the glittering event attracts thousands to a mad day of dressing up—and dressing down—at the city's **Flemington Racecourse**. Many in the crowd become so carried away with all the partying that they miss the main event.

Because of its small size and simple layout, Melbourne is ideal to explore on foot. (If you get tired, simply hop aboard a tram.) The **Bourke Street Mall**, with the ornate **General Post Office**, or GPO, at the western end is the hub of Melbourne's retail district, with major department stores, boutiques and souvenir shops. The **Royal Arcade** (1869) and **Block Arcade** (1892), both restored, offer a taste of 19th-century shopping. Nearby **Collins Street**, nicknamed the Golden Mile, is Australia's Wall Street and home of the **Melbourne Stock Exchange**. **Town Hall** and **City Square**, at the corner of **Swanston Street**, are popular venues for live entertainment, including lunchtime performances. At the top end of the boulevard—also known as the Paris End—is the entrance to the **Treasury** and **Fitzroy Gardens** and, a

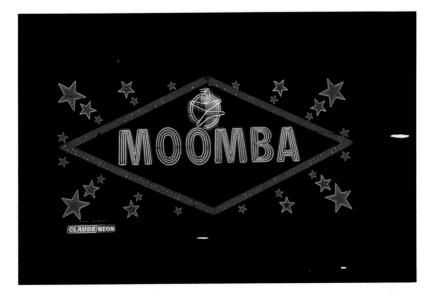

block north along Spring Street, **Parliament House**.

Opened as the colonial legislative assembly in 1856, the ornate Victorian-style building served as the Federal Parliament from 1901 to 1927 before the Australian capital moved to Canberra. Today, it houses the Victorian state Parliament and is a favourite site for rallies and demonstrations. Visitors are welcome to stroll up the grand staircase to the main entrance and examine one of the finest examples of parliamentary architecture. Across the street is 'the grand lady of Spring Street', the **Windsor Hotel**, built in 1883 and magnificently restored. Next door, in the same colonial style, is Melbourne's oldest theatre, the **Princess**, opened in 1887. The city's **Chinatown** district, originally established by Chinese gold-miners, stretches for three blocks down **Little Bourke Street**. The **Old Melbourne Gaol** in Russell Street is where Ned Kelly (see page 104) was hanged in 1880 and is now a museum.

Reflecting its founders' desire to recreate a taste of old England, Melbourne is famous for its parks and gardens. Although appearing slightly out of place in Australia, they are a refreshing collection of winding paths, ornamental ponds, flower beds and century-old exotic trees. **Fitzroy Gardens**, behind Parliament House, is now home to **Captain Cook's Cottage**, brought over piece-by-piece from Yorkshire in 1934. (Further east, surrounded by gardens, is the famous **Melbourne Cricket Ground**, the birthplace of Australian Rules

Sports

Australians have a justifiable reputation as sports fanatics. Much of this comes from their love of the great outdoors, drinking and gambling. If they are not actually playing a sport, Aussies are busy watching, listening to or debating the subject. Not long after I arrived in Australia, I joined a group of local journalists in the pub. Their conversation focused not on the weighty political and economic issues of the day but on an upcoming Rugby League match and the best prospects for the weekend's horse-racing Trifecta.

Except for horse-racing, spectator sports in Australia vary according to the season. Football dominates the winter months, when five different codes vie for the fans' attention. And of these, Australian Rules Football generates the nation's most passionate followers. A homegrown game combining elements of Gaelic football, rugby and basketball, 'Aussie Rules' has to be seen live to be fully appreciated. Played on the sporting world's largest football field, and with 18 men on a side, the game is a rough-and-tumble mixture of spectacular kicking, leaps, passing and tackling that goes on for a gruelling two hours. Goals are scored by kicking the ball, often from a considerable distance, through one of three goal posts at either end of the field. Aussie Rules is a virtual religion in Australia's southern states, and passions reach fever pitch in Melbourne during Grand Final Week at the end of September.

In New South Wales to the north, fans are almost as fanatical about Rugby League. A faster and more open game than Rugby Union, the game has 13 players to a side and is just as rough as American Football but without the help of helmets and padding. Union, still an amateur sport, also has its devoted followers, especially when international teams such as the New Zealand All-Blacks are visiting. While still relatively young sports in Australia, soccer and gridiron (American Football) are also growing in popularity.

Cricket reigns during the long summer months. Traditionally, this is when international teams tour the country, and there is nothing quite like a visit by the West Indies or England to arouse Australian patriotism. To the consternation of many traditionalists, one-day cricket matches—in which a win is guaranteed—have gained wide popularity in recent years. Tennis is another popular summer sport, with the Australian Open—one of the Grand Slam events—held in Melbourne every January, attracting top players from around the world.

Australians are world-famous as 'punters', or gamblers, and horse-racing is a year-round passion. There are race meetings literally every day around the country, with a massive network of betting facilities. At the top of the calendar is the Melbourne Cup, run on the first Tuesday of November, when all of Australia literally stops for its richest and most prestigious horse-race.

Football in 1858, the first Test Cricket match with England in 1877, and the Melbourne Olympics in 1956.) A couple of blocks to the north are the **Carlton Gardens** with its late Victorian-era **Exhibition Buildings**, built originally for the Centennial International Exhibition in 1888. But even more impressive are the **Royal Botanic Gardens**, across the Princes Bridge on the south bank of the Yarra River, and ranked as one of the finest landscaped gardens in the world. The gardens, designed by German botanist Frederick von Mueller, include the imposing **Shrine of Remembrance** to honour Australia's war dead and the **Myer Music Bowl**, popular for outdoor day and night concerts, particularly in summer. The **King's Domain Gardens** surround **La Trobe Cottage**, the original residence of the colony's governor, while **Como House**, in nearby **South Yarra**, is one of the city's most historic mansions, dating back to 1840. With its landscaped gardens of ponds, fernery and lawns, **Rippon Lea**, in the suburb of **Elsternwick**, is the city's best-preserved Victorian-era mansion.

Around Melbourne

Located southeast of the city, the picturesque **Mornington Peninsula** separates Port Phillip Bay from the smaller Western Port Bay to the east and fronts on to the stormy waters of Bass Strait. The long crescent of the bay offers calm-water beaches that are very popular in summer but the crowds rapidly diminish the further one travels down the Nepean Highway. Just south of Frankston, **Mt Eliza** — a bare 160 metres (525 feet) high — offers spectacular views out over both bays and the mostly rural hinterland. At the fishing town of **Mornington**, a **memorial** marks the visit of Matthew Flinders to Port Phillip Bay in 1802. The explorer was also the first European to climb **Arthurs Seat** further to the south, a hilltop now accessible by weekend chair lift. On the bay side, **Sorrento** was the site of the region's ill-fated first settlement the following year; little now remains of their presence except for a cemetery. At the tip of the peninsula, three kilometres (1.8 miles) away, the tiny settlement of **Portsea** offers both bay and ocean beaches. (A ferry service runs across the narrow and treacherous entrance to the bay, known as **The Rip**, to **Queenscliff**, site of a massive fort to protect the colony from a feared Russian invasion in the 1850s.)

On the ocean side, the windswept landscape consists of stark heath-covered sandstone cliffs with rugged headlands separating tiny beaches pounded by the heavy surf of Bass Strait. Swimming can be extremely dangerous. Australian Prime Minister, Harold Holt disappeared while swimming off this beautiful little beach on a Sunday morning in December 1967. His body was never found. Stretching off towards the

southeast is **Cape Schanck Coastal Park** where a well-kept walking track leads through the unspoiled bushland. At the Cape, a popular surfing spot, a lonely lighthouse overlooks tiny **Bushranger Bay** and **Pulpit Rock**. Further south is **Flinders**, at the entrance to Western Port Bay. (Ferries from Stony Point run to French Island at the centre of the bay and Phillip Island—see below.) Returning to Melbourne, the roads wind through hills and meadows given over to farming and grazing.

    Western Port Bay is much smaller (150 square kilometres, or 58 square miles) and different in character from Port Phillip Bay. Instead of fine sandy beaches, mangroves thrive along the mudflats and there are numerous sheltered creeks and harbours. The bay's most notable feature is **French Island** at its centre, capped by a solitary pyramid-shaped hill. Once a prison settlement, the island has avoided massive development and remains a mixture of farms and national parks. From Melbourne, the eastern shore of the bay is down the South Gippsland and Bass highways, the heavily travelled tourist route to **Phillip Island**. Straddling the entrance to the bay, the island is famous for its nightly parade of fairy penguins, the only members of the species to live so far north.

    After the Great Barrier Reef and Ayers Rock, Phillip Island is Australia's third-most popular tourist attraction. Everyone comes to see the penguins. But if these terribly cute animals were not such creatures of habit, they would do better to find another beach on which to come ashore. As hundreds of bused-in tourists, many of them Japanese, look on from flood-lit bleachers, the penguins splash ashore, take one look at the gawking crowd and scamper off into their nearby burrows. (The spectacle is worth seeing, but the discerning visitor cannot help but feel sorry for the penguins.) Afterwards, most tourists hop back on their bus and return to Melbourne. But there is a lot more to see. The small farming and resort island—roughly 20 by ten kilometres (12 by six miles)—is also home to free-ranging koalas, large colonies of fur seals and over 200 species of birds, including the unusual mutton bird. The island's 100 kilometres (62 miles) of shoreline varies from tranquil inlets to rugged headlands and rocky offshore islets. The motor racing circuit on the island was used in the famous Fred Astaire death scene from the film *On the Beach*. The principal town on the island is **Cowes** which, along with **San Remo** back on the mainland, provides a wide range of accommodation and restaurants. **Corinella**, now just a small fishing and holiday village on the east side of the bay, was the site of Victoria's second attempt at white settlement back in 1826. (Heading back towards Melbourne, the recently opened **Giant Worm** explains the lifestyle of the world's longest earthworm, creatures which grow to three metres (ten feet) in length and live in the hills around nearby **Korumburra**.)

The **Dandenong Ranges**, 35 kilometres (22 miles) east of Melbourne, offer a different range of scenery. An extension of the Great Dividing

Range running down the entire east coast of Australia, the Dandenongs feature majestic eucalypt forests and deep ferny gullies that provide sanctuary for a wide range of native wildlife such as parrots, lyrebirds, wombats and echidnas. Long popular for its cooler climate, the hills are also dotted with charming little villages with colourful flower and fruit gardens. Many have antique shops, arts and crafts studios and fine restaurants. The famous **Puffing Billy**, a vintage train run by volunteers, provides an unforgettable 13-kilometre (eight-mile) run through the cool forests. From **Mt Dandenong** (630 metres, or 2,067 feet), there are splendid views over the surrounding countryside and coastline and back towards Melbourne. At the northern end of the Dandenongs, the **Healesville Wildlife Sanctuary** provides a habitat for a wide range of native animals, including kangaroos and koalas, and is one of the few to breed the illusive duck-billed platypus in captivity. The wineries of the nearby **Yarra Valley**, Victoria's original wine-growing region, are the closest to Melbourne. A visit to the well-signposted vineyards, whose buildings date back to 1854, make a pleasant diversion—even if you do not drive away with a couple of cases of wine.

The Gold-fields

Located 112 kilometres (70 miles) northwest of Melbourne, **Ballarat** (population 78,000) is the gateway to the Victorian gold-fields. Spread through the low, tree-covered hill country that marks the western extension of the Great Dividing Range, the region is rich in history dating back to the colony's beginnings. Popular with tourists, it has managed to maintain much of its colonial-era charm. For the foreign visitor, the attractions offer a fascinating insight into Australia's past.

According to local stories, gold was first discovered in August 1851 when a prospector named James Esmond who was passing through the Ballarat area took shelter from a storm under some trees. Digging about his feet, he uncovered several pieces of gold. Word of the amazingly rich find soon spread, touching off a massive gold-rush that attracted thousands of diggers from Australia and overseas. At the height of the rush in the mid-1850s, some 60,000 persons were working the Ballarat fields. As the surface gold ran out, most of the men moved on, and companies were formed to exploit the underground veins of ore. The city's last mine closed down in 1918 after an incredible 650 tons of gold had been removed. Today, Ballarat's golden past lives on in its magnificent Victorian-era buildings, statuary and landscaped gardens. The **Sovereign Hill Goldmining Township**, located near the site of the original gold find, is a living museum recreating the city's first ten years of existence. East of Ballarat, a marble monument and diorama marks the famous **Eureka Stockade**, the scene of the armed rebellion by miners in 1854 (see above).

From Ballarat, the Midland Highway winds north through forest-covered hills and sheltered valleys dotted with once-thriving gold-mining towns. The countryside is pocked with old diggings, collapsed shacks and ghost towns. **Daylesford**, 47 kilometres (29 miles) to the northeast, survived the gold-rush and today thrives as 'The Spa Center of Australia' due to its numerous mineral springs. ('Drink it, bath in it, take some home,' boasts Victour.) The springs attracted many Swiss and Italian settlers in the late 19th century, an influence still visible in the town's architecture and traditions. (The typically northern Italian-style **Macaroni Factory**, which used the waters to add a distinctive taste to their pasta, is classified by the National Trust.) Further north, **Castlemaine** was once one of the region's busiest gold-mining centres and has some of Victoria's finest early buildings, most notably the Restoration-style **Market Museum**. Many have now been restored to provide bed-and-breakfast accommodation. At nearby **Maldon**, the National Trust thought so much of the quaint little town that they preserved the entire place in 1966. Its hundreds of buildings—and even a steam train—have been faithfully restored to their original condition.

With a population of 66,000, **Bendigo**, 155 kilometres (96 miles) northwest of Melbourne, marks the northern end of the gold-fields. (The Northern Highway links the city directly with the state capital.) If anything, Bendigo is even grander than Ballarat. The gold discovered here in 1852 was imbedded in quartz, requiring huge risk capital that made equally huge profits. Determined to recreate a taste of London, the city's millionaire miners named the main street **Pall Mall** and invested much of their earnings on ornate buildings, public gardens, statues and the arts. The slightly incongruous result is a 19th-century English city dropped into the middle of the Australian countryside. At the main intersection, appropriately named **Charing Cross**, stands the stately **Alexandria Fountain**, built to honour the popular Princess of Wales of that era. (Queen Victoria's grandsons personally inaugurated the statuary.) Along the main street, the most extravagant building is the five-storey **Shamrock Hotel**. Vintage trams, saved from closure by an emotional public outcry in the early 1970s, are now a leading attraction and take visitors down grand tree-lined boulevards to the **Central Deborah Goldmine**. The city is also the home of Australia's best-known pottery, **Bendigo Pottery**, which carries on another old English tradition and is open to the public.

The Coastal Areas

Melbourne and its vast Port Phillip Bay divide the 1,600 kilometres (1,000 miles) of Victorian coast into two roughly equal-sized regions. The **Southwest Coast** begins past the provincial city of **Geelong** (population 140,000), a mini-version of Melbourne, on the western side of Port Phillip Bay. The 320-kilometre- (199-mile-) long **Great Ocean Road** is the most spectacular coastal road in Australia. Built between 1916 and 1932 as a memorial to the nation's war dead, the winding two-lane highway clings to a ruggedly beautiful coastline flanked by the sharply rising forest-covered **Otway Ranges**. Between cliffs and deserted beaches are picturesque resort towns and quaint fishing villages, often set at the mouth of tidal estuaries. **Apollo Bay**, 185 kilometres (115 miles) southwest of Melbourne, is a thriving fishing port full of historic buildings and the gateway to windswept **Otway National Park**. (The region is located roughly due south of the gold-fields and accessible from there by a network of country roads running through the so-called lakes and craters area.)

West of **Cape Otway** and its lonely lighthouse, the scenery becomes even more spectacular as the road winds towards **Port Campbell National Park** and its famous sandstone rock formations. Best-known — and very much a pictorial symbol for Victoria and used in numerous television commercials — are the **Twelve Apostles**, lonely offshore sentinels that appear ready to collapse at any moment. The

park also includes **London Bridge** and **The Arch**, equally fragile-appearing natural arches. Nearby, **Loch Ard Gorge** is famous as the spot where only two survivors from a migrant ship stumbled ashore in 1878. West along the **Shipwreck Coast** to the South Australian border comes as something of an anticlimax. On the edge of a vast and fertile volcanic plain, the area is intensively farmed, supporting the large country towns of **Warrnambool**, once a whaling port, and **Portland**, site of the first permanent white settlement in Victoria and now its second largest. The original **Henty Homestead** is Portland's leading tourist attraction. Across the plain, **Hamilton** is the gateway to **The Grampians**, a geologically unique range with rare flowering plants and wildflowers, numerous native animals and Aboriginal art sites.

East of Melbourne, the coastline varies radically. **Wilson's Promontory**, 193 kilometres (120 miles) southeast of Melbourne, dominates the coast. First sighted by George Bass in 1798, the massive granite outcrop covered in coastal heathland is the most southerly point of the Australian continent. Exposed to the winds and waves of Bass Strait, the 'Prom' offers spectacular coastal and mountain scenery that has been protected since 1905 as a national park. Numerous walking tracks threading through the park lead to isolated beaches, bays and headlands. Sharp-edged mountains in the interior of the peninsula rise above 650 metres (2,133 feet). Camping is permitted at designated spots, and towns just outside the park provide motel accommodation and flats.

To the northeast of the promontory, and also accessible due east of Melbourne on the Princes Highway, is the '**Victorian Riviera**'. Boasting a milder climate than elsewhere along the Victorian coast, the region stretches all the way to the New South Wales border. The deserted beaches and sand dunes of **Ninety Mile Beach** provide a barrier to the famous **Gippsland Lakes**, a network of shallow lagoons and streams covering 36,000 hectares (88,960 acres) that are popular for cruising and fishing. The system empties into the Tasman Sea at **Lakes Entrance**, a picturesque fishing town at the northern end of the beach. Offshore, the drilling rigs of the rich Bass Strait oilfields are visible but intrude little on the immediate landscape. Heading east, the Princes Highway passes through thickly forested foothills of the Victorian Alps and estuaries that include the famous Snowy River. From the logging town of **Cann River**, a dirt road leads to **Point Hicks**, Captain Cook's landfall in 1770.

The Victorian Alps

Occupying the northeastern corner of the state, or roughly one-third of its total land area, the **Victorian Alps** are an extension of the Snowy

Mountains in neighbouring New South Wales. Although not as high as the latter, they cover a much larger area and offer visitors a less-spoiled environment. **Mt Bogong** (1,986 metres, or 6,518 feet) is Victoria's highest mountain and is surrounded by half a dozen others over 1,800 metres (5,908 feet) high. Known popularly as **The High Country**, the region is legendary for its mountain men, or rustic cowboys, immortalized in the film *The Man from Snowy River*. In more recent times, the mountains have become popular skiing destinations in winter. Much of the area remains primitive wilderness, its forest-covered peaks and ridges offering panoramic views out on to the flat plains of the interior. Rising from peaceful river valleys, the mountains are covered with giant eucalypt forests that give way at higher altitudes to the uniquely coloured and dwarfed 'snow gums'. The plateau is covered in unique Alpine vegetation. In summer, the invigorating air promotes hiking, fishing and horse-riding.

The grass-covered valleys below are dotted with some of Victoria's earliest inland settlements, many extending off the main track from Sydney, the Hume Highway. Closest to Melbourne, or about a three-hour drive to the northeast, the town of **Mansfield** is the gateway to this unique cowboy country with its Wild West collection of pubs and shops. (*The Man from Snowy River* and its sequel were shot at nearby **Merrijig**.) In the old days, this was also bushranger country. After holding up stage-coaches and other easy targets along the surrounding roads, these bandits would disappear back up into their mountain hide-outs. Their bravado earned them admiration as folk heroes—one reason why it often took the police years to catch them. Ned Kelly and his gang (see page 104) hid out in the region for two years before they were finally cornered at **Glenrowan**.

Wangaratta, 237 kilometres (147 miles) northeast of Melbourne, offers a double gateway—the High Country to the southeast and the state's finest vineyards to the north. **Beechworth**, only 36 kilometres (22 miles) to the east, is one of the state's best-preserved gold-mining towns, with more than 32 buildings classified by the National Trust. The Ovens Highway follows a river valley up past hulking **Mt Buffalo** to **Bright**, a quaint former gold town noted for its groves of exotic trees. From Bright, several roads lead up into the mountains and high plains above. Easily accessible Mt Buffalo, which stands 1,000 metres (3,300 feet) above the valley floor, offers spectacular views of the region. (The **Mt Buffalo Chalet**, a vast wooden structure built in the 1930s, is a ski and summer resort and worth an overnight stop.) Another winding road east from Bright passes over a summit where the western escarpment of the Snowy Mountains stands out sharply on the horizon. The appropriately named settlement of **Mt Beauty** marks the entry to **Bogong National Park** and the **Fall's Creek** ski resort.

Country Victoria

Victoria's Great Dividing Range and the Grampians in the west provide the state's major watershed, with rivers and streams to the north emptying into the **Murray River**. Originating in the Snowy Mountains, the river is Australia's longest and forms most of the state's border with New South Wales. The landscape across this northern section of Victoria is mostly flat and devoted largely to farming and grazing.

The region between **Wangaratta** and the border town of **Wodonga** offers a brief taste of the vast riverland to the west, especially for travellers en route between Sydney and Melbourne. (East of the twin towns of **Albury-Wodonga**, the waters of the Murray River, and the huge Snowy Mountains Project, are dammed up by **Lake Hume** to provide irrigation for the parched region.) Nearby **Rutherglen**, on the Murray River's southern bank, is the centre of Victoria's best wine-growing area. As elsewhere, visitors are welcome at the vineyards to sample the wines, with some providing fine country-style restaurants.

Further west, **Echuca** (206 kilometres, or 128 miles, north of Melbourne) became famous in the late 19th century as Australia's largest inland port for paddle-steamers plying cargo and passengers up and down the Murray River to South Australia. (During droughts, traffic simply stopped and waited for the waters to rise.) But by 1910, railways had replaced the river and the town stagnated. Today, several old steamboats and the old port have been restored into a tasteful tourist attraction. Cruises, some for several days, run the meandering tree-lined river, tying up along the riverbanks at night for barbecues and songs. Most of the tourists are Australians looking to discover their own heritage. But for the foreign visitor looking for something more off-beat, a cruise along the muddy Murray can be quite relaxing—and a great way to meet the locals. (Other cruises along the Victorian section of the Murray depart from Swan Hill and Mildura further downstream.)

The northwestern corner of the state, centred around the citrus-growing town of **Mildura**, is known as the **Mallee Country**, named for a tough dry-climate eucalypt which shoots out branches from far below the ground. The land here is marginal at best and heavily drought-prone, but the region has produced some hardy settlers who somehow make a living from grazing and growing wheat. Further west near the South Australian border, the land is mostly desert—a touch of the Outback that completes Victoria's well-rounded personality.

The Pub Owner's Wife

The pub owner's wife was in her mid-forties, her husband a little older.
Together they ran a pub on one of the roads in the Top End, southeast of
Darwin. Among clumps of pandanus and palms, it sat under a vast sky
and catered to a thirsty clientele. Their customers were truck drivers,
Aboriginal and white stockmen, miners passing to and from Darwin,
illicit tropical bird smugglers, bull catchers, buffalo shooters, aerial
musterers. Since it was a noisy pub, the pub owner and his wife lived in
a house some distance off, and the wife would walk down to the pub from
the house every evening to help out in the bar. It was a dark walk
through a sparsely populated landscape, and her husband considered it a
dangerous one. He could not say specifically who it was he feared would
attack her, but he was aware of the violence and madness which always
seemed close to realization in the humidity and endemic drunkenness of
the Top End. He therefore pressed her to carry a .25 Biretta with her
whenever she walked down to the pub at night. 'I'm not worried about
the blackfellers,' he told her, 'it's the mad white bastards that worry me.'

His fears had reasonable statistical grounds. The annual average for
murders in the Territory is fourteen times the Australian national mean;
the prevalence of fire-arms, geographic remoteness, grievances germinat-
ing richly beneath the humid sun and fed on liquor, the high rate of
individual eccentricity, the mysterious business of Aboriginal retribution—all that helped the figures along and made it wise for a woman
walking at night through a concentration of drinkers to go armed.

It became a habitual matter for the publican's wife to carry the small
revolver, though the pub owner himself may well have forgotten that he
had pressed the weapon on her.

Lately she approached the pub in the evenings with a certain sense of
grievance. Among the regulars were a number of hard-drinking women.
She was aware that intimate signals passed across the bar between some
of them and her husband. She hoped it was all just a bit of social byplay.
She had never seen anything more than that.

As well as her minor sexual suspicions, she hated the rowdiness of the
pub, the aggravation that prevailed there, the racial insults, the struggle

to get the aggressor and the drunk out of the door at closing time, the turning from an eventually closed and locked front door to see the swill, the vomit, the sometimes overturned furniture.

One night in 1980, carrying her bag, the Biretta half-remembered inside it, she strolled down as usual from the house to the pub. She passed through the screen of battered four-wheel-drives in front of the place, familiar vehicles, each of them matched to the face of some regular boozer already inside and settled down to an evening of hectic drinking. She went to the back of the pub and came into the bar through the office. From the office door she could not see her husband serving the customers. She presumed he was in the storeroom. She went out into the night again and saw the heavy door of the storeroom ajar, a little light spilling through it. Opening the door further, she saw her husband in there with one of the women customers.

The pub owner was of course astounded. He dragged his trousers up, belted them and walked towards her, beginning to speak. He discovered, before she did, that the Biretta was in her hand. As he reached the door she shot him through the wrist. The bullet passed through and hit his buckle. 'Bloody surprised he had his buckle done up,' some of the local people would say later. . .

. . .The pub owner's wife was paroled after nine months. She met her husband again. They were old-fashioned people, it was unlikely that, having both survived the shoot-out, they would separate and seek a divorce. The passionate shooting probably added something—a spice, a brio—to the middle reaches of their marriage.

They decided that the pub was not good for their marriage, and put it on the market, selling it easily. For, although it was what Australians call 'a blood house', a rough boozer, it was a gold mine. The former pub owner and his wife bought the local store, and can be found there behind that more prosaic counter today. When people come in and ask the wife to witness documents for them, she tells them with the pride appropriate to a survivor, 'No use asking me. I've got a criminal record.'

Thomas Keneally, Outback, 1983

Tasmania

A Different Australia

It is easy for visitors to Australia to overlook Tasmania. After all, mainland Australians do it all the time. A few years ago, for example, the state's citizens were mighty upset when a stylized map of Australia unveiled as the official symbol for the nation's much-touted Bicentennial in 1988 failed to include the island. Embarrassed officials quickly sent the logo back to the drawing board. (At the same time, newspapers and magazines—and guidebooks—whose maps of Australia inadvertently omit Tasmania can be guaranteed a host of angry letters to the editor.) As it rarely offers a news story, even foreign correspondents based in Australia tend to ignore Tasmania. And after living here for nearly 12 years, it was only in the course of researching this guide that I finally visited the island. It was very much a classic case of saving the best for last. Like most visitors to Tasmania, I came away totally charmed by this little-known part of Australia. It is the sort of place where people come to visit—and leave vowing to return permanently.

Located 240 kilometres (150 miles) south of Victoria across the stormy Bass Strait, Tasmania is refreshingly different from other parts of Australia. Visitors, especially other Australians, frequently comment that the island feels like another country. Indeed, in its appearance and character, Tasmania is about as far as one can get from the wide open spaces of the Outback and still be in the same country. The most widely heard local comparison is that it is a lot like New Zealand, which lies to the east across the Tasman Sea.

Only slightly larger than Sri Lanka, or the same size as England or Ireland (68,300 square kilometres, or 27,000 square miles), the apple-shaped island is mostly mountainous. Where the land has not been cleared for farming or timber, it is coated in lush—and frequently unique—vegetation. The state, Australia's smallest with only one percent of the country's land area, also includes the two Bass Strait islands of King and Flinders, each with a unique character of its own. Tasmania also boasts 'control' of unpopulated sub-Antarctic Macquarie Island.

Tasmania's extreme southerly position on the globe—roughly the same latitude as New Zealand's South Island or Argentina's Patagonia—gives it a cool and temperate climate. The weather is heavily influenced by its exposed position at the eastern end of the Roaring Forties, chill and fierce winds that blow across the Southern Ocean. In the early days of exploration and settlement, these trade winds were ideal accelerators for sailing vessels coming out from

Europe around the Cape of Good Hope. The danger, of course, was that they would crash into the place. And the island has plenty of shipwrecks to prove it!

There are four distinct seasons. In winter, snow covers much of the high ground and in summer, thanks to the latitude, daylight lasts until 9.30 pm. With the island's unique native deciduous trees, plus the many varieties imported by English settlers, spring and autumn offer their own special magic.

Tasmania gives a distinct impression of being on the edge of the earth. At Remarkable Cave, near Port Arthur on the Tasman Peninsula southeast of Hobart, is a notation that Antarctica is—only— 2,500 kilometres (1,500 miles) due south. Past the rough surf pounding the rugged coastline and the volcanic columns of Cape Raoul, the surging Southern Ocean gives the spot a real sense of drama. But onshore, this feeling has bred a cosy insularity that visitors find instantly comforting. In the hospitality stakes, Tasmanians are clearly the most welcoming of Australians.

This 'islandness' is accentuated by the drama of Tasmania's landscape. The topography was heavily influenced by the last Ice Age which ended only 20,000 years ago, and the countryside feels younger and more vibrant than on the mainland. The island's core of volcanic mountains was once heavily overladen with sheets of ice. As these retreated, they scoured the landscape and left behind some of the world's most spectacular mountain, river, lake and coastal scenery. Three vast areas of Tasmania's southwest are so unique by global standards that they have been listed on the United Nations' World Heritage list, in the company of sites such as the Grand Canyon, Mount Everest and Australia's own Kakadu.

Isolation from the Australian mainland has also given the island a unique collection of flora and fauna, such as the Huon pine and the Tasmanian Devil, or *thylacine*, a popular illustration on souvenir key chains, T-shirts and Cascade beer. A carnivorous marsupial whose coyote-like reputation for attacking sheep and chickens led to its widespread slaughter by Tasmania's European settlers, the Tasmanian Devil is now virtually extinct—despite occasional, but unconfirmed, sightings in wilderness areas. In Australian folklore, it is the equivalent of the Loch Ness Monster, Big Foot and the Yeti.

In these days when much of the world's natural environment is under serious threat, Tasmania still offers a refreshing dose of untouched wilderness. About 9,000 square kilometres (3,500 square miles) of the state is national park. Its wild southwest has one of the world's few remaining temperate rain forests which—even today— remains accessible only to determined bushwalkers or rafters. For

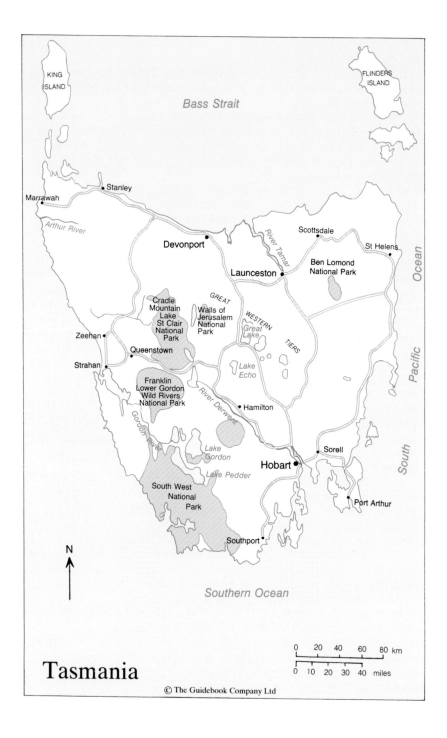

visitors in a hurry, however, there is a booming trade in aerial tours, with some offering pontoon-equipped planes that land on hidden harbours and lakes.

The Tasmanians themselves are also quite different from other Australians, who tend to regard them as a bunch of in-bred 'hillbillies'. Tasmanians, on the other hand, like to dismiss the rest of Australia as simply 'the other island'. The island's population of less than half a million, or 446,000 at the last census, is the most stable in Australia and has the country's highest percentage of native-born Australians. In a throwback to the days before Australia's more open immigration policy, Tasmanians remain predominantly Anglo-Saxon in origin. They have received few of the many non-English speaking settlers—eastern and southern Europeans and, latterly, Asians—who have migrated to the country since the Second World War. So, Tasmania feels much less cosmopolitan and easily fits that old cliché of being 'more English than the English'. In fact, with only limited opportunities available, Tasmania has long experienced a net out-migration to other parts of Australia. Despite having to cope with the nasty barbs, Tasmanians score highly in the list of the most successful Australians, among them noted Vietnam War cameraman Neil Davis and novelist Christopher Koch, best-known for his *The Year of Living Dangerously*. And while many do not remember him as an Australian, the Hollywood actor Errol Flynn was also born in Tasmania.

Because of its isolation and small population, Tasmania has largely missed out on the massive economic development that has transformed many cities and towns on the Australian mainland. (Although there is some manufacturing, most of the state's industries are extractive— timber, mining and fishing.) While this has left many Tasmanians feeling slightly 'neglected', it has been a blessing in disguise, especially with the growth of tourism. Instead of tearing down old buildings and homes for the sake of modernity, Tasmanians have saved a rich treasure of colonial architecture. (Visitors may wonder if they have ever torn anything down!) Today, many buildings—even entire towns—have been restored and turned into pleasant tourist attractions. Historic homes and buildings registered by the National Trust are particularly exciting. This rich man-made heritage, combined with its hospitable people and stunning natural environment, gives Tasmania a quaint old-fashioned atmosphere.

History

As elsewhere in Australia, the human habitation of Tasmania goes back to the dark days of pre-history. But even for the Aborigines, it was a remote spot and the last region to be settled. Although new evidence is constantly emerging, most anthropologists agree that Aborigines first settled the island about 20,000 years ago after crossing over from the mainland when the seas were more shallow. Another school of thought holds that, because of their unique characteristics, the Aborigines migrated by canoes or rafts from the Melanesian islands of the southwestern Pacific Ocean.

Isolated from the Australian continent, the Aborigines adapted to the harsh environment and survived as hunters and gatherers. Divided into five tribes over the island, they numbered between 3,000 and 5,000 when the first Europeans arrived. For Tasmania's Aborigines, the arrival—or invasion—of the Europeans doomed them to rapid extinction.

Although Spanish and Portuguese explorers may have passed by, it was the famous Dutch explorer-navigator Abel Tasman who is credited as the first European to discover the island. In 1642, as head of an ambitious expedition in search of the hypothetical 'South Land' and an eastward route to South America, Tasman stumbled on to the southwestern coast of Tasmania after a voyage across the Roaring Forties. He named the west coast peaks of Zeehan and Heemskirk after his two vessels and then explored the picturesque Tasman Peninsula southeast of Hobart. Near Dunalley, 36 kilometres (22 miles) east of the city, the explorer claimed the island for the Dutch, naming it Van Diemen's Land after the East Indies governor who had ordered the expedition. Ironically, Tasman and his officers then decided against further exploration around the island, missing out on Bass Strait, and instead headed out into the South Pacific where he discovered New Zealand, Fiji and Tonga. By the time he returned to Batavia, now Jakarta, Tasman had inadvertently circumnavigated the continent of Australia without seeing it. Not surprisingly, Tasman's superiors were hardly pleased at his mission's failure and, two years later, sent him out again. More than 100 years later, England's Captain James Cook was still searching for the mythical continent!

Van Diemen's Land, as Tasmania was known until 1856, was then visited by a succession of British and French explorers during the remainder of the 17th century. But few lingered in its often treacherous waters and easily accepted the notion that Tasman's discovery was the southeastern-most extension of New Holland, the Dutch name for the western and southern coasts of the continent. It was only after the British established their convict colony in New South Wales in 1788 that more detailed exploration of Van Diemen's Land finally took place. Heading out from Sydney in 1798, George Bass and Matthew Flinders (see page 44) were the first to determine that Tasmania was actually an island separated from the mainland by a

fairly sizeable strait, now named for Bass. They spent several months charting the coast before heading home.

As in most of Australia's other colonies, it was the fear of French colonization of the continent that finally led to the British settlement of Van Diemen's Land. The British also clearly saw some distinct advantages in the island's potential as a convict settlement. Under the command of Lt. John Bowen, the first shipload of convicts arrived at Risdon Cove in 1803 and, after less than a year, their settlement was moved west across the Derwent River to Hobart. (Risdon is now the site of a museum.) Two years later, the town of Launceston was established on the northern side of the island. While most of the early settlers, both convict and free, came from the notorious penal colony on Norfolk Island (see page 44), they were soon joined by convicts and immigrants brought directly from Britain. At first, the island was administered by New South Wales, but in 1825 Van Diemen's Land was declared a separate colony.

The European settlement of Tasmania produced some of the most notorious chapters in Australian history, for both the convicts and the Aborigines. British officials soon found the island an ideal spot to keep convicts busy—and under control. For the convicts, however, a court sentence of transportation to Van Diemen's Land was the next thing to a death sentence. As vividly portrayed in Marcus Clarke's classic, *For the Term of His Natural Life*, it was a time of harsh and often cruel justice. This was especially so for those convicted of serious crimes in Britain or Australia, who were sent to remote prison settlements such as Sarah and Maria Island where they spent their days at hard labour.

At Sarah Island on deceptively peaceful Macquarie Harbour on the west coast, prisoners in the 1820s worked from dawn to dusk, often in freezing water, cutting down forests of giant Huon pine, constructing boats and building the settlement. When it and Maria Island became too difficult to administer, authorities in 1830 established the ultimate prison settlement at Port Arthur on the Tasman Peninsula. To prevent escape, the peninsula's only link with the outside world, a narrow strip of land, was guarded by dogs, and convicts were told that the surrounding waters were shark infested. Over the next 47 years, Port Arthur—described in more detail below—became a notoriously efficient symbol of Britain's penal system.

In the context of the Dickensian Age, however, such treatment was not unusual and, today, it is easy to overemphasize the cruelty of the system. The vast majority of convicts completed their sentences and, with a small grant of land in still-virgin country, settled down in another part of the island. In the early days, most convicts were simply 'assigned' as servants to free settlers where, unless the boss was particularly tough, life was relatively tolerable. Others were assigned to government work-gangs to build the colony's infrastructure of roads, bridges and public buildings. After 1840, all convicts went through Port Arthur. Anxious to finish their sentences, and with a bit of help from the lash, the convicts built modern Tasmania. Today, it is difficult to gaze for long at a lovely building before one's mind wanders back to what it must have been like for those tough men and women. Of course, there were always those who quite relished a life of crime. Often openly assisted by remote settlers, many of them ex-convicts themselves, these Tasmanians were some of Australia's most colourful bushrangers, outlaws who—as in America's Wild West—roamed the countryside holding up stagecoaches, banks and inns. Pick up a tourist brochure in Tasmanian settlements such as Hamilton and you will soon learn which bushranger once roamed the region. It took a major military operation—and a few public hangings—finally to bring some law and order.

A different sort of law and order was applied to Tasmania's Aborigines. In one of the saddest chapters in Australian history, they were literally hunted down and shot in what became known as the 'black war'. Others died of disease or hunger. When officials finally stopped the massacre in 1847, there were only 44 Aborigines left out of an estimated 3,000 to 5,000 at the start of the century. They were moved first to Flinders Island and then to Oyster Cove, near Hobart. When the last full-blooded male Aborigine, 'King Billy', died in 1869, scientists collaborated in a bizarre incident to cut off his head for study. Truganini, a grand dame of her tribe when she died in 1876, is now widely remembered as 'The Last Tasmanian'. The extermination of this ancient race remains a sensitive subject today and it is hardly surprising that perhaps Australia's most militant Aborigines are from Tasmania—in this case, mixed-race descendants of that proud people.

But from the point of view of the early settlers, this was the God-ordained price that had to be paid for taming the raw and primitive island. Far from the motherland, and terribly homesick, they created a clone of Old England in the far southern seas—a land of small villages, farmers' cottages and provincial towns. Their efforts have left behind an incongruous mixture. (A scene looks almost right, even down to the hawthorn hedges and rock fences, and then you suddenly spot the gum trees!)

These early settlers worked hard, and, by the 1820s, the colony was exporting wheat and wool to New South Wales. Whaling—much of it right off Hobart—also developed early into a major coastal industry. Timber and shipbuilding were also important. By 1853, free settlers were doing well enough to lobby successfully for an end to transportation. But long-term prosperity has always eluded the island, and the economy has jumped erratically from boom to bust. Even the corporate-like name change to Tasmania in 1856 failed to improve things, sparking off instead a depression that lasted 25 years! That bust ended with a mining boom in the 1880s after the discovery of a treasure of copper, gold and zinc in Tasmania's 'Wild West'. But the miners' appetites were voracious, as illustrated by the desolate landscape around Queenstown where pollution literally destroyed the environment.

Since the Second World War, Tasmanians have pinned their hopes for economic growth on the island's vast forests and hydroelectric potential, as well as the development of downstream processing plants and manufacturing. Because of its climate and rich soils, farming and orchard growers have been able to diversify into a wide range of produce which has pushed aside the apple as its most famous crop. (Interestingly, Tasmania is about the only place where opium poppies are legally grown—not under tight security but in sweeping fields along the northwest coast.) But work remains a problem for many Tasmanians and, in recent years, the state has consistently scored the nation's highest unemployment rate. Lately this bust has been exacerbated by a growing conservationist sentiment that has forced the government to adopt a more thoughtful attitude towards the rate and extent of development. But Tasmanians remain bitterly divided between developers and conservationists. Even the most casual visitor to Tasmania will quickly pick up the burning environmental issue of the day, whether it be a new pulp mill, a new logging concession or yet another dam. After seeing the island, it is easy to agree with those who want to keep Tasmania just as it is.

Getting Around

The only international flights into Tasmania are a limited service by Australian Airlines from Christchurch, New Zealand, to the capital, Hobart. But there are regular flights from Sydney and Melbourne into Hobart, Launceston and Devonport. In addition, there is a car ferry service across Bass Strait from Melbourne to Devonport.

Tasmania can be divided roughly into four regions. On a map, the island looks small, but Tasmania is bigger than it looks. With an abundance of sights along the way, travel always takes longer than expected. There is nothing quite as frustrating as pulling into a town right at sunset, looking for accommodation. So, it is best to take plenty of time. The visitor needs at least a week, ideally two, to appreciate Tasmania fully.

With its network of excellent, signposted roads—graded A to C according to their condition and importance—the island is ideal for the self-driving visitor. (Sites of historical and geological importance are also well marked, a rare tourist feature in Australia.) The highways in Tasmania have the added advantage of not being nearly so crowded, and therefore dangerous, as on the mainland—especially useful for those who have never driven on the left-hand side of the road before. All major car rental agencies operate in the state and, in Hobart and Launceston, there is cut-throat competition between 'rent-a-wreck' companies. Self-contained vans and caravans can also be hired. Organized tours range from simple bus tours through to elaborate adventure holidays featuring four-wheel driving, hiking and rafting. Buses also travel regularly around the island, but there are no passenger train services. Several companies also provide scenic flights, by aircraft or helicopter, and both river and ocean cruises. Tasmania is famous for its fishing, especially trout in the state's vast network of natural and artificial lakes.

Through Tourism Tasmania, the government's official travel agency, accommodation can be booked around the island, allowing the traveller to plan a relaxed itinerary between overnight stops. Still largely unique to Tasmania, there is a wide network of colonial-style and farmhouse accommodation, even 'homehosting' in towns or country, to supplement more ordinary motels and hotels. Renovated with modern kitchens and toilets, and reasonably priced, these old homes are a joy to stay in. In the little country town of Hamilton west of Hobart, for example, we found our key hanging on the door in an envelope with a brief note of welcome. Inside the sandstone cottage, built in 1845, the atmosphere was like a warm and cosy cocoon out of the past, and we immediately wanted to extend our stay. Tourist accommodation throughout the island is often simple, but always clean and comfortable.

Tasmania is famous for its seafood, especially its scallops and crayfish (lobster), and boasts some of Australia's finest restaurants. Incredibly, Tasmania has 600 licensed restaurants and taverns, or one for every 700 people. Many are in colonial-era buildings where the ambience and service are as good—sometimes better—than the food. Mutton birds, venison and quail are also particular specialities. Trout, introduced last century, and Atlantic salmon, now grown commercially, are also delicious additions to many menus. There is even a small wine industry (still only appreciated locally), a unique alcoholic cider and two local beers, Cascade and Boag's. Depending on the time of day, tea rooms and old pubs always make pleasant stops. Be warned, however, that some places—such as the zinc mining town of Rosebery on the west coast—offer little more than hamburgers and roast chicken.

In and Around Hobart

Set at the foot of towering **Mt Wellington** (1,270 metres, or 4,600 feet), the state capital of Hobart is clearly one of the world's loveliest cities—even if other Australians do not quickly agree. Straddling the mouth of the **River Derwent**, a fast-flowing stream coming out of the **Central Plateau** to the northwest, this city of 178,000 looks out over a vast estuary divided into an assortment of bays by mountainous peninsulas and islands. The surrounding shoreline, mostly heavily wooded, is marked by sandy inlets and rocky outcrops. This is Hobart's 'front-yard', a watery playground for sailing, water sports and fishing. Onshore, the port of Hobart—deep enough to handle ocean liners—is right next to the city. Tree-lined suburbs spread out along the bays and up the hillsides. The climate is notably mild, cool in summer and rarely freezing in winter. In the winter months, Hobart's imposing setting is made even more dramatic by the fields of snow atop Mt Wellington.

Founded in 1804, Hobart proudly wears its mantle as Australia's second-oldest city. With many of its colonial-era buildings preserved, plus its statuary and lush parks, the visitor feels like he has stepped back in time. But everything is still in working order and the atmosphere is quaintly vibrant. The city boasts one of the world's finest collections of Georgian architecture. Fine old public buildings, most of which are built of sandstone carved by convicts, still dominate downtown. In the suburbs, Georgian mansions and Victorian terraces are found alongside more modern but tasteful wooden and brick cottages. The business district, located just back from the waterfront, retains most of its turn-of-the-century utilitarian buildings and adds to the city's old-fashioned atmosphere. But aside from the **Elizabeth Street Mall** and the **Cat and Fiddle Arcade**, which all souvenir-hunting tourists must visit, this district is the least attractive part of Hobart.

The best place to start a tour of Hobart is at **Constitution Dock**, along the waterfront. Famous for its rowdy welcome parties every New Year's Eve at the end of the gruelling Sydney-to-Hobart and Melbourne-to-Hobart yacht races, the dock is surrounded by early 19th-century warehouses and public buildings, most notably the squat two-storey **Customs Building**. (The main eyesore is the recently built **Sheraton**, an ultra-modern establishment that looks oddly out of place, although not enough to ruin the atmosphere.) On the water, there are floating fish shops, ocean-going yachts and cargo vessels. From the western end of the dock, near a small collection of historic vessels, there is a public ferry to the eastern shore. Several companies offer a variety of cruises out into the vast estuary. The longer trips feature sumptuous meals of crayfish and excellent views of the city and surrounding countryside.

Further on, a short stroll past the sandstone **Parliament House** leads to **Salamanca Place**, a vast tree-lined square facing old stone warehouses that once serviced cargo vessels docked nearby. Today, most of the buildings have been renovated and converted into a tasteful collection of shops and restaurants. On Saturday morning, the square turns into a vast open-air market featuring high-quality arts and crafts—and the occasional antique. Behind this, reached by **Kellys Steps** or side streets, lies Australia's first suburb, **Battery Point**, where the narrow streets wind past a magnificent mixture of Georgian mansions and Victorian terraces. Many of these, such as **Barton Cottage**, have been converted into tourist accommodation, and the village-like atmosphere makes Battery Point the most attractive place to stay in Hobart. The most significant buildings are **St George's Church**, the **Maritime Museum, Arthur's Circus** and the **Van Diemen's Land Folk Museum**. For history buffs, walking tours take in these and other highlights of the area.

Out of the downtown area, but still a healthy walk or jog away, the **Queen's Domain** is widely regarded as one of Australia's loveliest botanic gardens. It offers a mixture of native and exotic trees and

flowers, including a spectacular display of begonias in summer. The vast parklands look out over the narrow mouth of the Derwent and the sweeping **Tasman Bridge**, a city landmark that collapsed dramatically in 1974 when struck by a freighter. Rebuilt over the next three years, the bridge provides high-speed access to the city's eastern suburbs, the airport and southeast Tasmania. Just beyond the Queen's Domain in the suburb of **New Town** is National Trust-registered **Runnymede**, a single-storey stone villa built in 1840 and one of Tasmania's grandest historic homes. Of more modern vintage, and a popular attraction especially for Australians, is the **Wrest Point Casino**, which overlooks the estuary about ten minutes south of downtown.

But to fully appreciate Hobart's setting, a drive to the top of **Mt Wellington**—either in your own car or a tourist bus—is a definite must. After passing through hillside suburbs, the road rises through dense temperate rain forest and then into the stunted alpine vegetation above the snow line. From the summit, the view is spectacular and takes in a vast area of southeastern Tasmania, from Hobart and its suburbs directly below, across the islands and peninsulas of the estuary to the Tasman Sea and to the valleys and mountains of the interior. For the energetic, there are walking trails leading to the adjoining national park or back down the sharp face to the city. One entrepreneur even hires out bicycles for those who want to coast back down. In winter, the peak is closed off and visitors should visit **Mt Nelson,** lower and closer to the city, which also offers extensive—but less dramatic—views.

Outside of Hobart, only half an hour's drive to the east over the River Derwent, is **Richmond**, one of Tasmania's most attractive historic towns. It is located in low hill country along the Coal River. Richmond was the site of Australia's first bridge in 1823, opening up the region to the east. During the 1830s, it was an important military post and convict station along the road to Port Arthur. But with the opening of the **Sorell Causeway** to the south in 1872, Richmond—once ranked as the colony's third-largest town—turned into a quiet rural backwater. Thankfully, much of it has been preserved.

Richmond Bridge is the town's most famous landmark and, although not as perfect as the one in Ross due to settling, the wavy stone bridge provides a lovely—but slightly haunting—backdrop to the town. Legend says that the ghost of a cruel overseer, beaten to death and then buried in the foundation by convicts, still lingers along the creek. The convict past lives on most dramatically, however, in nearby **Richmond Gaol**, first opened in 1825 to house convict labourers and those en route to Port Arthur. The rooms and cells have been studiously restored and catalogued by the curator. Take a walk into one of the men's solitary cells, for example, and close the door behind you—the total darkness, and stuffy air, quickly sends a chill down your back. Nearby, the Flogging Yard, with its wooden 'triangle' where convicts were strapped down, causes more goosebumps.

Outside the gaol, the town itself makes a fascinating stroll. Restored buildings are now galleries, arts and crafts boutiques and restaurants. The Georgian-style **Prospect House** on the edge of town offers fine meals and colonial accommodation. The **Bridge Inn**, one of Tasmania's earliest pubs, also provides a friendly atmosphere for tea, a meal or just a cool beer.

Closer to Hobart, **Risdon Cove** is worth a brief stop on the way either to or from Richmond. This was the site of the first English settlement of Tasmania before it was moved across the river to Hobart. There is a museum and interpretation centre, plus replicas of the original slab huts built at the settlement.

Further out of the capital, there are several attractive destinations within easy driving distance. But for a rich mixture of stunning natural scenery and convict history, the best destination—many say in the entire state—is the **Tasman Peninsula** and **Port Arthur**. (Richmond makes a convenient stop en route, as does Dunalley, where a monument marks Abel Tasman's landing in 1642.) Located about 100 kilometres (62 miles), or a pleasant hour and a half's drive through farming country southeast of Hobart, the entire peninsula—sealed off at Eaglehawk Neck—was turned into a penal colony in 1830 and, over the next 47 years, processed some 12,500 convicts. Although badly damaged after its closure by fire, storms and neglect, Port Arthur's remaining buildings and ruins were recently restored and stabilized in a seven-year government-funded programme that has made it one of Australia's best historic sites. For Australians keen to rediscover their heritage, the visit is very much a pilgrimage.

There is a distinctly eerie feeling to Port Arthur, especially when grey clouds shroud the surrounding forested hills and chilly winds blow in from the sea. Adding to the mood is the settlement's park-like atmosphere, with tall rows of elms and other imported trees adorning the well-manicured lawns. There is even an ornamental garden and cricket pitch that date from those early days. The beautifully proportioned **church**, dating from 1834 and never formally consecrated, is the best-known of Port Arthur's buildings, but there is enough for three or four hours of sightseeing. Other buildings of particular note are the **Penitentiary**, an engineering feat in its day but now little more than four-storey-high walls, and the **Model Prison**, a well-preserved radical institution where prisoners were forced to wear hoods and remain totally silent. More time is needed for a cruise to the

Aborigines on the east coast

We got ready a few cartridges as fast as we could, and set out towards the place where we had seen the aborigines. It was now only nine o'clock. We had gone only a few steps before we met them. The men and the youths were ranged in the front, nearly in a semicircle; the women, the children and then the older girls were a few paces behind. As their manner did not indicate any hostile design I hesitated not to go up to the oldest, who accepted, with a very good grace, a piece of biscuit that I offered him, of which he had seen me eat. I then held out my hand to him, as a sign of friendship, and had the pleasure of seeing that he understood my meaning very well, he gave me his hand also, at the same time inclining himself in a little sort of bow, at the same time as he did this he raised his left foot, which he carried backward in proportion as he bent his body forward. All these motions were accompanied by a very pleasant smile.

My companions seeing this, also advanced up to the other males of the tribe, and immediately the best understanding prevailed. They received with a show of great joy the neckcloths that we offered to them. Then the young people approached near to us, and one of them had the generosity to give me a few small shells, of the welk kind, pierced near the middle, and strung like a necklace. This ornament, that he seemed to call 'canlaride', was the only one that he appeared to possess, and it had been worn round his head. A handkerchief supplied the place of this present, gratifying the utmost wishes of his savage heart, when he advanced towards me I tied it round his head for him, and his countenance expressed the greatest joy, as he lifted up his hand to feel it again and again. . .

# of Tasmania, 1792

. . . It appeared very astonishing to us that at that high latitude, where, at a period of the year so little advanced as the present, we needed all the clothing that we could wear, that they did not feel the necessity for wearing clothes. Even the women for the most part were entirely naked, as well as the men. Some of the women only had the shoulders, or part of the back, covered with a kangaroo's skin, worn with the hair next to the body, only two had this form of covering and each of these had an infant at the breast. . .

I had given several things to them without thinking, or expecting anything in return; but I wished to get a kangaroo's skin. Among the aborigines that were around us I could see only one girl who had one. I made signs that implied that if she gave it to me she could have a pair of pantaloons instead, but she ran away to hide herself in the woods. The other aborigines appeared truly hurt at her refusal to give it to me, and called several times for her to come back. At length she yielded to their entreaties, and came to bring me the skin. Perhaps it was from timidity or only that she could not prevail on herself to part with the 'garment'. In return she received the pantaloons, less useful to her, according to the customs of the ladies of this country, than the skin, which served to cover the shoulders, which are the particular part, at least among the females, that have to be hid. We showed her the manner of wearing the panta-loons; but notwithstanding this, it was necessary for us to put them on for her ourselves. To this she yielded with the best grace in the world.

Jacques-Julien Houtou de la Billadiere, 1755-1834

Isle of the Dead, just off **Point Puer,** where nearly 2,000 convicts and settlers are buried, or to the other islands. A seaplane service, the price of which depends on the number of passengers, also operates out over the picturesque peninsula from Port Arthur.

With numerous natural sites and other convict complexes around the rest of the Tasman Peninsula, the visitor is well-advised to stay overnight rather than rush back to Hobart. (There is a wide range of accommodation, including colonial-style.) This allows braver souls to take in nightly 'ghost tours' through the old ruins of Port Arthur. It also allows more time to explore the peninsula's stunning scenery of plunging cliffs and pounding surf, such as the volcanic spires of **Cape Pillar** or **Cape Raoul,** or to enjoy a swim at **Pirate's Bay** along spectacular **Eaglehawk Neck,** where patrolling dogs and guards once kept convicts from escaping the peninsula. The bays to the west, protected from the surf and part of the River Derwent's vast estuary, offer fine sandy beaches and glorious fishing. At nearby **Penzance,** site of Australia's very first motel, there is a rich collection of coastal features with names like **Tasman's Arch,** the **Devil's Kitchen** and the **Blowhole.** Well-marked walking trails lead off from here and other points around the peninsula.

Another pleasant destination out of Hobart is the so-called **Southern Region** which takes in the **D'Entrecasteaux Channel,** the **Huon River Valley** and the **Hartz Mountains.** Because of its proximity to Hobart, the area is now popular with commuters who can enjoy a country-style existence. The region—perfect for day trips—offers a rich mixture of scenery, especially in spring (September to November) when its legendary apple trees are in bloom. Beginning immediately south of **Kingston,** headquarters of Australia's Antarctic programme, the sheltered waters of the Channel—named for the French explorer Bruni D'Entrecasteaux who visited in 1792—were a killing ground for whalers in the early days of the colony but are now best known for their crayfish and scallops. Separating the coast from **Storm Bay,** part of the vast Derwent estuary, is lovely **Bruny Island** with its mixture of beautiful beaches, forest-covered mountains and rich history. Reached by a half-hour car ferry from the fishing town of **Kettering,** the 55-kilometre- (34-mile-) long island—actually two submerged mountaintops—is linked by a narrow isthmus known as The Neck, a favourite haunt of the tiny fairy penguin. Visitors should keep in mind that a serious look around Bruny Island and the adjoining coastline along the Channel Highway can take the better part of a day.

Further to the south, the **Huon Valley** offers a different flavour, with its quaint villages surrounded by apple orchards, dairy farms and thick forests. Typical of many parts of Tasmania, it has a wide, and slightly dizzying, variety of attractions within a very small area. **Franklin**, once designed as a major port, has a fine collection of colonial architecture. Inland from **Geeveston**, the **Hartz Mountains National Park** provides a taste of Tasmania's southwest with its alpine vegetation, tarns and waterfalls. The park's spectacular heights provide views over this still untouched wilderness and out towards the peaks of Bruny Island and the estuary. A sealed road leads on through **Dover**, the most southerly town in Australia, and to **Southport**, a quaint fishing village and popular holiday resort. For train buffs, a tourist railway that was once used to haul limestone makes a lovely run along the coastline from the gem town of Lune River, while inland are **Hastings Caves** and **Thermal Springs**. A passable dirt road then leads on to **Cockle Creek**, another fishing and holiday village which is also the starting point for the famous coastal walk into the southwest wilderness. Again, there is enough here to keep the visitor busy for most of the day.

Another region worth visiting, especially en route to Tasmania's 'Wild West', is the **Derwent Valley**. Settled in the early days of the colony, the region's quaint villages of stone houses give it a distinctly English look. The banks of the swiftly flowing River Derwent are lined with exotic trees that are especially beautiful in autumn. The cultivated land is dominated by vines of hops, an ingredient in beer. **New Norfolk**, 45 minutes northwest of Hobart and the region's largest town (population 10,000), was settled by convicts from Norfolk Island in 1813 and contains a rich collection of historic buildings, including Australia's oldest continuously operating pub, the **Bush Inn**, and **St Matthew's Church of England**, the state's first church. The **Old Colony Inn**, set in lovely gardens, is well known for its meals and teas. Further upstream, **Salmon Ponds** is where Australia's first trout were successfully bred in 1864; with its museum and breeding tanks, it makes a pleasant stop.

From **Bushy Park**, where hops were first introduced in 1822, a highway leads to **Lake Pedder** and **Lake Gordon**, two large man-made lakes built to generate electricity and now popular with anglers for giant trout. More importantly, this region is also the main gateway to the **South West National Park**, Tasmania's largest wilderness area and part of the UN-registered World Heritage. (An alternative entry point, as noted above, is through Cockle Creek, south of Hobart.) Dominated by quartzite and dolerite peaks, the park is a mixture of button-grass meadows and thick temperate rain forest. From either the **Gordon Dam** or **Scotts Peak Dam**, there are stunning views out over the rugged country. (The latter point is also a start-to-finish point of the park's main walking trail.) The main disadvantage of this diversion, however, is that the traveller has to backtrack to the River

Derwent before continuing. Those in a hurry are better advised to skip the area; there is better scenery further to the west.

The tiny country town of **Hamilton**, located on the **Lyell Highway** 70 kilometres (43 miles) from Hobart, maintains its quaint old-world charm and makes a pleasant overnight stop. Among the colonial buildings, **St Peter's Church** (1836) certainly has the most character. Set on a hilltop overlooking the valley and ranges beyond, the small church—built with only one door to keep all the convicts inside during services—has a rustic simplicity. A plaque on the wall honours the two sons of the local shire clerk who were killed at Gallipoli in 1915. A stroll through the graveyard behind opens up more local history, including the unmarked graves of forgotten convicts. Elsewhere in Hamilton, there is a mix of small stone cottages and grander houses. **Glen Clyde House**, once an inn, has been beautifully restored into a gallery and tea rooms.

The West Coast

Strictly speaking, this region refers to the wild west coast of Tasmania. But as the Lyell Highway (A10) winds its way west to **Queenstown** and **Strahan,** it skirts the southern part of the island's most imposing physical feature—the **Central Plateau**—and a destination in its own right.

Uplifted by volcanic activity nearly a billion years ago, this vast plateau acts as Tasmania's watershed, with streams running off in virtually all directions. Also known as the '**Land of 3,000 Lakes**', the plateau shows the scars of the last Ice Age with its glacial lakes, sweeping meadows and sharp ridges and valleys. Particularly unusual are the 'skittleballs' that litter the landscape, the result of a volcanic lava flow some 23 million years ago. Swept by fierce winds, the highlands are covered in snow in the winter and support distinctive alpine vegetation such as buttongrass and 'horizontal scrub'. The chilly lakes are literally brimming with trout—imported, of course—and are an angler's paradise. Although some of the region has now been opened up for hydroelectric projects, much remains accessible only on foot.

Tasmania's Central Plateau can be approached from several directions; the Lake Highway, unsealed for about 50 kilometres (30 miles) around **Great Lake**, actually crosses its eastern edge. The descent—or ascent—over the northern escarpment is quite spectacular, with its plunging waterfalls, sheer volcanic cliffs and long views out towards Bass Strait. (Two other well-known destinations in the north, **Cradle Mountain** and the **Walls of Jerusalem National Park**, are discussed below.) For the traveller heading towards the West Coast, however, the best taste of the plateau comes around **Lake St Clair**, a short drive northwest of **Derwent Bridge**, a settlement that is little more than a grocery store. (With a regular bus service, it is also a popular spot for backpackers heading into the highlands.) The lake, formed by glacial action, is Australia's deepest and is surrounded by spectacular mountain scenery, including Tasmania's highest peak, **Mt Ossa** (1,617 metres, or 5,900 feet), which forms part of the vast **Cradle Mountain–Lake St Clair National Park**. A cruise out into the lake or a stroll along the shore makes a nice break. (Lake St Clair is also the start of a trail that crosses the park to Cradle Mountain—a five-day hike.)

West of Derwent Bridge, the landscape becomes even more scenic as the road passes through the **King William Range** and then descends steeply into the headwaters of the famous **Franklin River**. Showing the effects of glaciers that once covered this region, the valley walls rise sharply from swift-flowing streams coloured a distinct brown from the buttongrass meadows above. Dense forests line the streams and lower valley floors, giving way to alpine vegetation above the snow line. To the south sprawls the **Franklin Lower Gordon Wild Rivers National Park**, a favourite destination for determined rafters and hikers and one of the last temperate wilderness areas in the world.

After this awesome scenery, the road descends into the lunar landscape surrounding **Queenstown**. The discovery of copper here in the early 1870s opened up this once-pristine region to some of the most rapacious mining ever seen. Crude sulphurous smelting, a heavy appetite for firewood, and bushfires combined to destroy all trace of greenery and left the valley a virtual desert. It is easy to see why the Tasmanians call this region their 'Wild West'. Such mining methods halted 30 years ago, and today the town has a bizarre appeal as an example of what man is capable of inflicting on the environment. As the largest town on the West Coast (population 3,700), Queenstown provides accommodation and an excellent base to visit old ghost towns and the wilderness beyond. The town's museum, located in an old pub on the main street, has an excellent exhibit of old photographs from Queenstown's booming mining days, and a park across the street features an old cog railway that once hauled copper ingots to the coast. Because all the rails were ripped up, the train—known as the ABT— now has nowhere to go. Instead, taped sounds from the old days blare out over giant loudspeakers. Both highways leading south from the town follow the abandoned rail line, giving visitors an appreciation of the engineering challenges involved in opening up this once-thriving mining region.

The port of **Strahan**, an hour's drive from Queenstown over a
winding ridge-top highway, makes a more pleasant stop, especially
overnight. Located at the northern end of **Macquarie Harbour**, site of
a harsh penal colony in the 1820s, the town later thrived as a port
during the tin and copper mining days. In the early 1980s, Strahan was
the marshalling point for conservationists who, after Canberra's
intervention, successfully saved the nearby Franklin River from being
dammed for a hydroelectric scheme. Today, the fishing town of only
400 residents is undergoing extensive renovation as a tourist attraction.
    The surrounding region offers a rich mixture of scenery and history.
Along the coast, breakers blown across the Southern Ocean by the
Roaring Forties smash into a long slow curve of **Ocean Beach** and
provide an appropriate name for the harbour's treacherous entrance,
Hell's Gate. The sunsets along the coast are particularly beautiful.
Inside the harbour, cruises take visitors to the haunting ruins of **Sarah
Island**, once home to several hundred convicts, and then up the
Gordon River. Lined by sharp cliffs covered with thick forests of Huon
pine, the river offers a unique reflective quality attributed to the high
content of buttongrass in its brown waters. The cruise offers a
memorable glimpse into a still largely untouched wilderness.
    Heading north from Strahan, the road winds along the coast and,
near the **Henty River**, passes through an eerie landscape of 30-metre-
(100-foot-) high sand dunes that advance at the speedy rate of one

metre (three feet) a year. The road then moves inland to **Zeehan**, a well-preserved tin mining town that prospered in the late 19th century. With its **School of Mines Museum** and quaint atmosphere, it makes a pleasant stop. From here, you can either rejoin the A10 highway for the North Coast or explore the wild and unpopulated coastal region to the northwest. But with few roads, much of Tasmania's West Coast remains quite inaccessible—unless you are a keen bushwalker or have your own boat. This is bound to change in the coming years, however, with the construction of a highway linking Zeehan with the northwestern corner of Tasmania.

The North Coast

Fronting on to Bass Strait which separates Tasmania from the Australian mainland, the North Coast has its own distinctive character. With the three sizeable towns of Launceston, Devonport and Burnie, the region is the most heavily populated in the state. In their outlook, its residents are more oriented towards Melbourne—across the strait—than to Hobart. (Despite its small size, Tasmania has a north–south rivalry that has frequent political and economic implications.) While the built-up areas are industrialized, and the hinterland is rich in forests and minerals, it is the region's rich soils that have long provided Tasmania's most consistent wealth, with many farmers and graziers tracing their ancestry back to the original settlers. With its tapestry of crops and pastures, colonial-era farm houses and towns, and even fences made of rocks, the atmosphere along the northern coast is heavily English. Moving inland, the farmlands, rugged headlands and white beaches of the coast give way to thick native forests, hidden waterfalls and gorges, and soaring mountains.

At the western end of the coast, known more formally as the **North West Coast** or **Circular Head**, the historic port of **Stanley** (population 600) is one of the most picturesque towns in Australia and well worth an overnight stop. Driving clockwise around Tasmania, it is a leisurely half-day drive from Strahan and Queenstown; from the other direction, it is roughly one day from Launceston. Located at the tip of a peninsula dominated by a volcanic plug known as **The Nut**, Stanley was founded in 1826 as the main port for the Van Diemen's Land Company, which was granted extensive lands and dominated the area's early development. When gold was discovered in neighbouring Victoria in the 1830s, the area boomed from exports of beef, mutton and potatoes. Later, much of the company's lands were sold off to private farmers, although it continues to own a sheep station at Woolnorth, near the northwestern tip of the island. The town continued to prosper, but when nearby Smithton replaced Stanley as the principal port earlier this century the town declined in importance. It was only saved by extinction in recent years by old-timers determined to preserve its unique heritage.

Now classified as a historic town, Stanley retains its strong 19th-century colonial flavour and boasts a quaint collection of restored churches, buildings and homes. Among these is a simple weatherboard house where Joseph Lyons, the only Tasmanian to become an Australian prime minister, was born. Many of the buildings are open to visitors, while some—such as popular Laughton House—provide colonial accommodation. Near Stanley's port where freighters still call, visitors should not miss **Hursey Seafoods** overlooking **Marine Park**. While you are waiting for your fish and chips, the friendly staff will identify the live fish—many unique to Bass Strait—in the shop's large holding tanks. (Tasmania's succulent crayfish occupy other tanks.) Nearby, a chairlift and a walking trail take visitors to the top of **The Nut** with its magnificent views of the town and coastline, a rich mixture of rugged headlands, crescent-shaped beaches, and farmlands. The walk around the grass-covered top, now home to flocks of sheep and a muttonbird rookery, takes about half an hour. On a hill just north of Stanley is **Highfield**, the original headquarters of the Van Diemen's Land Company. With its convict-built homestead and support buildings now undergoing restoration, it makes for a fascinating insight into the life of a once all-powerful company.

Set amidst pastures and low hills, the coastal town of **Marrawah** is famous for the giant waves that crash in from the Southern Ocean, its lonely beaches and rocky headlands. Just to the south is the broad and swift-flowing **Arthur River**, still relatively unknown as a tourist destination. A pleasant five-hour cruise operates upriver four days a week and runs 18 kilometres (11 miles) to the juncture with the **Frankland River**, where lunch is served in a forest clearing. Although mostly unpaved, other roads lead further south along the coast or inland through forested foothills and grassy plains.

East of Stanley, the main highway passes through rich rolling farming country, while along the coast there are picturesque little holiday settlements, such as **Boat Harbour Beach**, lapped by the calm waters of Bass Strait. **Rocky Cape National Park**, once a favourite hunting ground for cave-dwelling Aborigines, makes a brief but pleasant diversion, as does nearby **Table Cape**. Located atop a sheer cliff, Table Cape features one of Tasmania's earliest lighthouses and overlooks the town of **Wynyard**. But this charming countryside soon disappears and, for 70 kilometres (43 miles), the road passes through one of the most polluted and densely populated regions of Tasmania. This is especially so around **Burnie**, where effluent from pulp mills and other factories makes swimming a real health hazard.

Devonport, with a population of 24,000, is the state's third-largest city and, as the terminus of the vehicular ferry from Melbourne, is a well-known entry point for many visitors. But, except as a spot for a quick meal at the local Kentucky Fried Chicken, there is little to see.

While the high-speed Bass Highway, or Route 1, continues to Launceston, 100 kilometres (62 miles) to the southeast, a better—and more scenic—alternative is to head south over a network of secondary roads to the northern edge of Tasmania's **Central Plateau.** The wild alpine country around **Cradle Mountain,** with its glaciated valleys and lakes, is well worth the winding two-hour drive from the coast. Accommodation at the **Cradle Mountain Lodge,** nine kilometres (six miles) from **Dove Lake,** is first-class. Visitors have a choice between self-contained cabins with their own fireplace or the main lodge. An overnight stay allows plenty of time for bush walks in the national park and a rare opportunity to see Tasmania's unique nocturnal animals, such as wombats, spotted tailed quolls and possums, in the wild.

Another road—and an ideal detour en route to Launceston—leads through rolling farmland to **Sheffield.** Set against the backdrop of **Mt Roland,** which rises sharply to 1,230 metres (4,500 feet), the town is famous for its murals of colonial scenes on the sides of old buildings. From atop a range to the south, there are stunning views of the **Great Western Tiers,** a massive kilometre- (0.6-mile-) high escarpment forming the northeastern corner of the Central Plateau. An unpaved road leads past waterfalls and caves to the appropriately named **Walls of Jerusalem National Park.** Continuing to the east, the main road (B12) passes through gently rolling farmland and tiny settlements where colonial homes are surrounded by hawthorn hedges. **Mole Creek** offers several attractions, including limestone caves, a colonial farm and honey production, although the nearby wildlife park is slightly disappointing. This scenic detour ends at **Deloraine** (population 5,000), a lovely town dating from the 1830s located along the tree-lined **Meander River,** where the road rejoins the Bass Highway. The town is also the juncture of the Lake Highway which rises sharply up the Great Western Tiers on to the Central Plateau and then continues south towards Hobart.

Launceston, 50 kilometres (30 miles) to the east, is Tasmania's second-largest city, with a population of 65,000. As an inland city, its character is quite different from Hobart. Located 65 kilometres (40 miles) upriver from Bass Strait, it was founded in 1805—Australia's third-oldest city—and, thanks to the region's fertile soil, prospered quickly. Originally known as Patersonia, after its founder Colonel Paterson, the settlement was later renamed for the Cornwall birthplace of the colony's governor. Launceston, the state's leading commercial centre, sits at the head of the broad **Tamar River Valley** at the juncture of the **North** and **South Esk**, its residential suburbs spreading out over the surrounding hills and valleys. As one of the principal entry points into Tasmania, along with Hobart and Devonport, the city is the first stop for many visitors and, even if you are just driving through, it is well worth an overnight stop.

The well laid-out downtown district is a mixture of parks, fine colonial-era buildings and homes, many now restored, and several churches—perfect for an early morning stroll. A short drive or walk to the west, **Cataract Gorge** is the city's most famous natural attraction. Here, hidden in a deep gorge between steep cliffs, the waters of the South Esk meet the Tamar in a surprisingly dramatic setting. The surrounding park has a first-class restaurant, a chairlift over the gorge, and walking trails down to the stream where swimming and boating are allowed.

Closer to the city, drop by **Penny Royal World**, a historic tourist village on the site of an old windmill, and the nearby **Gunpowder Mill**. For those with time, a tiny steamboat runs excursions on the Tamar and the gorge. The city has several fine restaurants and, like Hobart, there is a casino—this one in a country club outside the city.

From Launceston, the traveller has several choices. A one-day drive up the **Tamar Valley** to historic **George Town** on Bass Strait passes through orchards, farmlands and mining country. The Tasman Highway heads east through hilly farming country, the town of **Scottsdale** and then to the East Coast. Or there is the busy Midland Highway which goes south to Hobart, about two hours away, passing through the most Australian-looking countryside in Tasmania—wide valleys of grazing sheep and crops. The highway, which opened not long after settlement began, is rich in history. Its roadside inns, stone villages and military towns are very English in appearance.

The best stop is at **Ross**, established in 1821 on the border of what was then the island's two counties, and later an important coach changing station, military garrison and stock market. Most of the town's colonial buildings have been preserved and restored, with many turned into tea rooms, restaurants, and antique and arts and crafts shops. **Ross Bridge** is the town's most famous landmark, far outshining its counterpart at Richmond (see page 140), Tasmania's first. Opened in 1836, the beautifully proportioned bridge built by convicts is covered in finely carved images of Celtic symbols, animals and figures. A further 90 kilometres (56 miles) to the south is **Oatlands**. The **Callington Mill**, built in 1836, and the town's fine collection of Georgian buildings are worth a brief stop. From here, Hobart is less than an hour's drive away.

The East Coast

There is enough in the regions mentioned above to keep the average visitor occupied for at least a week. But for those with just a bit more time, even an extra day, a diversion down the East Coast opens up another distinctive part of Tasmania. From the north, access is via Launceston, or turning east off the Midland Highway at Conara, the Tasman Highway continues south to Sorell, near Hobart.

Uncrowded and still largely untouched by development, the region is a popular holiday spot with Tasmanians themselves who have long dubbed it their 'Sun Coast'. Certainly, the coastal scenery is among the most beautiful in Australia, with fine beaches, spectacular headlands and forest-covered hills. The coast—lapped by the waters of the Tasman Sea—is also dotted with small settlements, many dating back to the early whaling days or later timber and mining booms. South of **St Helens**, the largest town on the coast, there is a string of beach resorts, such as **Sacamandar**, **Falmouth** and **Four-Mile Creek**, which make a pleasant midday stop. Further on, and just south of the fishing town of **Bicheno**, the **Freycinet Peninsula**—named for the French explorer—is famous for its red granite cliffs and mix of rich blue seas and secluded beaches. For the visitor who does not mind a bit of hiking, the national park is one of Tasmania's scenic highlights.

Nearby **Swansea**, looking out over **Oyster Bay** to the peninsula, makes a good overnight stop before continuing on to **Triabunna**. From here, cruises operate to **Maria Island**, 13 kilometres (eight miles) away, which was named by Abel Tasman in 1642. After the closure of Sarah Island in Macquarie Harbour (see page 148), the island served briefly as a convict colony before Port Arthur was opened. At **Darlington**, the island's only settlement, visitors can see relics from the convict period and then explore the wooded hills and beaches.

South Australia

A Mediterranean Outback

South Australia is not well known as a tourist destination, although the state has recently begun to promote itself with the slogan 'Surprise Yourself!' It's not a bad slogan. And for the overseas visitor, unless your trip coincides with the Adelaide Grand Prix, the most pleasant surprise is how uncrowded the state is, especially compared to Australia's more popular tourist spots.

South Australia's atmosphere and charm are unlike anywhere else in the country. Heavily influenced by its desert and semi-desert climate, the lifestyle is easy-going and the pace slow and relaxed. In the Mediterranean-style climate of the south, the temptation to slow right down should come easily to visitors looking for a quiet and out-of-the-way destination. In the heat of midday, for example, there is nothing quite as refreshing as walking into a colonial-style house now converted into a first-class restaurant where the air is several degrees cooler than outside and the atmosphere instantly relaxing. In many places, the dining rooms open on to a cosy courtyard shaded by grapevines. It is the perfect setting for a meal and a glass of chilled wine.

South Australia's fame as the country's leading wine producer has given the state a special style that seems to permeate everything. (The state also boasts a stylish beer known as Coopers, a tasty ale that completes its fermentation inside the bottle.) It is a lifestyle that South Australians are meticulous to preserve but don't mind sharing with visitors. Spared the rash of commercial and tourist developments in other parts of Australia, South Australia has kept much of its old-fashioned atmosphere.

With an area of 988,182 square kilometres (381,400 square miles), South Australia covers roughly one-eighth of the Australian continent and, after Western Australia and Queensland, is the third-largest state. Much of it is desert, with two-thirds unsuitable for either farming or grazing, and 99 percent of its 1.4 million residents live below the 32nd Parallel, just north of Port Augusta. But even in settled areas, the desert looms large, especially when the dry hot winds are blowing from the interior. Much of the land is flat, with undulating hills. North of Adelaide, these rise sharply to form the spectacular Flinders Ranges.

Where there is sufficient rainfall or irrigation (80 percent of the state receives less than 250 millimetres, or ten inches, a year), much of the land has been cleared for pasture and wheat, with the remaining eucalypts surviving as windbreaks and on hilltops. In late spring and summer, the vast landscape turns into a shimmering mixture of golden

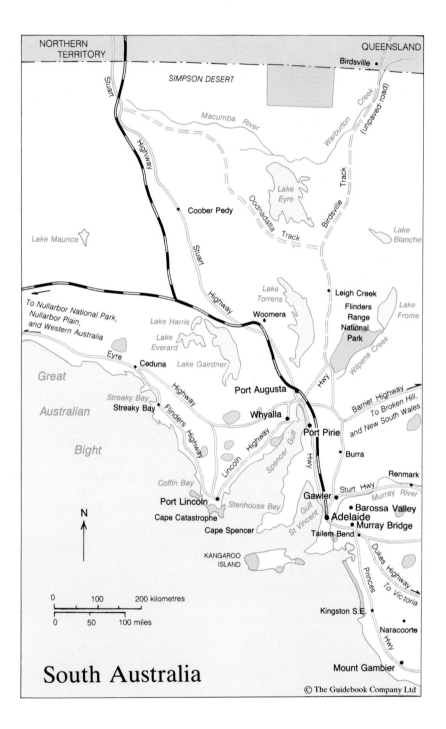

South Australia

fields and lines of grey-green gum trees under a cloudless blue sky. Along the coastline, this typical South Australian scene mixes with the turquoise-blue waters of the Southern Ocean, while inland the backdrop is of dark mountain ridges. Along the muddy Murray River, the state's only major water course, the mixture of colours includes the startling green of irrigated crops and fruit trees. In the more rainy and fertile southeastern region of the state, the landscape is lush and similar to that in neighouring Victoria.

The largely unsettled northern region of the state offers a wide variety of Outback scenery, ranging from Sturt's Stony Desert in the northeast through the wasteland of salt lakes, such as Lake Eyre and Lake Torrens, in the centre, to the flat grasslands and undulating hills towards the northwest. Elsewhere, the massive sand dunes of the Great Victorian Desert intrude into the northwestern corner of South Australia. The Nullarbor Plain (Latin for 'no tree') straddles the border with Western Australia and fronts on to the stark limestone cliffs of the Great Australian Bight. But these regions are hardly pristine. Railways, paved roads and dirt tracks cross these remote areas to tiny opal-mining towns and huge cattle and sheep stations, or ranches. In many places, only ruined homes and towns remain of once-bold dreams to settle what remains a most inhospitable land. But certainly the oddest intrusion of man into the region is the famous Dog Fence. Winding over a distance of 9,600 kilometres (6,000 miles), this constantly patrolled barrier was constructed earlier this century to keep dingoes, or wild dogs, from attacking sheep in the south. It is impossible to miss, even from the air.

History

The Dutch were the first Europeans known to have sighted the coastline of what is today South Australia. By the early 17th century, they were well established in the spice-rich East Indies, now Indonesia, and began to explore the shores of what they named 'New Holland' (see page 13). In 1627, Dutchman François Thyssen sailed south from Batavia, now Jakarta, to take a closer look, but he saw nothing of immediate economic value and sailed home.

It was the French who were to play a more serious role in South Australia's settlement by Europeans. When Captain Matthew Flinders (see page 44) was circumnavigating the continent in 1802, happily naming everything in sight after places in his home county of Lincolnshire, including present-day Port Lincoln on the Eyre Peninsula, he encountered the French explorer Captain Nicholas Baudin who was charting the same coastline. For Flinders, the encounter had serious strategic implications, as England and France were technically at war. The news of Baudin's visit—and especially fears that it would lead to French colonization—soon led New South Wales' officials to order the establishment of English settlements outside of Sydney. Convicts and their minders were sent to Victoria and Tasmania the following year; South Australia had to wait another three decades.

The British continued to explore South Australia's coastline, but it was not until Captain Charles Sturt made his epic voyage in 1830 from New South Wales down the Murray River to its mouth that settlement of South Australia was considered seriously. Sturt, who nearly died while exploring the desert regions of northern South Australia, returned to Sydney and recommended the speedy establishment of a colony. When his tales of a 'well-watered land' reached England, the 'systematic colonizers', led by the Quaker minister Edward Gibbon Wakefield, proposed the creation of a self-supporting colony of free settlers. Convicts would be banned, and the money raised from land sales would be used to bring in equal numbers of religious-minded young men and women. (Wakefield's views also inspired the colonization of New Zealand in 1840.) After heavy lobbying by both land speculators and idealists, the English Parliament finally passed the South Australia Act in 1834 authorizing the bold experiment. On 28 December 1836, 200 settlers gathered under a gum tree in what is today the Adelaide suburb of Glenelg as the colony of South Australia was formally proclaimed.

The colony's early days were a disaster, largely because of continuous quarrelling between the two distinct authorities—one government, the other corporate—charged with developing the settlement. They even disagreed on where to put the colony's capital city and what to name it. These disputes, which soon saw the recall of the first two South Australian governors, Hindmarsh and Gawler, were only settled when Captain George Grey took over in 1842. England assumed full control of the colony the following year. Meanwhile, more migrants arrived. As planned, most of the new settlers came from devoutly religious and hard-working British stock. Several thousand German Lutherans also arrived, fleeing persecution in their homeland, and were soon clearing the ground for South Australia's best-known industry, its wine-making.

By 1844, thanks to the successful early cultivation of wheat and the birth of a wool industry, South Australia was paying its own way. Copper discoveries near Adelaide, some worked by Cornish migrants, added to the colony's early prosperity. When the Victorian gold-rush began in 1851, local entrepreneurs were well-placed to supply the gold-fields with food, equipment and the odd digger. They constructed paddle-steamers and pioneered a romantic era of transport up the muddy Murray River to the neighbouring colony. By 1860, South Australia's population was nearly 100,000.

A desire to expand farming and grazing lands also led to some of Australia's most heroic feats of exploration. But the news from outside the Adelaide and Murray River regions was hardly encouraging. Explorers returned with tales of an unfriendly land of burning sun, vast deserts and stark lakes of salt. Their sentiments were reflected in some of the early names for the colony's geographical features, such as Mt Hopeless and Mt Disappointment in the northeast. In 1840, the explorer Edward John Eyre, after whom Lake Eyre is named, attempted to find a stock route across the southern edge of the continent to Western Australia. More than a year later, Eyre and an Aboriginal named Wylie were the only survivors to stumble into King George's Sound, at present-day Albany. For the entire distance of 800 kilometres (500 miles) across the Nullarbor Plain, Eyre found not a single stream or river. (Today, his transcontinental route is remembered as the Eyre Highway—and it is still a tough journey, even by car.)

Attempts to find a route to Australia's northern coast also met with bitter disappointment. In the mid-1840s, Charles Sturt made several attempts, only to turn back for lack of water. Passing through the northeastern corner of South Australia, he found the Stony Desert and a seascape of undulating sand dunes in both directions. 'A country such as I firmly believe has no parallel on earth's surface,' Sturt wrote in his diary in 1845 before turning back. (Today, the Birdsville and Strzelecki Tracks—both unpaved roads—pass through the region.) Australia's most famous tragic explorers, Robert O'Hara Burke and William John Wills, died near Innamincka in the same region after reaching the Gulf of Carpentaria in 1861. Success finally came to South Australia's most famous explorer, John McDouall Stuart, who—after two failed attempts—finally crossed the 'dead heart' of the Australian continent in 1862. But the journey had taken its toll. His health ravaged, Stuart died only four years later with his sight and memory gone. (The Stuart Highway, linking Adelaide with Darwin, the capital of the Northern Territory, now bears his name.)

Largely on the basis of Stuart's exploration, South Australia successfully took over the administration of the Northern Territory in 1863, an awkward and expensive annexation that continued until 1911. In an attempt to control the southern colonies' telegraph trade, South Australia pushed through the famous Overland Telegraph to Darwin in 1872. Completed in record time, the project also saw the introduction of camels into the Outback. Brought in from Afghanistan

A welcome sight in the desert—a farmer's water tank on the Nullarbor Plain, South Australia

along with their handlers, they quickly became a widely used form of transportation up until the 1920s. When the camels were replaced by the motor vehicle, they were simply turned loose. But instead of dying off, they proliferated as giant pests. When a narrow-gauge railroad was completed to Alice Springs in 1929, those pioneering days were recalled in its name—the *Ghan*.

From the reports of those early explorers, it was hardly surprising that most of the colony's settlers decided to keep their expansion to more immediate areas in the south. The Yorke Peninsula, northwest of Adelaide, was settled early by wheat farmers and sheep graziers and then boomed in the 1860s with the discovery of rich copper deposits. Port Lincoln, at the tip of the Eyre Peninsula to the west, was one of the colony's earliest settlements and, because of its magnificent Boston Harbour, was briefly considered as the capital. By the mid-1840s, settlers were moving into the peninsula's interior. In other parts of the colony, the southeastern region around Mt Gambier was first opened up by overland pioneers from Victoria. Along the Murray River, the thriving riverboat trade helped to create new farming towns, their crops dependent on irrigation. Even Sturt's discouraging discoveries in the far northeast were put to use when the Birdsville Track became an important stock route from southwestern Queensland during the 1880s.

Because of its unique origins, South Australia was spared many of the political quarrels and social divisions that nagged the other Australian colonies. Representative government was granted in 1857 and the colony soon earned a reputation for enlightened legislation. South Australia, for example, originated the now widely used Torrens Title System and the first use of 'easy credit' in real estate dealings. (It also introduced Australia's first income tax.) When droughts in the mid-1880s forced many off the land, the government introduced scientific farming methods, including new drought-resistant strains of wheat and the use of phosphate fertilizers. The same period also saw wide-ranging social reforms such as the eight-hour day, workers' compensation, and the vote for women. Meanwhile, railroads—using two different gauges—reached into many of the settled regions. And when the rich deposits of silver, lead and zinc were discovered at Broken Hill in western New South Wales in 1885, most of the financial and employment benefits went to South Australia.

After Australia's federation in 1901, the state moved to diversify its economy away from its almost exclusive dependence on agriculture. That dependence continues, primarily in wheat and sheep, but today South Australia also earns a living from fishing, mining, processing and light manufacturing. (Mitsubishi, for example, has its Australian car assembly plant outside of Adelaide, and a Technology City has been established to attract high-tech industries.) Given their harsh physical setting, there is something at first terribly incongruous about some developments, such as the so-called Iron Triangle—Port Pirie, Port Augusta and Whyalla—at the head of Spencer Gulf and the Moomba Gas Field just off the Strzelecki Track in the northeast. Other remote regions have served a more deadly purpose. Between 1953 and 1957, the British tested six nuclear bombs in the desert wilderness around Maralinga, north of the Watson siding on the *Trans-Australia* railway. The tests left a painful legacy on the land's traditional Aboriginal owners and on hundreds of Australian and British servicemen who worked at the site. (Despite an expensive clean-up, the area remains off limits.) The Woomera Prohibited Area, a vast swath of salt-pans and scrubland northwest of Port Augusta, was a testing range for British-made rockets after the Second World War and continues to see experimental work by the Australians. Near Woomera, on the edge of the zone, is the top-secret—and highly controversial—American-run 'spy base' at Narrungar, linked into a web of stationary early-warning satellites. Further north, Roxby Downs is the site of the world's largest uranium mine; an entire airconditioned town has been created in the desert for its miners.

Getting Around

Adelaide has only a limited number of international flights, although that is starting to change, and there are regular domestic flights to the city. As it is, many overseas visitors transit briefly through Adelaide airport en route from Melbourne or Sydney to Alice Springs and Ayers Rock, or even on flights to Perth. Similarly, the *Indian-Pacific* and *Ghan* railways and interstate bus lines pass through the city. So, it is easy to rearrange your itinerary to stop over for a few days.

Getting around South Australia does present a few challenges, however. Around Adelaide, renting your own car or signing up for a tour opens up a wide range of day trips, but unless you are a determined long-distance driver, the more remote sights are best reached by aircraft, bus or train.

The government-funded travel agency, Tourism South Australia, operates travel centres in Sydney, Melbourne and Adelaide. (As a reflection of the relatively few number of foreign visitors, the government has no overseas offices, but a good travel agency should be able to help.) These centres offer a wide range of services, including transport to and around the state, plus accommodation. Tourism South Australia also provides a particularly rich selection of privately run tours to all parts of the state. Most of the excursions are quite

imaginative, and many provide a mixture of road, rail, air and even
water travel. The tours range from busy one-day tours around
Adelaide to more relaxing Outback camping safaris ranging from five
days to two weeks. For the more adventurous, operators organize
camel safaris through the Flinders Ranges, retracing the footsteps of
Burke and Wills, as well as whale watching and caving along the
Nullarbor cliffs and four-wheel-drive crossings of the Simpson Desert.

For visitors who are planning to do their own driving in Australia,
several paved highways connect South Australia with other states. The
easiest itinerary is to include Adelaide as the western leg of a trip
taking in Sydney and Melbourne, following the coastline on one leg
and returning through the Outback. But such trips should only be done
in a trustworthy vehicle as the distances between stops, especially
inland, are enormous. (More than the speedometer, drivers should
keep a close eye on the car's temperature gauge.) In many areas,
kangaroos are a serious traffic hazard, especially at night. Visitors are
cautioned, however, against venturing too far down dirt roads without
a fully equipped four-wheel-drive vehicle and plenty of water.

Adelaide

When South Australia's first Surveyor-General, Colonel William
Light, chose the site for the colony's capital not long after the arrival
of the first settlers in late 1836, he was already prepared for the
inevitable 'knockers', or detractors. 'The reasons that led me to fix
Adelaide where it is,' Light wrote in his journal, 'I do not expect to be
generally understood or calmly judged at present.' Today, visitors to
Adelaide—named for the wife of King William IV—cannot fail to be
impressed by the genius of Light's planned city.

Set on the **Torrens River** plain between the **Gulf of St Vincent** and
the **Mount Lofty Ranges**, the centre of Adelaide (population 980,000)
is a square-mile grid of wide streets and fine buildings. Surrounding the
city on all sides is a green belt of parklands containing gardens, lakes
and playing fields. Inside the city itself, there are five squares, or small
parks, set with trees, shrubs and lawns. (At **Light Square**, in the
northwestern section of the city, the remains of the city's founder are
buried.) The design gives Adelaide a distinct small-town atmosphere.
From the corners of this central area, broad tree-lined boulevards link
the city with its surrounding suburbs.

Adelaide has been spared the high-rise developments that have
afflicted most other Australian capital cities. And despite the
construction of some modern buildings, the city has retained much of
its colonial-era atmosphere. With tall buildings concentrated in its
northern section along **King William Street** and **North Terrace**, much

of Adelaide is a modest collection of low-rise commercial buildings, hotels and homes. Interspersed around the city, and reflecting the piety of its early settlers, are the numerous churches that have earned Adelaide the nickname 'City of Churches'. Helped by the Mediterranean-style climate, the city boasts a sophisticated charm. And compared to other Australian cities, its residents have a strong sense of propriety and decorum. Adelaide is the only city, for example, where people queue, or line up, with such precision for the bus.

On the cultural side, Adelaide has long touted itself as 'The Athens of the South', highlighted by its colourful Festival of Arts held in March of every even-numbered year. Modelled on the Edinburgh Festival in Scotland and strongly supported by the community, the festival attracts well-known overseas and local guest artists to a two-week feast of music, ballet, art, theatre, opera and other entertainment. Like Edinburgh, there is even a 'fringe', offering an alternative mix of entertainment that often surpasses the main event. Reflecting how wine and culture go together, especially in the country's leading wine-producing state, the Barossa Valley Vintage Festival is held on alternate years. Together, these two colourful events have earned South Australia the name 'The Festival State'.

In more recent years, the city has turned to other activities to glamorize its image, although not always with universal public support. To the dismay of many residents, the ornate **Adelaide Railway Station** was refurbished and converted into the state's only legal casino in 1985. But the move has at least rejuvenated a previously deteriorating section of the city, including the construction of a new hotel and convention centre. At the same time and after years of lobbying, Adelaide joined the prestigious **Formula One Grand Prix** circuit, receiving instant international exposure for the city. The race, run on a street circuit on the eastern side of the city, attracts thousands of motor racing fans from Australia and overseas every November. (As the last race of the season, however, the championship has frequently already been decided elsewhere, taking away much of its dramatic appeal.) Residents continue to have mixed feelings about the effect of the race on Adelaide's normally tranquil environment. As the tourists arrive, many residents simply leave town for the duration.

Adelaide's simple layout makes the city ideal to explore on foot— although a midday stroll in summer can work up quite a thirst. (One advantage of South Australia's climate, however, is that the heat is dry, with very low humidity.) The best advice is to keep a leisurely pace and take time to explore some of the sights described below. A stroll through the city's surrounding parklands is particularly pleasant in the cooler early morning or evening hours. Adelaide and its suburbs are also serviced by an excellent public transportation system, including the German-built **Busway**, featuring high-speed buses running on concrete tracks. (The Busway, still largely experimental, runs along the River Torrens northeast of the city.)

Victoria Square, at the centre of Adelaide, is a good place to begin a walking tour. The square's main feature is a modern **fountain**, opened in 1968, honouring South Australia's three main rivers—the Murray, Torrens and Onkaparinga. The wide tree-shaded square is surrounded by several colonial-era structures, such as the **General Post Office** (GPO) with its striking **Victoria Tower**, two solid-looking court buildings, and churches.

At the southern side of the square, the city's only surviving tramline offers a pleasant 20-minute ride to the beachside suburb of **Glenelg**, site of the colony's founding in 1836. Located next to Adelaide's most popular beach, the suburb features tree-lined parks and restored colonial-era buildings. The suburb's top attraction is a full-scale replica of the **HMS** *Buffalo*, which features a museum and restaurant open seven days a week. The **Old Gum Tree**, where the colony was proclaimed, is located in MacFarlane Street, surrounded by modern buildings. (Buses and taxis also link the suburb with the city.)

Just north of Victoria Square on the east side of King William Street, the **Adelaide Town Hall** is built in 16th-century Renaissance style and features the carved faces of Queen Victoria and Prince Albert, an impressive clock tower and courtyard entryway. Completed in 1874, the building has a grand marble staircase leading to a large hall used for concerts and theatre. A couple of blocks up and on the other side of the street is the elaborate Renaissance-style **Edmund Wright House**, built in 1876 and renowned for its richly decorated gilded ceiling, one of the finest in Australia. Surrounding these two historic structures is a mix of more utilitarian buildings, most dating from earlier this century. Adelaide's main shopping district centres around the popular **Rundle Mall**, opened in 1976 and featuring restaurants, boutiques and department stores. (Shopping arcades and alleys lead off the mall into other neighbouring streets.)

For some reason, the streets on both sides of King William Street have different names. The street across from the mall is called **Hindley Street**, the heart of the city's entertainment and dining district. At night, the street becomes a blaze of neon lights and frenzied activity as pedestrians crowd the sidewalks. In the street, youngsters from the suburbs cruise by in their souped-up cars, engaging in occasional drag races. With a mixture of everything from restaurants and espresso bars to strip shows and amusement parlours, the street has a distinctive personality. But only a block further down is a quiet district of fine restaurants.

North Terrace marks the city's northern boundary, flanked on one side by commercial buildings and on the other by Adelaide's most important public institutions. Just west of its intersection with King William Street is **Parliament House**, an impressive Roman-style building constructed of South Australian marble and granite. Although officially opened in 1889, it was not completed until 50 years later. Next door is the recently restored **Old Parliament House**, built in 1855 and now a museum of the state's political history. (Open seven days a week, the museum also features a well-made audio-visual documentary of South Australia's history.)

Just to the west is the **Adelaide Casino**, located in the city's magnificently restored railway station. Despite its critics, the casino is easily Australia's most elegant, and a visit is well worthwhile even if you don't plan on gambling. Open from 10 am to 4 am during the week and continuously at weekends, the casino features 98 gambling tables, an excellent restaurant and five bars. Hindley Street, with its mixture of nightlife and restaurants, is only a short walk away.

To the east of the intersection of North Terrace and William Street, a number of elegant public buildings are interspersed between lawns, gardens, trees and memorials. These include **Government House**, the residence of the state's governor-general, the **University of Adelaide** and the **State Library**. The area is also rich in museums. The **Art Gallery of South Australia** and the **South Australian Museum**, both open daily, are worth visiting, especially for their collections of Aboriginal and Australian art. The **Royal South Australian Society of Arts Gallery**, located inside the **Institute of Technology**, features exhibitions of local artists. (The best place to see and purchase Aboriginal arts and crafts is the **New Gallery of Aboriginal Art** at 28 Currie Street, one block south of Hindley Street.) At the eastern end of North Terrace, **Ayers House** is a magnificently restored colonial mansion constructed between 1846 and 1876 which now houses two first-class restaurants.

Each of Adelaide's surrounding parklands, designated by its point on the compass, has its own distinct characteristics. **North Parklands**, which begins at North Terrace, stretches across both sides of the River Torrens to North Adelaide. Just north of Parliament House is the

Driving West

As a foreign correspondent living in Australia, most of my travels around the country over the past 12 years have been on assignment. I have seen some fascinating places, many too difficult for the average tourist to reach. Among my favourites: the three-day Indian–Pacific rail trip from Perth to Sydney, a four-day 'road train' journey over the then-unpaved Sturt Highway from Adelaide to Alice Springs, and a two-week DC-3 tour around northeastern Australia, with a flight over Ayers Rock at sunset.

Then, there was the time I drove from Sydney to Perth. In mid-December 1986, I was assigned to cover the America's Cup races off Perth. It was a long posting, and we decided the best way to travel the 4,200 kilometres (2,600 miles) to Australia's west coast was by road. The first order of business was to service our aging Australian-built Ford Falcon station wagon. Then, just in case we met a kangaroo, I had a giant set of 'roo bars' installed on the front of the car, complete with floodlights. With most of our luggage in an oversized roof rack, the six of us piled in and aimed the car westward over the Blue Mountains. Our plan was to arrive in Fremantle in time for Christmas.

An anonymous American tourist once said, 'Driving across Australia is like driving back and forth across Nebraska for a week.' That is a slight exaggeration, but the transcontinental drive is still hard work. It was only a decade ago that the highway was finally paved for its entire distance, and today it is a two-lane highway all the way to Perth. We took a fairly leisurely five days; the record is 36 hours.

By late afternoon of the first day, we had cleared the Great Dividing Range and the land was levelling out into scattered low hills covered in grey-green eucalypt forest and golden fields of wheat awaiting harvest. As the sun set, the landscape took on a distinct purple tinge. Colourful native birds came out to feed along the tree-covered roadside. We refuelled at West Wyalong where the young attendants were anxious to close and head off to a local dance. 'No, there is no Wyalong, only a West Wyalong,' they explained laconically, 'but we don't know why.' But they had enough time to chat and, after offering us a free beer, the conversation turned to supercharged Corvettes and their dreams of visiting Disneyland. Two hours down the highway, we stopped at Hay for the night and woke up to a flat landscape of dry fields and scruffy trees.

By early afternoon, we had crossed the muddy Murray River—surprisingly small for Australia's mightiest river—and were driving through Mildura and its fields of irrigated citrus trees. The straight road passed through the tiny Outback of northwestern Victoria, an undulating ochre-coloured countryside dotted with clumps of mulga trees. Outside, the temperature was above the old 'century mark' (100°F, or 38°C), sending the engine's temperature gauge to a dangerously high level. We flipped off the airconditioner, slowed down and cracked open the windows. A blast of hot desert air swept into the car, putting us into a groggy mood. When we crossed the South Australian border two hours later, we were forced to give up our fresh fruit to the border health inspectors but were soon compensated as we met the Murray River once again and even more citrus orchards. At a roadside stall in Berri, one dollar bought us a bag of the most delicious oranges we had ever tasted. An hour later, we farewelled the now-majestic river and headed through wide fields of ripening wheat, then over the Mount Lofty Ranges and into Adelaide. Entranced by its layout and relaxed atmosphere, we immediately fell in love with the place.

We were barely one-third of the way to Perth and the car's overheating radiator was now a serious worry. It was also Saturday morning. Back in Sydney, they would simply tell you to come back on Monday, but in the friendly manner typical of small towns in Australia the local Ford dealer rang around until he found an open radiator shop. As we chatted amiably, he installed a reconditioned 'heavy-duty' radiator and soon had us back on the road.

Heading north from Adelaide, we skirted the turquoise-blue Gulf St Vincent, then passed through a desolate countryside of rolling hills and salt lakes before emerging along a narrow coastal strip between the vast Spencer Gulf and the soaring foothills of the Flinders Ranges.

After refuelling at the industrial town of Port Augusta at the head of the Gulf, we turned west into a forbidding landscape which instantly brought home the immensity of the driving task ahead. We were crossing a virtually treeless reddish-coloured plain dotted with rocky outcrops such as Iron Knob, a rich source of ore for the nearby steel foundry at Whyalla. Compared to the first two days of our journey, the road traffic was noticeably lighter and we were overwhelmed by a feeling of isolation and melancholia which persisted as we entered the state's richest wheat-growing area at the northern end of the Eyre Peninsula. Along the highway and adjacent rail line, small settlements dominated by huge grain silos appeared to be trapped in a time capsule. Stopping at tiny Poochera, where I had spent three days waiting for my road train years before, I caught up with news of old acquaintances. Pulling into the seaside town of Ceduna after 10 pm, we checked into a motel only to be kept awake half the night by a noisy rock band in the local pub.

Waking up a bit cranky and irritable, we made an early start for what we knew would be the most gruelling part of our trip—crossing the legendary Nullarbor Plain. But an hour out of Ceduna at the old township of Penong, famous for its many windmills and charming old buildings, we made a brief detour down a dirt road to Point Sinclair. A stark windswept headland, it overlooks the eastern end of the Great Australian Bight and Cactus Beach, a popular—terribly isolated—surfing beach. Just inland from the coast, the landscape is a mixture of high vegetation-covered sand dunes and large salt pans, including the oddly coloured Pink Lake. Back on the highway, we spotted one of the area's road signs warning drivers to beware of kangaroos, wombats and wild camels. Soon, we had left behind the wheat fields and moved inland through undulating countryside covered in remarkably thick eucalypt forests, part of the large Yalata Aboriginal Reserve.

Then, quite suddenly, we entered the vast and treeless plain known as the Nullarbor—Latin for 'no tree'. Once the floor of an ancient seabed, the limestone plain stretches far inland and is covered in light scrub and dotted with caves, many of them quite vast. We were now roughly half-way across the continent and, hardly surprisingly, the petrol at the plain's only settlement, Nullarbor Station, was the most expensive of the entire journey. Nearby, we drove just off the highway for a spectacular view of the famous Nullarbor Cliffs. Although it was summer, cold winds off the Southern Ocean and the Bight quickly had us scrambling for our jackets before strolling across to look down over the sheer cliffs to the pounding surf below. After a couple of stops, we crossed the Western Australian border at Eucla, where a road leads down to the Old Telegraph Station along the Bight. Opened in 1877 and once a busy link with the rest of Australia, the haunting ruins of the station today lie mostly buried by sand dunes.

But such scenic diversions were rare. For most of the time (hour after hour), we kept moving west at a steady 120 kilometres (75 miles) per hour, or slightly above the speed limit. Our only stops were to refuel, to grab another cup of coffee or a quick meal and to switch drivers. Conversation became as repetitious as the surrounding countryside and even our cassette collection was becoming boring. By the afternoon of the fourth day, the trip had turned into an exhausting marathon and our patience was running thin. After crossing into Western Australia, we found the time difference had given us an extra two and a half hours. In a burst of adrenalin and chatter, we pressed on into the night. With our bright floodlights illuminating the road far ahead, we passed through the tiny settlements of Cocklebiddy, Calgunia and Balladonia and along one of the world's longest straight stretches of highway (145 kilometres, or 90 miles). Pulling into the old gold-mining town of Norseman after 10 pm, we had clocked up a record 1,200 kilometres (750 miles) during the day. But as we began looking for a place to stay, we found every motel in town had posted its 'No Vacancy' sign and closed down for the night. Thanks to the attendants at the local petrol station, we finally found a guesthouse and, after rousing the owner, settled in for the night.

After a hearty breakfast, we resumed our journey and by midday arrived in the famous gold-mining town of Kalgoorlie. But away from the coast, the soaring desert temperatures took their toll. The car's airconditioner simply gave up and my wife was feeling alarmingly faint.

We pulled into an airconditioned shopping centre and debated whether to check into a motel or continue the 600 kilometres (370 miles) to Perth. We decided to proceed. Soon, the hot Gold-fields were behind us, and, after passing through the heart of Western Australia's wheat belt, we cleared the Darling Ranges and descended into Perth just as the sun was setting over the Indian Ocean.

Settling into our place in Fremantle, we quickly concluded that the trip was definitely worth doing—but only once. Our plan was to sell the car and then fly back to Sydney in comfort. But six weeks later, my wife and I turned the car around and did the trip all over again. The second time was a breeze!

Festival Centre, Adelaide's best-known landmark. Occupying a two-hectare (five-acre) site overlooking the river, the performing arts complex features a concert hall, theatres and an open-air amphitheatre built to provide a range of venues for the biennial **Festival of Arts**. But the centre provides a wide range of quality entertainment throughout the year. (Visitors should check what's on in local newspapers or at the centre's box office.) Further down the slope, **Elder Park** is a departure point for cruises up the river to the **Adelaide Zoo**, best known for its collection and breeding of colourful native birds, and the adjoining **Botanic Gardens**, with its 16 hectares (38 acres) of Australian and exotic plants. Walking paths along both sides of the river offer a relaxing break from the city.

On the other side of the **Adelaide Bridge**, the **Adelaide Oval** is one of the world's finest cricket grounds. In the summer months, both international and domestic cricket matches are held here. The atmosphere is quite congenial, and a lazy day, or even just a few hours, at the Adelaide Oval makes a pleasant break. (If you are not familiar with cricket, this is a good place to pick up a few lessons from the friendly fans.)

North Adelaide, part of Light's original plan and also surrounded by parklands, rises on a slope above the River Torrens. The suburb has a totally different character from the city, reflecting its role as Adelaide's first bedroom community. Instead of institutional and commercial buildings, the suburb is a collection of gracious homes, cottages and apartments. (Many have now been converted into offices.) Most reflect South Australia's particular architecture—wide verandas against the desert heat, corrugated tin-roofs, and walls of sandstone or bluestone, a volcanic rock—and sit in well-shaded yards kept alive by constant watering. The pace of North Adelaide is notably slower than the city next door and, in recent years, has become quite a trendy neighbourhood. The buildings have been carefully restored and, especially along **Melbourne Street**, now serve as antique shops, swish boutiques and restaurants. Many of the restaurants have courtyard or sidewalk tables frequently shaded by sprawling grapevines. The suburb also has several comfortable old pubs, most featuring restaurants and live music. The area offers a quiet and more relaxing alternative to downtown's Hindley Street.

Of course, there is a lot more to Adelaide than downtown and its quaint northern neighbour. As in other Australian capitals, the city's suburbs sprawl over a vast area from the coast up into the tree-covered Adelaide Hills. Older suburbs have the flavour of North Adelaide, with gracious old homes set in leafy gardens along tree-lined streets. Up in the hills, people seeking a more rural lifestyle have moved into old farmhouses or built their own dreamhouse, then commute to work on the plains below. Others prefer the city's coastal suburbs with their 32 kilometres (20 miles) of beaches. But there are also some grimly depressing and stifling suburbs such as those around the satellite town of Elizabeth, 20 kilometres (12 miles) northeast of the city. (Built in the 1960s to house mostly English migrants for the city's manufacturing industries, the homes were all built to the same plan and, because of their location, catch the full brunt of the hot desert winds.)

Around Adelaide

The Adelaide region offers a wide variety of attractions. One of the most popular—and closest—destinations is the **Adelaide Hills**, less than half an hour east of the city, where winding roads link tiny villages nestled in lovely valleys. From **Mt Lofty** (711 metres, or 2,334 feet), the highest point in the ranges, there are spectacular views of the Adelaide region and a large botanical garden containing a mixture of native and exotic trees. The hills and its villages offer a cosy and comfortable atmosphere and endless places to stop and linger. The highlight of any visit is **Hanhdorf**, the oldest-surviving German settlement in Australia and only 35 kilometres (22 miles) southeast of the city. Settled in 1838 by Prussians, the village has been faithfully restored and maintains its very strong German character with its bakers and wurst-makers and a wide variety of arts and crafts. Overseas visitors will particularly enjoy a visit to the Hanhdorf Academy and Art Gallery. Its large collection of original paintings includes several by Sir Hans Heysen, one of Australia's most famous German migrants. (Coach tours also visit the hills, with many taking in further destinations north and south of the city.)

But no visit to South Australia is complete without a visit to one of its famous wine-growing districts. The **Barossa Valley**, an hour's drive northeast of Adelaide, is Australia's largest and most famous wine-producing area. Surrounded by gently rolling hills, the valley is like a piece of southern Germany dropped into one of the most beautiful parts of South Australia. Surrounded by fields of grapevines, the valley's small towns are a colourful collection of historic buildings and churches that reflect its settlement by religious and political refugees from Prussia and Silesia in the early 1840s. While the valley's unique dialect, known as Barossa *Deutsche*, has now largely disappeared, German tradition lives on in the art of wine-making, fine food and hospitality.

The ideal time to visit the valley is during the biennial **Barossa Vintage Festival**, beginning on Easter Monday in every odd-numbered year. The colourful festival celebrates the end of the year's vintage and

brings together all the villages and towns of the valley for a busy week of entertainment, food and, of course, wine-tasting. Billed as the world's largest wine festival, the event attracts thousands of visitors. But unless you have made specific plans to attend, or are just plain lucky, most overseas visitors will miss out on this biennial Festival. The valley's joyful mood does linger on, however, through a busy calendar of other events such as the Oom Pah Festival every January, a Hot-air Balloon Regatta in May, and a Classic Gourmet Weekend in August. Wine shows also take place in several towns throughout the year.

There are several ways of visiting the Barossa Valley. The easiest is to catch a day-tour with one of three Adelaide bus companies which, for about A$30, includes a visit to a major winery, a wine-tasting and lunch. But more serious wine buffs might prefer to rent their own car and spend a day or two exploring the valley's wineries, restaurants and towns at a more leisurely pace. There are also regular bus services to and around the valley, chauffeured tours, or groups arranged by Tag-Along-Tours at Angaston. (Another way of getting around the compact valley is to hire a bicycle or a horse, or simply to walk.) The valley also offers a wide range of accommodation, from modern motels and homestyle hotels to quaint cottages and grand homes set amidst the vineyards.

Whichever way you choose to see the Barossa Valley, you will be entranced by its relaxed and friendly atmosphere. There are more than 50 wineries in the valley, ranging from the giants of the Australian wine industry to numerous family-run vineyards and exclusive wine-makers. Almost all provide wine-tastings and bottle sales, and several offer dining facilities. **Orlando**, where German-born Johann Gramp planted the Barossa Valley's first grapes back in 1847, is easily the best known, followed by well-established wineries such as Seppelts, Penfolds, Krondorf and Wolf Blass. But it is often the smaller wineries that offer the most character and the best opportunity to meet the wine-makers themselves. The tasting rooms at the **Holmes Springton Winery**, for example, are located in an old blacksmith's shop and you can join the wine-maker over a light lunch. At **Chateau Yaldara**, visitors are ushered into the antique ballroom of a French-style chateau for wine-tastings. And at the **Maxwell Meadery** at **Dorrien**, fermented honey is the speciality. There are many more, of course, and much of the fun of visiting the Barossa lies in discovering them.

Adding to the valley's enchantment are its quaint villages and towns which have changed little over the years. **Angaston**, in the northeastern corner of the valley, has a touch of northern England in its sandstone architecture, while other towns such as **Bethany**, **Tanunda** and **Lyndoch** reflect their strong German origins. In Tanunda's **Goat**

Square, for example, the site of the town's early market is surrounded by original stone cottages built in the early 1840s. Old churches and cemeteries tell much of these communities' early history. The settlers' traditions have also lived on in their appreciation of fine food. For those anxious to sample their wine purchases over a picnic, drop into a town and pick up freshly baked German-style bread and sausage before heading off to a secluded park. And for those who prefer a good restaurant, the choice is enormous. The **Marananga Restaurant and tea-rooms** is set in an old stone cottage, while the nearby **Pheasant Farm Restaurant** serves the best game food in the state. Another well-known restaurant is the **Landhaus** in Bethany, a former shepherd's cottage that has been converted into a small motel.

Wine is also grown in the **Southern Vales** district south of Adelaide. Although not as compact as the Barossa Valley, there are more than 40 wineries, some with restaurants, scattered through the picturesque region of rugged coastline and gentle hills. Only half an hour south of the city, **Reynella** was the site of the colony's first commercial winery back in 1839 and makes a pleasant stop. Now owned by one of Australia's leading wine-makers, Thomas Hardy and Sons, the winery is a collection of well-preserved stone buildings, including a grand English-style mansion, surrounded by beautifully landscaped gardens. Most of the wineries, however, are located further south around the quiet town of **McLaren Vale** where both sides of the valley are covered in vines. In contrast to the Barossa, however, there are a lot of small boutique wineries, a fact that greatly increases the visitor's chances of meeting individual growers. (The popular tourist slogan down here is 'Meet Your Maker'.) The colourful **Bushing Festival** every October marks the release of the year's vintage.

The Southern Vales are also the gateway to the beautiful **Fleurieu Peninsula**, named by the French explorer Baudin back in 1802 and site of some of the earliest settlements in South Australia. (Winding roads criss-cross the peninsula, making the region ideal to explore in your own car, although day tours take in a pleasant variety of destinations.) Along the peninsula's rugged windswept coastline, there are literally dozens of uncrowded beaches. One of the most spectacular is along the peninsula's southern shore, where **Waitpinga Beach** clearly lives up to its Aboriginal name meaning 'windy place'. Overlooked by towering cliffs, rough breakers out of the Southern Ocean pound a shoreline backed by huge sand dunes. For hikers, the woodlands along the cliffs offer spectacular views out to sea and conservation parks full of wildlife. Opened up early for its rich farmland, the peninsula's rolling hills are dotted with more than a dozen quaint towns with beautiful old stone buildings, churches and monuments. **Strathalbyn**, about an hour's drive southeast of Adelaide, is one of Australia's loveliest country towns. Settled by devout Scots in the early 1840s, the town offers a touch of Scotland with its well-preserved buildings and parklands along the banks of the River Angas.

At the southeastern corner of the peninsula overlooking **Encounter Bay** and the mouth of the Murray River is historic **Victor Harbour**. Originally a whaling station, the port prospered from the 1850s onwards as a transshipment point for trade along the river up into Victoria, New South Wales and Queensland. In those days, an 11-kilometre (seven-mile) horse-drawn tramway—Australia's first railway—carried cargo between Victor Harbour and **Goolwa**, a port just inside the treacherous sandbank that marks the river mouth. From there, a fleet of riverboats headed across vast **Lake Alexandrina** and up the Murray into the Australian interior. But by 1900, the river trade had virtually ceased and Victor Harbour turned into a popular resort and retirement community. The main tourist attraction is **Granite Island**, site of the town's once-thriving port facilities and linked to the mainland by a long causeway. Today, the island is a sanctuary for wallabies and fairy penguins and can be reached by restored horsedrawn trams. Just south of the town is the brooding hulk of Rosetta Head where Flinders and Baudin had their dramatic meeting in April 1802. For visitors keen to relive the romantic days of river travel, the modern paddle-wheeler *Murray River Queen* conducts two- and five-day trips out of nearby Goolwa. Shorter half-day cruises are offered on the wood-burning paddle-steamer *Mundoo* and the more conventional *Encounter* and *Aroona*.

Although coach tours and driving your own car are the most common ways to see the Fleurieu Peninsula, a great alternative—especially if you like old steam trains—is to catch the **Victor Harbour Tourist Railway**. In what is billed as the world's longest regularly-run tourist rail service, the restored steam train travels the 260 kilometres (162 miles) from Adelaide to Victor Harbour nearly every Sunday between April and November. (Because of the very real danger of bushfires, the train does not run during the summer months.) For the bargain price of only A$25, the train runs through the beautiful Mount Lofty Ranges south of the city to Golway and then along the tops of sand dunes to Victor Harbour. On alternate Sundays, tourists can leave the train and, for an additional charge, either board a paddle-wheeler on Lake Alexandrina or visit a winery followed by a short cruise up the Murray River. The train is run by volunteers and attracts keen 'steam buffs' from all around Australia, a naturally congenial lot who make overseas visitors feel instantly welcome.

A Horseless Carriage

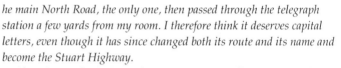

*T*he main North Road, the only one, then passed through the telegraph station a few yards from my room. I therefore think it deserves capital letters, even though it has since changed both its route and its name and become the Stuart Highway.

Along it, one day in December 1907, came travellers who caused more excitement among the whites and more panic among the blacks than anything else during our stay there.

Natives rushed to the station office with the news that on the track a few hundred yards away there was a "buggy going all by hisself, him got smoke coming out longa him." We showed little consternation, and that perplexed them, but it was only because we had advance word from telegraph stations to the south that Mr Harry Dutton, of Anlaby, Kapunda, and his colleague, Mr Murray Aunger, were on the way in the first motor car to attempt to cross Australia.

We had seen one or two of these horseless carriages in Adelaide during a holiday in 1904, so we knew what to expect in a physical sense as well. I had even had a ride in one at Glenelg. In those days riding in a car was roughly the same as riding in an aeroplane in the 1930s and in a space capsule in the 1960s. I remember that it had high seats arranged back to back, which meant a hair-raising experience for the rear seat passengers. But to most of the men in Alice Springs at that time the car was a novelty, the first they had seen, and the natives couldn't have been more terrified of the Devil himself.

The camp on the river bank broke into pandemonium. I've never seen such panic: elderly lubras, clasping their precious dogs, scrambled up *trees like teenagers, making sure that they would be well out of range of the smoking monster if it should come their way: infectious dread spread among hundreds of mangy dogs which howled piteously; piccaninnies cowered or yelled with fright. But finally almost every soul on the station came to stare and wonder and give a welcome to the first motorists, while keeping their escape routes open in case the monstrous thing should belch and roar as it had on arrival.*

Thirty or so horses in the stockyard were as frightened as the natives and galloped around madly; one, shut in the small breaking-in yard, jumped the six feet high rail fence, raced westwards, and wasn't found until many days later.

Only the old men of the tribe, the Aranda Elders, were unmoved, or pretended to be. I suppose they had to put on a brave face in front of the others. They glanced disdainfully at the smoking buggy and then returned to their accustomed contemplation of the surrounding tribal land.

Les Spicer, one of the operators, asked an old patriarch named Billy what he thought of the car.

Billy thought about the question for a long time. Then he spat disgustedly, albeit eloquently, and said, "I reckon might-be that white-feller properly Number-One fool. Him make'im anything like buggy-longa-smoke. But he can't make'im rain, eh?"

And that was that.

Doris Blackwell & Douglas Lockwood, Alice On The Line, *1965*

One of the best-kept secrets of the Adelaide region is **Kangaroo Island**, just off the western tip of the Fleurieu Peninsula. The island offers a near-perfect mix of surf, sand, sun and scenery—plus lots of native wildlife. Although only a half-hour flight or a six-hour ferry trip from Adelaide, Kangaroo Island—Australia's third-largest island—has maintained its splendid isolation without succumbing to over-development. Much of the island's 4,350 square kilometres (1,680 square miles) is wilderness and national parks, while its rugged coastline offers a stunning mixture of white sandy beaches, plunging cliffs and offshore reefs. The most dramatic scenery is around the island's southwestern corner, where the full fury of the Southern Ocean smashes into the pitted limestone cliffs of **Cape Du Couedic** and the strangely shaped **Remarkable Rocks**. In contrast to this ferocity, the island's northern shore overlooks a string of quiet and sheltered beaches on the **Investigator Strait**.

Kangaroo Island has a rich—and sometimes brutal—history. Although traces have been found of old campsites and tools, mystery still surrounds what happened to the island's original Aboriginal inhabitants, all of whom had disappeared when Flinders visited in 1802. Noting how easily his men were able to slaughter kangaroos for food, he named the island after the animal. Later, the Frenchman Baudin, whom Flinders met at nearby Encounter Bay, visited and named many of the coastal features. (**Frenchman's Rock**, near **Penneshaw**, marks one of their stops on the island.) These two European visitors were followed by a motley collection of sealers and whalers, including a sealing expedition from the United States in 1803 which inspired the name **American River** at the eastern end of the island. Later, the island's coves and bushland became home to a savage collection of escaped convicts, deserters and shipwrecked sailors who were finally brought under control by the legendary 'Governor Wally', a tough-minded farmer. When the formal settlement of South Australia began in 1836, his brutal reign ended. But life was tough for those early colonists and, because of poor soil and water, many soon moved on to the mainland. Because of its treacherous coastline, Kangaroo Island also became a notorious graveyard for ships, with more than 60 wrecks dotting its shoreline.

Today, the island's most exciting attraction—thanks to its isolation from the mainland and the lack of predators such as dingoes and foxes—is the abundance of easily approachable wildlife in virtually undisturbed bush. At **Seal Bay**, for example, visitors can wander among the browsing seals or even go surfing with them. At other locations, kangaroos, wallabies, koalas and emus vie for your attention. There are more than 200 species of birds, including black cockatoos, pelicans and fairy penguins. In spring, when wildflowers proliferate, the island is particularly attractive. For overseas visitors, the island provides a rare opportunity to experience the diversity of the Australian wilderness—all in one location.

One-day tours fly visitors to the island and take in the most important sites by four-wheel-drive vehicle for about A\$200. (There are even special charters which fly visitors in just for dinner at one of the island's top seafood restaurants!) Package tours are also available, ranging from two days to one week, with arrivals on the island by air or sea. (The most upmarket of these is an eight-day tour that combines four-wheel driving with camel- and horse-riding, and even a bit of sailing; accommodation is in refurbished lighthouses and farmhouses.) For self-drivers, ferry services to the island depart from **Port Adelaide** and **Cape Jervis** on the Fleurieu Peninsula. (The latter journey takes about an hour across the **Backstairs Passage**.) Almost all of the roads on the island are unpaved, and drivers are warned against driving too fast on the gravel surface.

Most of the accommodation on Kangaroo Island is located in the three coastal resorts at its eastern end—**Kingscote**, **Penneshaw** and **American River**—and varies from luxury resort hotels and motels to holiday flats and caravan parks. (Camping is also permitted at limited places around the island.) Away from these three towns, accommodation is available in self-contained cabins and cottages and in refurbished homesteads. Swimming, diving and hiking are favourite activities here, although many visitors come just for the incomparable fishing, especially the famous King George Whiting, tuna and crayfish. Not surprisingly, the island's restaurants offer some of the best seafood in Australia.

The Flinders Ranges

Beginning along the coast 250 kilometres (155 miles) north of Adelaide, the **Flinders Ranges** offer some of Australia's most spectacular mountain scenery. Named by Captain Flinders, who first sighted them in 1802, the razor-edged ranges stretch northwards for 800 kilometres (500 miles) into the heart of the Outback. The Flinders Ranges have a unique and awesome beauty. Rising sharply into the bright blue sky from the dry and rocky flatlands, the rugged peaks, gorges and valleys offer an incomparable mixture of contrasting colours, vegetation and wildlife. After the rains in spring, the entire region is covered in a carpet of wildflowers. Although the geological forces that formed the present landscape are relatively recent (about 60 million years ago), they have exposed some of the earth's most

ancient rock formations. Most of the rocks in the region are from 500 million to one billion years old. But around the northern town of Arkaroola, geologists have discovered granites that are even older— 1.5 billion years old. Elsewhere in the ranges, palaeontologists in the late 1940s discovered important fossils of jellyfish and worms, marking the evolution—about 600 million years ago—of more complex animal forms.

In more recent times, the Flinders Ranges' numerous waterholes and abundant native wildlife supported Aboriginal tribes who left behind a rich legacy of cave-paintings and rock art. In virtually every corner of the Flinders, the evidence of the Aboriginal Dreamtime is visible, often in places of extraordinary beauty. During unusually wet seasons in the 1840s, European farmers moved into the region, only to be forced out several years later when the usual dry conditions returned. A mining boom, mainly in copper, also ended in disaster. Their legacy is found in the many ruined homesteads and abandoned towns scattered throughout the ranges. Today, people are returning not to tame the land but to enjoy its beauty and tranquillity. It is open to question how long it will be before someone decides to ruin everything by dropping a five-star hotel into this stunning wilderness. For the moment, though, it is still well worth visiting. The Flinders Ranges are a leisurely day's drive or quick flight north of Adelaide.

Located in its central section, **Wilpena Pound**, 420 kilometres (260 miles) north of Adelaide, is the best-known feature in the Flinders Ranges. Appearing at first glance like a collapsed volcano or meteorite crater, the Pound is a huge plateau encircled by sheer cliffs that rise over 1,000 metres (3,282 feet) from the surrounding flatlands. Inside this large natural amphitheatre, measuring 16 by six kilometres (ten by four miles), the densely wooded floor is home to thousands of birds and other native animals. According to Aboriginal legend, Wilpena Pound—meaning 'place of bent fingers'—was formed when two huge snakes attacked a tribal initiation rite and devoured most of the participants. Then, stretching themselves out in a circle around the ceremonial ground, the snakes willed themselves to death to form the surrounding walls. The point where their heads barely touched is the narrow gorge that provides the only entrance into the Pound. Scientists have a much less colourful explanation, describing the feature as the result of 'variable weathering among different rock formations'. As the more resistant quartzite was lifted and tilted, erosion weathered away the softer deposits below, leaving the Pound's magnificent walls.

The best way to appreciate the full magnificence of this geological wonder is to take a 20-minute scenic flight from a dirt airstrip near the **Wilpena Pound Resort**, a quaint motel and camping complex located just outside the structure. Back on the ground, a short road from the resort runs beside Wilpena Creek with its lush mixture of red river gums, reeds and bulrushes and up to a carpark that marks the beginning of a walking track into the Pound itself. Even a brief visit inside takes a couple of hours and, properly equipped with water and a snack, it is easy to spend all day exploring. (Visitors are cautioned, however, to stick to the marked trails.) The inside of Wilpena Pound makes a stunning contrast to the dry and sparsely covered land outside. The valley floor is thick with vegetation, such as red river gums and native pines, which changes to shrubby plants and small trees as one moves up the gently rising slopes to the surrounding peaks. The more exposed ridgelines are home to wild grasses, flowering plants and 'blackboys'.

Several trails lead up the slopes to what are among the highest peaks in the Flinders Ranges. (**St Mary's Peak**, at the northwestern end of the Pound, is the highest at 1,170 metres, or 3,840 feet, but several others are only slightly lower. The easiest climb, however, is **Wangara Hill**, just inside the entrance above the old Hill homestead.) The reward from the top is a superb view over the entire region. The valley floor is criss-crossed by a network of trails. Here, the most rewarding trek is to the rugged and spectacular **Edeowie Gorge** at the northwestern end of the Pound.

Not surprisingly for such a lovely piece of real estate, Wilpena Pound did see some attempts at European settlement. For several years in the 1850s, the valley was used as a stock-run before droughts forced its closure. Then, in 1899, the Hill family moved into the Pound and, much to everyone's surprise, successfully grew wheat which they hauled out over a log road they constructed through the gorge. But in 1914, the Hills' fragile link to the outside world was washed away in a flood and they abandoned the Pound. All that remains of their experiment is an old stone cottage just inside the entrance and cleared lands where wheat once grew. Today, the Pound and other surrounding areas are protected as the **Flinders Ranges National Park**.

With its variety of accommodation, Wilpena Pound is an excellent base for further exploration. (Although the road to Wilpena is paved, the surrounding dirt and gravel roads—with their rough surfaces, dry creek crossings, and blind curves and crests—require extreme caution, especially after a rainstorm. For the self-driver, most roads are suitable in conventional vehicles.) Nearby, up a dirt track that passes through thick native pine forests with the higher ranges in the background, is **Sacred Canyon**, with a distinctive collection of Aboriginal carvings. But the most scenic trip runs north from Wilpena through the **Bunyeroo Valley** and on to the **Aroona Valley**. Particularly beautiful in spring when flowers cover the valley floors and hillsides, the road winds past rugged mountains and through narrow gorges. The mountains—actually sharply tilted layers of sediment—offer a rich mixture of colours and support a straggling collection of trees and bushes. At cooler times of the day, groups of red kangaroos graze along the valley floors. At the end of the lovely Aroona Valley, only a cellar and foundations remain from a hilltop homestead built in 1851. From here, another road leads west through the famous **Brachina Gorge** which cuts a rugged path through the **Heysen Ranges**. Along both of these roads, scenic lookouts provide panoramic views of the breathtaking landscape. Further north, and also worth visiting, are the old copper-mining settlements of **Blinman** and **Parachilna** which are now heavily reliant on tourism for their survival. Although little more than 'one-pub towns', they offer much character and old-fashioned hospitality.

Given its huge spread, there is a lot more to see in the Flinders Ranges. (Most guided tours run for five days, although the above itinerary can be done by the self-driver in half the time.) In the Ranges' southern section, close to Adelaide, the highlight is **Mt Remarkable National Park**, with its lush vegetation, pools and creeks, and spectacular **Alligator Gorge**. But with its more temperate climate and denser settlement, you would do better to bypass this section for points further north, such as the wild and rugged northern section of the Flinders Ranges around **Arkaroola**. From here, convoys of four-wheel-drive vehicles head off along narrow trails on Ridge Top Tours which provide spectacular views of the desolate flatlands and salt lakes of the Outback.

Outback South Australia

When it comes to the Australian Outback, I will openly admit a bias to the South Australian version of this legendary region. It was here, in 1980, that I had my first Outback experience, riding as a passenger from Adelaide to Alice Springs on one of Australia's famous 'road trains'—powerful trucks that pull two or three trailers. In those days, the **Stuart Highway** was unpaved to the Northern Territory border and had a well-deserved reputation as the longest and roughest stretch of road in the country. It was not unusual for flash-floods to wash away the road, stranding vehicles for days or even weeks. We were more fortunate, although it was hardly an easy trip. For three long days and nights, Malcolm Anderson—a veteran Outback 'truckie'—nursed our heavy load over 1,000 kilometres (620 miles) of bone-jarring corrugations, or parallel ridges, several inches high, that made up much of the road's surface. For most of the trip, talcum-like 'bulldust'

swirled into the cabin, choking the lungs. And at one middle-of-the-night stop, our truck broke down with a dead battery. The unflappable Malcolm suggested we gather more wood for our campfire and lay out our sleeping-bags. Gazing up at the star-filled sky, we settled into easy conversation as we waited for someone to come along. Many hours later, and just as dawn was breaking, we finally heard another vehicle approaching. In courtesy typical of the Outback, the driver stopped and, after a jump-start from his battery, soon had us on our way.

The trip was a magnificent introduction to the scenery, pace and hospitality of the Australian Outback. Like many other first-time visitors, I expected to find little more than a flat, featureless wasteland. Instead, as the miles slowly went by, I became entranced not only by the variety of scenery but also by the Outback's many moods. Heading north from **Port Augusta**, the blazing white salt-pans and rocky ochre-coloured mesas give way to flat scrubland flanked by heavily weathered mountain ranges. Around the opal-mining town of Coober Pedy, the landscape turns to undulating grassy plains dissected by dry creek beds shaded by majestic ghost gums. In the early morning and late afternoon, kangaroos graze by the roadside, while overhead giant wedged-tail eagles—the state's official symbol—soar looking for prey. The mood and colours constantly change, depending on the time of day and the cloud cover, and add to the Outback's feeling of mystery.

In 1987, the Stuart Highway was finally paved and today's visitors along what old-timers affectionately called 'The South Track' have it a lot easier. But the temptation now is to rush through, usually en route to Ayers Rock and Alice Springs in the neighbouring Northern Territory, without pausing to appreciate the serenity and natural beauty of the Outback. There is also the danger of missing out on those hardy and colourful souls who make this vast region their home, living either on vast cattle stations or in tiny roadside settlements. Often laconic and secretive, these characters take their time warming to strangers. But once the ice is broken—usually over a cold beer—they are often the most hospitable and friendly Australians you are likely to meet.

With a population of about 4,000, the largest settlement along the Stuart Highway—and one well worth visiting—is **Coober Pedy**. Located 850 kilometres (530 miles) northwest of Adelaide, the town is South Australia's largest and oldest opal-mining centre, dating from 1915. At first sight, Coober Pedy—Aboriginal for 'white man in a hole'—hardly makes a favourable impression with its clapboard buildings set in a dusty lunar-like landscape. There is a real 'last frontier' feel about the place. But there is another side to this Outback town. With summer temperatures soaring as high as 45°C (113°F), most of life takes place underground. Homes, shops, museums, churches and now a luxurious four-star hotel have been carved out of the soft rock, making Coober Pedy one of Australia's most unusual towns. More than 30 opal-mines surround the town, and there are guided tours of the mines where most of Australia's unique rainbow-coloured gems originate. 'Noodling', or hunting for opals in piles of waste mining material, is a favourite pastime. But at the risk of touching off an argument, or worse, visitors are warned to check with the owner beforehand. It is much safer to browse through one of the town's many opal shops.

The Stuart Highway is certainly the most convenient way to visit the South Australian Outback. You will need to take proper precautions, however, such as refuelling at every opportunity and watching your engine's temperature. Unfortunately, road trains normally do not carry passengers, but regular coach services travel up the highway. More comfortable, however, is a ride from Adelaide to Alice Springs on the *Ghan*, a modern replacement of the famous train which now runs roughly parallel to the highway. Air services also link the capital with Coober Pedy.

Three other main routes cut through the South Australian Outback, each with its own character and history. All are unpaved and lonely, however, and because of the danger of breaking down are not recommended for visitors travelling on their own. (Hardly a year passes without another tragic tale of travellers perishing in the Outback after their vehicle broke down or became bogged; even experienced travellers are advised not to make the trip during the hot summer months.) But with their wide variety of attractions, these more remote areas are definitely worth visiting with an experienced tour operator. By day, four-wheel-drive vehicles explore the sights—such as inhospitable deserts, the great salt lakes and hidden waterholes, and oases—and then camp for the night under the stars.

Running roughly parallel to the Stuart Highway, the **Oodnadatta Track** follows explorer John McDouall Stuart's successful transcontinental journey to Darwin in 1862 and was later the line for the famous Overland Telegraph and the legendary *Old Ghan* railway. After running past the western side of the Flinders Ranges, the dirt road passes near **Lake Eyre**—a vast salt lake where the late Sir Donald Campbell set the world land speed record in his jet-powered *Bluebird* in 1964. (The lake, which is actually below sea level, has only filled three times in the past 200 years, most recently in early 1989.) Further north, and roughly due east of Coober Pedy, **William Creek** is one of the country's quaintest Outback settlements and consists of little more than a pub and petrol station. In more recent years, the town made the headlines after Australia's telephone company spent A$1 million installing what it boasted was the world's loneliest telephone booth. **Oodnadatta**, roughly 1,000 kilometres (620 miles) northwest of Adelaide, was long an important rail junction along the *Old Ghan*. The town has real Outback character and is well worth visiting. (A passable dirt road links the town with Coober Pedy.)

Elsewhere in the Outback, the **Birdsville Track** heading up to the northeastern corner of the state is easily one of Australia's most famous Outback roads. The track was built to drive cattle from southwestern Queensland down to Port Augusta, a role that continues today by road train. Today, a run up this track—and the **Strzelecki Track** further to the east—is worn like a badge of honour by four-wheel-drive enthusiasts. Although a two-day trip, officials warn travellers to take along enough supplies for a week in case sudden rain makes the tracks impassable.

Western Australia

Australia's 'West Coast'

Until Australia won the America's Cup—the yachting world's most coveted trophy—back in 1983, few outsiders had even heard of Western Australia. Perth millionaire businessman Alan Bond not only ended the Americans' 132-year domination of the Cup but almost single-handedly put the city and state on the world map. By the time Australia defended the America's Cup in the Indian Ocean waters off the nearby port city of Fremantle four years later, thousands of overseas and domestic visitors had discovered the state's unique beauty and charm. Even Dennis Conner, the irascible American skipper who had lost the Cup in 1983 and then decisively wrested it back in Perth, was so impressed with WA (as the state is popularly known) that he readily agreed to star in a series of tourist promotion commercials with the catchy slogan 'Say G'day to WA'.

Isolated by vast deserts from the more populous eastern side of the continent, Western Australia is like a nation apart, with a very different atmosphere and appearance from the rest of the country. Its isolation has also given the state a unique and exciting collection of plant and animal life, particularly its incredible wildflowers which festoon the countryside every spring. On first impression, Perth could be said to resemble Southern California—before it was overwhelmed by people, freeways and smog. (Even the ocean is in the right direction!) Blessed by gentle sea breezes off the Indian Ocean, the climate is agreeably Mediterranean—warm and dry in summer and mild and rainy in winter. The endless sun-drenched beaches, a gentle hinterland and fine food and wines have combined to give Perth the most casual lifestyle of any capital city in Australia.

Western Australia covers roughly one-third of the Australian continent. With 2.5 million square kilometres (nearly one million square miles), the state is Australia's largest. The contrasts in topography and climate are equally vast. Much of the state's interior comprises hot and inhospitable deserts, such as the aptly named Great Sandy Desert in the north and the Great Victorian Desert in the southeast. At the same time, however, these inland regions have yielded tremendous mineral wealth, most notably in the rich gold-fields around Kalgoorlie, 600 kilometres (370 miles) east of Perth. But closer to its often-rugged 12,000-kilometre- (7,500-mile-) long coastline, the landscape varies dramatically across the spectrum, from the temperate south through to semi-desert and WA's lush tropical north.

The southwestern part of the state around Perth is one of the most beautiful and unspoiled places in Australia. Washed by dark blue

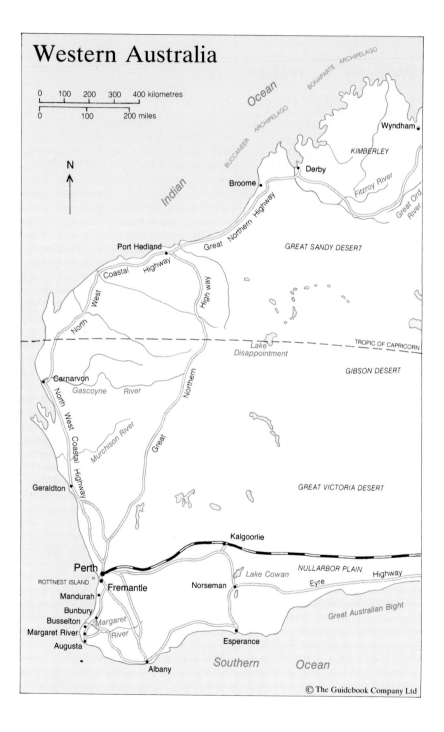

ocean waters, the coastline offers an endless collection of largely deserted golden beaches interspersed with granite headlands and tidal estuaries. Inland, beyond windswept sandhills and heathlands, the rolling hills are covered in dense forests of eucalyptus trees, including varieties unique to Western Australia, such as the majestic Jarrah and Karri. Hidden away in these lush forests are spectacular caves, tiny creeks and an assortment of wildlife. Where the land has been cleared by settlers, there are small farms and vineyards. The region is dotted with quaint towns still largely untouched by massive tourism.

The countryside north of Perth presents a very different side to Western Australia. In contrast to the lush southwest of the state, this is one of the most remote and harshest regions of Australia. Stretching for thousands of kilometres, the northwestern bulge of the continent—known as the Gascoyne and Pilbara—is mostly semi-desert, with no permanent rivers or lakes and only a handful of settlements. But for visitors who love wide open spaces and easy fishing, it is an ideal destination. Under the often cloudless skies, the turquoise-blue waters of the Indian Ocean, dotted with coral reefs and tiny islands, lap gently on dazzling white sandy beaches which stretch to the horizon. At Monkey Mia on Shark Bay, some 800 kilometres (500 miles) north of Perth and one of the long coastline's few indentations, wild dolphins wander close to shore to be hand-fed and stroked by the locals.

Despite its remoteness, this region is home to some of Australia's most ambitious mining projects. Off the modern port of Karratha lie the recently tapped gas reserves of the Northwest Shelf, reputedly the world's largest, while inland the red ranges, plateaus and gorges provide vast reserves of iron ore. Huge open-pit mines, mining towns, railways and ports are scattered incongruously across the two billion-year-old landscape. Just to the north, the busy pace of the Pilbara gives way to the tranquillity of Eighty Mile Beach, one of the longest uninterrupted stretches of sand in the world.

Then, moving on to the far tropical north of Western Australia, the Kimberley region provides some of Australia's most spectacular—if still difficult to visit—scenery and offers some of the country's most exciting adventure holidays. Stretching from the romantic pearling town of Broome to the Northern Territory border, this region is a savannah-covered plateau dominated by the King Leopold Range and a collection of smaller ranges. Ancient rivers have sliced through the rugged red ranges, opening up lush gorges teaming with freshwater crocodiles and other wildlife. Jutting into the Timor Sea, the Kimberley coastline is easily the most rugged in Australia, consisting of drowned river valleys that stretch far inland and feature some of the most extreme tides in the world. (When the tides drop, typically 12 metres, or 40 feet, the waters rush into the sea like waterfalls.) Lonely and remote, with most areas accessible only by boat, the coastal region is also home to Australia's famous—and extremely dangerous—saltwater crocodiles.

Considering its huge size, Western Australia has a remarkably small population of only 1.5 million. The vast majority, or just over one million, live in and around Perth, while the remainder are scattered in small fishing, farming and mining towns or live on vast cattle stations, or ranches. (There is also a sizeable Aboriginal population, most of whom live on remote reserves or as 'fringe-dwellers' on the edges of towns in the cēntre and north of the state.) Unlike the more populous eastern states, most of the population are of Anglo-Celtic origin, although recent years have seen a growth in migrants from southern Africa and Asia. Much like the American West Coast since the Second World War, the state has also experienced a rise in settlers arriving from other parts of the country.

Both old and new Western Australians (known affectionately as 'sandgropers') revel in their isolation from the rest of the continent. They are fiercely proud and easily the most parochial Australians. They also tend to resent 'easterners', whom they have long labelled 't'other siders', and are fond of pointing out that it was Western Australians—not Australians—who won the America's Cup. Some of this sentiment, of course, comes from the feeling that their very existence is often ignored by the rest of the country. (One way of attracting attention is their occasional threat, mostly in jest, to secede from Australia and form their own separate country!) But there is little question that their isolation has created a unique mentality. When 'sandgropers' gaze outwards, it is more likely to be towards Asia and southern Africa than towards the rest of the country. Considering the high price of air fares to the east coast, the sentiment is easy to understand. Most people find it much cheaper to take their holidays in Bali.

But it is not only isolation that has given Western Australia such a unique character. It is still very much a pioneering country; there is a distinct 'buzz' about the place. The state is incredibly rich in natural resources, such as gold, iron ore and diamonds, and their exploitation over the years has produced a boom mentality that makes 'sandgropers' surely the most optimistic of all Australians. Perhaps it is no accident that the state has produced more millionaires per capita than any other part of Australia. The unmatched climate and scenery is just frosting on their cake. And they are not shy about enjoying it. One millionaire I met—now in his fifties and a keen surfer since his youth—still relaxes by taking on the huge waves near Margaret River, southwest of Perth.

Like Tasmania, overseas visitors can easily overlook Western Australia. But for those who can take the time, the state is a refreshing contrast to the rest of Australia and, thanks to its isolation and frontier spirit, they are guaranteed a friendly and hospitable welcome. It is not hard to ignore the locals' frequent grousing about 'easterners'. In fact, after a few days in this special part of Australia, you will probably even agree with them.

History

While it is likely that Aborigines moved into the Kimberley region not long after their migration from Asia about 40,000 years ago, their migration into the other parts of this vast state took some time. Living as nomadic hunter-gatherers, they gradually moved southwards and, by approximately 25,000 to 30,000 years ago, had occupied the entire region. For thousands of years, thanks to their physical isolation from the rest of the world, the Aborigines held undisputed control and developed their unique culture.

In more recent historical times, Asians may have visited the Western Australian coastline, but, unlike the Macassars in the neighbouring Northern Territory, they had no visible impact and developed no lasting links. Similarly, in the early 16th century, Portuguese navigators on their way to the Spice Islands—today's Indonesia—are believed to have spotted the western and northern parts of the state, later naming the region 'Jave le Grande'.

The first recorded landing by Europeans on the coast of Western Australia (and Australia itself) was by the captain of a Dutch trading ship, Dirck Hartog, in October 1616. Landing on an island that now bears his name in Shark Bay, 830 kilometres (515 miles) north of Perth, Hartog marked his brief visit by taking a pewter dinner plate from his ship, scratching a rough inscription on it and then nailing it to a post. (None the worse for wear, the plate was found earlier this century at what is today called Cape Inscription and is now on display at the State Museum in Amsterdam.) The Dutch named the continent New Holland and followed up Hartog's visit with further explorations by others, including Abel Tasman (see page 130) in 1644, but they saw little of economic value along the barren coastline. Instead, the coast of New Holland became a shipping hazard for vessels making their way around the Cape of Good Hope and across the Roaring Forties before taking a sharp left turn north to the East Indies. Many simply did not make that tricky manoeuvre, and even today, marine archaeologists continue to find the remains of these ships.

The poor prospects for trade and colonization were confirmed by explorers from other nations. When the English buccaneer William

Dampier landed near Broome in 1688, the sight of the Aboriginal inhabitants of the northwest coast prompted his famous line about their being 'the miserablest people on earth' and little different 'from brutes'. (See page 13.) When French explorer Bruni d'Entrecasteaux visited the coastline over 100 years later, he also saw little of value — but plenty of places in desperate need of names. From Cape Bougainville at the tip of the Kimberleys to Esperance and the Archipelago of the Recherche in the state's southeast, his visit of 1792 lives on in the names of literally dozens of places.

When the British established the colony of New South Wales on Australia's east coast in 1788, they left New Holland unclaimed, believing it to be a separate continent. But after Matthew Flinders proved otherwise in his epic circumnavigation of Australia between 1802 and 1804 (see page 44), official thinking began to change. As elsewhere, the fear of French colonization — especially in the wake of d'Entrecasteaux — finally prodded Sydney into the establishment of a small convict settlement at King George Sound, site of present-day Albany, in 1826. The following year, the governor of New South Wales sent Captain James Stirling to survey the Swan River region, the site of present-day Perth. Stirling was so impressed that he offered to return and establish a settlement. Although at first reluctant, pressure from a syndicate of investors and colonists eventually forced London's approval, and on 2 May 1829 Captain Charles Fremantle arrived to take formal possession of what had once been New Holland. With Stirling as the colony's lieutenant-governor, the first batch of officials and settlers from Britain arrived the following month on the *Parmelia* (now the name of the local Hilton Hotel). The towns of Perth and Fremantle were founded shortly afterwards.

The colony's early days were difficult. The sandy soils around Perth were less than ideal for agriculture, and there was not enough labour to work the widely scattered land grants. Discouraged by the rough conditions, many settlers packed up and moved to the eastern colonies. But the more adventurous pioneers found fertile soil on the eastern side of the Darling Ranges and around Geraldton to the north, although the labour shortage continued to plague the infant colony. The problem was only solved in 1849 when London yielded to public pressure from the colony and agreed to the transportation of convicts to Western Australia. (Ironically, as we have seen, public pressure in the eastern colonies at this time had already forced an end to the practice.) The convicts' cheap labour, plus hefty grants from the British government, led to a rapid expansion of settlement. By the time transportation ceased in 1868, the last Australian colony to do so, almost 10,000 convicts had arrived in Western Australia. But the colony was finally on a firm footing.

Although not as dramatic as elsewhere in Australia, exploration also played a key role in the colony's expansion. By the 1860s, pastoralists were moving into the northwest. They were quickly followed along the coast by pearlers who in turn attracted a colourful work force of Malays, Islanders and Chinese. Elsewhere in the colony, systematic surveys identified new areas for farming and grazing. But explorations towards the east—such as the Forrest Brothers' epic walk from Esperance to Adelaide in 1870—found little more than desert and only reinforced Western Australia's isolation from the rest of the continent. (Until the opening of a railroad between Perth and Sydney in 1970, ships remained the main link with Australia's east coast.)

While agriculture was crucial to the colony's early economic growth, it was gold that assured Western Australia's long-term prosperity. Small discoveries in the Kimberley and Pilbara regions in the 1880s touched off a gold-rush that by the end of the century had spread to the incredibly rich Eastern Gold-fields around Coolgardie and Kalgoorlie. Some 200,000 'diggers' from the eastern states and overseas rushed into the region, and soon the desolate countryside was dotted with prosperous gold towns. (Today, most are little more than ghost towns, but the gold-rush continues in several centres using underground mining techniques and huge work forces.) The gold-rush also spawned a vast collection of public works projects such as the improvement of Fremantle harbour, the Perth-to-Kalgoorlie railway and even a 483-kilometre- (300-mile-) long pipeline to bring water to the parched gold-fields.

The influx of gold-miners also had political ramifications. When negotiations with the other Australian colonies began in the late 1890s, agricultural interests in Western Australia were strongly opposed to Federation, fearing a loss of revenue from customs duties. But the large number of miners helped to tip the balance in favour of the proposal, paving the way for the creation of the Commonwealth of Australia—and the colonies' independence from Britain—in 1901. As a concession to hurt feelings in the west, the new federal government promised to fund a transcontinental railway, although that feat took nearly 70 years.

As noted earlier, the state's relations with the rest of Australia have never been smooth and, in the years since Federation, have flared regularly. Most of the time, these have involved disputes over funding and taxes. During the Great Depression, tempers rose over the federal government's high tariff protection for manufacturing industries, a policy which many in the west saw as disadvantaging farmers. In a referendum in 1933, Western Australians voted by a two-to-one

margin to secede from the Commonwealth. In the end, despite an appeal to the British Parliament, nothing came of the move and the state's secession movement waned with the threat of Japanese invasion during the Second World War. (Like Darwin in the Northern Territory, the port of Broome in the far north of the state was bombed by the Japanese, although not with the same intensity.) Post-war prosperity from the expansion of agriculture and mining and a rapidly growing population further dampened the state's secessionist sentiment. Today, secession—once approved overwhelmingly—may be a dramatic-sounding threat, but little else.

Western Australia is certainly rich enough to survive as a separate country. While agriculture—primarily wheat, wool and cattle—remains an important part of Western Australia's economy, mining has taken on growing importance in the past 30 years. Beginning in the early 1960s, the rich iron-ore deposits of the Pilbara found a ready market in Japan and other Asian markets, turning the region into one of Australia's largest earners of foreign exchange. The state also boasts lucrative deposits of bauxite, nickel and other exotic minerals, huge reserves of natural gas and, since the 1980s, the world's largest

diamond mine. (While mostly industrial, the Kimberley diamonds include the rare 'pink diamond', a nice souvenir if you can afford it.) Manufacturing has progressed less dramatically, and the state remains heavily dependent on goods freighted in from the more populous eastern states. In Western Australia, the boom mentality remains deeply entrenched. But there is growing concern for the state's fragile environment, especially its great southwestern forests.

Getting Around

Because of its isolation and vast size, Western Australia requires a bit of effort to reach and get around. There are three main regions to the state, although the vast desert interior, including the Eastern Gold-fields, almost qualifies as a region on its own. For the visitor with only limited time, like a couple of weeks, the most highly recommended destinations are the Perth region in the south and the Kimberleys in the far north.

The easiest way to visit Western Australia is simply to fly into Perth. As an international gateway into Australia, this is especially convenient for visitors arriving from or departing for Europe, Asia or southern Africa and involves little extra cost. Australia's domestic airlines also provide regular flights to Perth from the east coast. (Air fares are relatively high, but visitors holding tickets purchased overseas are entitled to a 25 percent discount, with further reductions for advance bookings.) Another pleasant, though more expensive, alternative is the four-day *Indian-Pacific* rail journey from Sydney, which allows visitors to see a wide chunk of the southern part of Australia in airconditioned comfort. Finally, there is National Highway 1, roughly paralleling the train line, which is traversed by regular transcontinental bus services. For the self-driver (see box), the road trip can be quite an adventure, but it requires at least four or five days. Once in Perth, the most satisfactory means of exploring the region is to hire your own car. Rail, bus and air services—including guided tours— are also available.

To reach the Kimberley region in the state's tropical north, the state airline, Ansett WA, runs daily flights from Perth to Broome, Derby and Kununurra and then on to Darwin in the Northern Territory. This enables visitors to schedule brief stopovers for sightseeing along the way and is especially easy for those on round-Australia air passes. (Ansett WA also sells a Kangaroo Air Pass, which offers vast discounts over long distances.) And as noted in the Northern Territory chapter, access into this region is easily arranged out of Darwin by either air or road.

Because of the vast road distances, air travel is also the best way to see other parts of this far-flung state, with Ansett WA and other regional airlines providing regular flights to, for example, the Gascoyne and the Pilbara regions. There is a daily train service to Kalgoorlie in the heart of the Eastern Gold-fields as well as air and bus services.

The Western Australian Tourism Commission runs a network of tourist centres in all the country's major cities, including Perth, and these are an excellent starting point—even if you have only decided after your arrival in Australia to visit the state. (The WA Tourism Commission also has overseas offices in London, Los Angeles, Tokyo, Hong Kong, Kuala Lumpur and Singapore.) Staff will cheerfully book accommodation and arrange itineraries, including rental cars and local tour operators. (Within the state, there is also a wide range of equally helpful local tourist offices.) But visitors should be warned that during the springtime wildflower season, between August and November, when much of the state's desert interior is covered in flowers, bookings can be quite heavy. (This is especially true on the *Indian-Pacific* rail line which, if you can get a seat, provides a broad vista of this annual phenomenon.) Accommodation ranges from Perth's collection of first-class hotels through to more moderately priced, but comfortable, motels around the state.

Western Australia is rightly famous for its seafood, such as western rock lobster, prawns, scallops and southern bluefin tuna. In the tropical north, the luscious barramundi is a special favourite. (South of Perth, marrons—a delicious freshwater lobster—are grown commercially.) The state also produces some of the country's finest wines, with the best coming from the Margaret River district. It has also made a name for itself in beers. Australia's current boom in 'boutique breweries', or pub-brewed beers, began at the Sail and Anchor Hotel in Fremantle in the lead up to the America's Cup races. Perth is also where Alan Bond started his now massive brewing empire. (His flagship beer, Swan, is produced locally, but for a tasty bitter, try Emu Export.) Alone among Australia's capital cities, Perth has a long-established tradition of dining 'alfresco', a relaxing Mediterranean touch that goes perfectly with the climate and the local ingredients. Out of town, especially in the southwest, the countryside is dotted with old-fashioned country inns that offer everything from Devonshire teas to local specialities. And, especially in the state's more remote areas, visitors will always enjoy dropping into rustic old pubs and meeting the local characters.

Perth

Straddling the broad reaches of the **Swan River** between the Indian Ocean and the Darling Ranges, Perth is the capital of Western Australia and has a population of 1.1 million. Many people still recall astronaut John Glenn's description of Perth in 1962 as 'The City of Lights' when everyone turned their lights off and on to salute his passage overhead as the first American to orbit the earth. But a more common and accurate description of Perth is 'The Most Isolated City in the World', something that is easily palpable to arriving visitors and adds to the city's special ambience. With its blue skies and dry climate, Perth boasts more days of sunshine that any other Australian capital city. Irrigation and the occasional heavy winter rains give Perth a garden-like appearance, with a rich collection of landscaped parks and gardens. For many residents, life revolves around the out-of-doors, especially along its unspoiled beaches and waterways; Perth has more boats—and yacht clubs—per capita than any other city in the world.

Perth and the neighbouring port of **Fremantle** were established in 1829 when a group of English settlers arrived on the *Parmelia*. When they found the sandy soil unsuitable for crops, they soon moved up the Swan River to the fertile flats around **Guildford**, now a quaint historic town on the northeastern edge of the city. Perth itself was founded

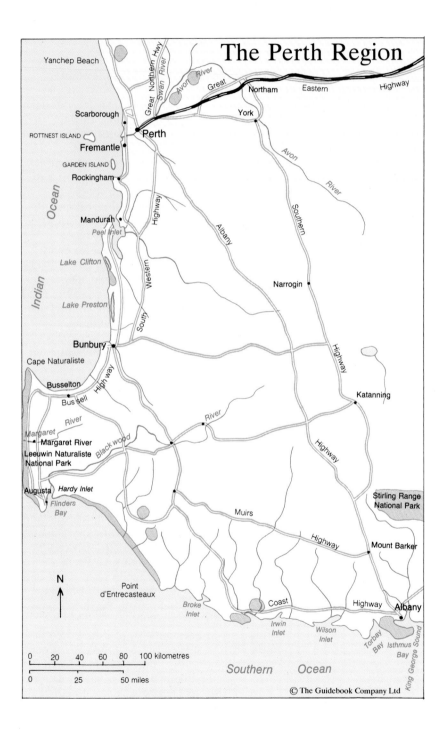

The Perth Region

Yanchep Beach

Great Northern Hwy

Swan River

Avon River

Great

Avon

Northam

Eastern

Highway

Scarborough

York

Perth

ROTTNEST ISLAND

Fremantle

GARDEN ISLAND

Rockingham

Avon

River

Southern

Indian

Ocean

Highway

Albany

Mandurah

Peel Inlet

Lake Clifton

Western

Narrogin

Lake Preston

South

Highway

Bunbury

Cape Naturaliste

Busselton

Bussell

Katanning

High way

River

Margaret

River

Blackwood

Margaret River

Leeuwin Naturaliste
National Park

Highway

Augusta

Hardy Inlet

Flinders
Bay

Stirling Range
National Park

Muirs

Highway

Mount Barker

N

Point
d'Entrecasteaux

Broke
Inlet

Coast

Highway

Albany

Irwin
Inlet

Wilson
Inlet

Torbay
Bay

King George Sound

Isthmus
Bay

| 0 | 20 | 40 | 60 | 80 | 100 kilometres |

| 0 | 25 | 50 miles |

Southern   Ocean

© The Guidebook Company Ltd

along the northern bank of the river in August 1829, mainly as an administrative and business centre for the fledgeling colony. It grew slowly in those early days but became firmly established with the gold-rush days of the 1880s and '90s. Gradually, suburbs on both sides of the Swan have joined Perth with Fremantle, 20 kilometres (12 miles) away at the river's mouth, although each retains its own unique character. In more recent years, residents have also moved into the foothills of the Darling Ranges and into coastal areas north and south of the city.

Since the beginning of the state's mineral boom in the 1960s, downtown Perth has rushed headlong—some would say headstrong—into the modern age. Many of its colonial-era buildings were demolished, and the skyline today is dominated by glass, steel and concrete skyscrapers. (The best illustration of this rampant development ethic is the **Barracks Arch** at the western end of St George's Terrace. Once the entrance to a large military parade ground, the lonely arch now overlooks a busy six-lane freeway.) But despite these modern intrusions, it has not spoiled the city's magnificent physical setting. Just east of downtown, the Swan River broadens into a wide estuary, its waters frequently as flat as glass. Then, as the river nears **King's Park**, a prominent cliff at the city's western end, it narrows sharply before passing into an even larger estuary further downstream. Along the northern bank of this first lagoon, known as **Perth Water**, a wide strip of parklands (complete with cycle paths) separates the river from the city itself which is located on a slight ridge. Across the Water, and reached by bridge or ferry, is **South Perth**, a popular residential area.

Although there are other more relaxing options, most visitors stay in Perth's downtown hotels where exploring the city—which runs only ten blocks by four—is as easy as strolling out the front door. While the massive redevelopment of the city has given it a slightly impersonal air, there is still a lingering charm about the place. Thankfully, not all of Perth's colonial-era buildings were destroyed during the building boom, and there remain some excellent examples of architecture from the period that are worth visiting.

The best place to start a walking tour is on **St George's Terrace** at **Pier Street**, site of **The Deanery**, built in the late 1850s as the residence of the Anglican Dean of Perth and one of the few remaining buildings from that period. (Unfortunately, it is not open to the public.) Across the street and set in its own grounds is **Government House**, the state governor's official residence. Built in a Romantic style with Gothic arches and turrets, the house was completed in 1864 and resembles a Down Under version of the Tower of London. In the adjacent **Stirling**

Gardens are two other fine examples of colonial architecture, the Georgian-style **Old Courthouse** (1836) and the classic **Supreme Court** (1897).

From here, a short stroll either through the parklands or along Barrack Street and then across busy Riverside Drive leads to the banks of the Swan River. From **Barrack Square**, on the water's edge, there is a wide range of river cruises either up to the **Swan River Vineyards** or down to Fremantle and on to **Rottnest Island**. (There is also a regular ferry service to South Perth, site of the city's zoo and an old flour mill built in 1835.) The cruises range from several hours to a full day and, in the case of the Fremantle route, offer the option of returning by other means.

Back along St George's Terrace, heading west past Barrack Street, is one of the city's more incongruous sights—**London Court**, a Tudor-style shopping arcade; built in the 1930s, it is complete with carved woodwork, wrought-iron, hanging signs and even a replica of Big Ben. (Perhaps because it is so out of place this far from England, visitors cannot help wandering into the arcade for a look.) At the corner of the Terrace and William Street, the city's main north–south artery, the **Palace Hotel** is another odd sight. When developers planned to demolish this grand old hotel and replace it with yet another skyscraper in the early 1980s, residents signalled that they finally had had enough. Their compromise can be seen today—the preserved and restored façade of the hotel, backed by the highest building in Perth. Further up the Terrace, cheek by jowl with modern buildings, are the **Old Perth Boys School** (1854), now a gift shop for the National Trust, and the **Cloisters** (1858), a former school noted for its fine brickwork.

The **Hay Street Mall** is the place to go for shopping and souvenir hunting. A network of arcades leads off the Mall in several directions, and there are a wide range of boutiques, shops and galleries. (The sole agent for Argyle diamonds is Charles Edward Jewellers, in the **Piccadilly Arcade**.)

Out of the downtown area, but still a brisk walk or short taxi ride away, are several other sights worth seeing. For a view of the city and its immediate environs, head to **King's Park**, with its walking tracks, botanical gardens and natural bush. The clifftop park, which covers 400 hectares (990 acres) in West Perth, is particularly attractive in the spring when Western Australia's famous wildflowers are in bloom. (The annual **Wildflower Exhibition** on the last weekend of September is extremely popular.) For those interested in history, the **Western Australian Museum**—located in **Northbridge** just north of downtown—offers a wide range of exhibitions, plus the **Old Gaol**, a Georgian-style stone prison from the convict days. Northbridge is also the centre of the city's nightlife, when its large concentration of ethnic restaurants, nightclubs and piano bars bring out the crowds. For gamblers, the **Burswood Island Casino and Hotel** complex—opened in 1986 in time for the America's Cup races—operates round the clock, seven days a week, and is only a five-minute taxi ride from the city.

For a dramatic contrast to modern downtown Perth, visitors should head down the river to the port-city of **Fremantle**. (It is about 20 minutes away by car via the Stirling Highway and can also be reached by bus, train or boat.) Located at the mouth of the Swan River and lapped by the turquoise-blue waters of the Indian Ocean, Fremantle has a graceful charm and beauty that is downright seductive. Widely regarded as the best-preserved 19th-century port city in the world, 'Freo' (as it is known affectionately by the locals) has jealously preserved its rich heritage of colonial buildings and atmosphere since long before Australia won the America's Cup in 1983. Much of this came from the area's traditional working-class orientation, primarily dockworkers and fishermen. Attracted by the cheap rents and quiet atmosphere, artists and writers moved into Fremantle in the 1970s, reinforcing the community's desire for conservation. For many years, the city remained a quiet backwater, best known to outsiders for its cheap Italian-run sidewalk cafés and restaurants.

Little was done with Fremantle's rich collection of classic buildings until the port was named as the site for the America's Cup defence in the (southern) summer of 1986–7. (Interestingly, Bond's club, the posh Royal Perth Yacht Club, is actually located on the Swan River near the city; they quickly built an annexe at Fremantle to host the event.) Some old-time residents disagree, but that decision was the best thing that ever happened to Freo. From 1983 onwards, millions of dollars from the federal and state governments and private investors were spent restoring the city to its former glory. In a burst of energy and a lot of paint, the city's old buildings (many of them classified by the National Trust) were meticulously restored to become museums, art galleries and commercial enterprises, such as hotels, restaurants and pubs. Any new buildings were required to blend into the surroundings. (More money went into expanding the nearby boat harbour—already home to a large local fishing fleet—to handle the nearly 20 12-metre (40-foot) racing syndicates who participated.) When the yacht racing finally got underway, Fremantle had a new lease on life—without affecting its essential character.

The unmatched glamour and colourful crowds of the America's Cup are now only a memory. Life has returned to a more sedate pace, and many locals swear the place is better than ever. Although there are motorized trams, Fremantle is the perfect place to stroll around and

explore. With the **Round House**, a former gaol, atop **Arthur Head** at its western end, **High Street** has a particularly rich collection of old buildings, including a couple of grand old pubs. The nearby **Western Australian Maritime Museum** contains relics dating back to the 1600s, including parts of the famous 1629 Dutch wreck **Batavia**, and is a must for the visitor. (The museum is open Monday–Thursday, 10.30 am–5 pm, Friday–Sunday, 1–5 pm.) For lunch, walk around to the waterfront where there are several seafood restaurants. **Lombardo's** is famous for the best fish and chips in the state. (A bit further away in **East Fremantle**, the **Oyster Beds River Restaurant** is one of Perth's best.) Another worthwhile stop is the **Fremantle Markets**, a historic marketplace built in 1897, which offers a wide variety of arts and crafts or just a good snack. (It is open Friday and weekends.) Next door is the **Sail and Anchor**, Australia's original pub brewery, with 14 different beers on tap. (But watch out for a potent brew called 'The Dog Bolter'.) With its abundance of hotels and restaurants, you may decide that Fremantle is a more relaxing alternative to Perth.

There are several other attractions not far from the city. (Many can be reached by public transport or tours, although having a car greatly increases the options.) Between Perth and Fremantle, there are several lovely suburbs, such as restored turn-of-the-century **Subiaco** with its boutiques and restaurants and the grand mansions of the *nouveaux riches* in **Dalkeith** and other riverside suburbs.

But visitors should not miss Perth's famous Indian Ocean beaches. Only 15 or 20 minutes from downtown, they stretch for 30 kilometres (19 miles) north from Fremantle and are so numerous that one is reserved solely for dogs and another for nudists. The more popular beaches, such as **Cottesloe**, **Scarborough** and **Trigg Island**, are next to shopping centres offering snacks, meals or just a quiet drink. A visit by boat or air to **Rottnest Island**, 20 kilometres (12 miles) off the coast, is worthwhile—if only to see its unique 'quokkas', the small friendly marsupials responsible for the island's Dutch name. Popular as a weekend retreat for the locals, the island also features historic buildings, secluded beaches and quiet coves.

Inland, the scenic **Swan River Valley**, 20 kilometres (12 miles) northeast of Perth, offers the closest wineries to the city, while the nearby **Darling Ranges** provide spectacular views of the coastal plain.

The Great Southwest

Within a day's drive of Perth, there is a wide choice of places to see. But whichever direction you go, one big advantage is that you can plan an itinerary that involves little or no backtracking and catch a nice mixture of coastal and inland regions. (The WA Tourism Commission produces an excellent booklet entitled *The Weekend Holiday Book*, which provides even more details and destinations.) Weekdays are the best time to head out of town, although with the state's small population and vast space, travelling at weekends is never as crowded as it is 'back east'. Unless you have planned a pressing game of blackjack the same night back at the casino, the best strategy is to toss your suitcase in the car and take your time. (And don't forget your swimming gear!)

This highly recommended region covers the southwestern part of the state (see Perth Region map). Blessed with a temperate climate, it takes in an incredibly rich mixture of scenery, from the sweeping farmlands around Perth to the rugged indented coastline. Strictly speaking, the region ends at the port of **Albany**, 400 kilometres (250 miles) southeast of the capital, but it is well worthwhile heading east to lonely **Esperance** and then north to the gold-fields region around **Kalgoorlie**. From there, you can join the Great Eastern Highway back to Perth, 600 kilometres (372 miles) away.

Heading south from Perth along the Mandurah Road, the coastline becomes increasingly beautiful, and there are frequent temptations to stop. About 50 kilometres (31 miles) south of the city is historic **Rockingham**, which was briefly considered as the site for the colony's capital in 1829 after the first settlers landed on nearby **Garden Island**, now an important naval base. The town sits on a peninsula overlooking the calm turquoise-blue waters of Cockburn Sound and the islands of Shoalwater Bay. A ferry service operates to **Penguin Island**, a habitat for fairy penguins from March to December. Another 25 kilometres (16 miles) further south, **Mandurah**, with its beaches and large estuary, known as the **Peel Inlet**, is a favourite weekend spot for Perth residents and well known for its fishing and crabbing. (Because of their proximity to Perth, both of these destinations are worth considering as separate day trips.)

South of Mandurah, the land becomes less densely populated, and, moving inland, the road passes through a stretch of forest and farmland before arriving at the historic township of **Australind**, on the eastern shore of **Lake Leschenault**, a lovely estuary. The town was founded by the London-based Western Australian Land Settlement Company in 1839 for English pioneers who would then trade with India, thus its name. Some 400 families arrived but, after much hardship, the project was abandoned after only a few years. Today, a monument beside the estuary relates the town's sad history. Nearby there are a couple of historic buildings—**Henton Cottage**, and a former workman's cottage that is now the **'smallest church in Australia'**.

Bunbury, another ten minutes down the road, survived to become the region's largest commercial centre and port (population 22,000). It is worth taking a quick drive around the older parts of the city, including Ocean Drive with the impressive **Bunbury Lighthouse**, before continuing into the southwest.

After Bunbury, the road follows the gentle curve of **Geographe Bay**, named after his vessel by the French explorer de Freycinet in 1803, and passes through flat dairy country and the quaint riverside hamlet of Capel before arriving at the seaside town of **Busselton**, 254 kilometres (157 miles) south of Perth. Protected by Cape Naturaliste to the northwest, the waters of the bay are calm much of the time and perfect for swimming, sailboarding and fishing. Founded in 1832, Busselton was one of the earliest settlements in the state, and its historic buildings give the town a special charm. With its wide range of accommodation, including guesthouses, and several fine restaurants, the town is a pleasant place for an overnight stop and a good base from which to explore the nearby coastline.

At **Cape Naturaliste**, another 30 kilometres (19 miles) away past lovely **Dunsborough**, the unmatched beauty of this region becomes apparent. With its rich variety of scenery, it is also known as the Cape of Contrasts. On one side of the cape are white sandy beaches overlooking the calm and clear turquoise-coloured waters of Geographe Bay. At **Bunker Bay** and **Shelley Beach**, the trees reach right to the water's edge. On the other side are the pounding breakers of the Indian Ocean and scruffy wind-swept vegetation. At the oddly shaped **Sugar Loaf Rock** on the ocean side, huge freak waves frequently send visitors scrambling for cover. Several trails wind through the area, including one from the lighthouse overlooking the cape that leads down on to massive sand dunes that jut out into the ocean.

That breathtaking introduction to Western Australia's southwest is enough to enchant even the most jaded world-traveller, and the mood lingers on further south into the heart of the Margaret River district. Sticking out like a defiant fist into the Indian Ocean, the 64-kilometre- (40-mile-) long coastline—most of which is protected as the **Leeuwin-Naturaliste Natural Park**—consists of tough granite headlands, sandy bays and estuaries formed by several streams and rivers. (Although swimming can be hazardous, the surfing here rates among the best in the world.)

Adding to the coast's stark beauty and feeling of isolation, there are only a handful of tiny settlements such as **Quininup** and **Gracetown**. **Prevelly Park** is particularly lovely, with its distinctive Greek Orthodox church built as a memorial to Australian troops who died in that country in the Second World War. From the nearby estuary and the pounding surf, travel eight kilometres (five miles) inland to the town of **Margaret River**. This is the region's largest settlement; with its historic buildings and other attractions, it is a popular holiday resort and home to a thriving arts and crafts industry. Originally developed for its dairy land and farming, the district is now famous for its many wineries, regarded as the best in the state. Just south of town, the **Leeuwin Estate Winery** offers wine tastings and delicious meals in its heavily timbered main hall. One of the state's cultural highlights is the outdoor concert staged here each January, when a visiting overseas orchestra entertains, accompanied by laughing kookaburras in the surrounding gum trees.

Between Margaret River and Augusta the land is less developed, and many areas remain in their original state with dense forests of giant Karri trees and literally hundreds of limestone caves; the **Mammoth**, **Lake** and **Jewel caves** are the most interesting and accessible. Scenic roads, some unpaved, lead through the forests, with turnoffs to isolated beaches such as **Hamelin Bay** and **Cosy Corner**. At the southern end of this region, the town of **Augusta**, founded in 1830 and the state's third-oldest settlement, is ideally sited beneath a low range of hills and overlooks the tranquil Blackwood River and Hardy Inlet on one side and broad ocean beaches on the other. The lookout atop **Green Hill** provides views of the immediate coastal region and across **Flinders Bay** far to the southeast to the sand dunes and forests of the **D'Entrecasteaux National Park**. The region is popular with holidaying Western Australians for its fishing, swimming and boating, and visitors can hire boats or catch a cruise far up into the vast inlet. But for a dramatic setting, it is hard to top nearby **Cape Leeuwin**, named by the Dutch and the most southwesterly point of Australia. Here, below the towering limestone lighthouse (open Tuesday– Sunday), the massive swells from the mighty Indian and Southern oceans meet and crash spectacularly on the massive granite outcrops. On a sunny day, it is comfortable to just lie down on the warm rocks and become absorbed by the sounds and atmosphere. The nearby **Old Waterwheel** is an unusual attraction. Erected to provide a water supply for the lighthouse keepers late last century, the now unused wooden wheel is slowly turning to stone.

From Augusta, which is 317 kilometres (196 miles) south of Perth, you can either return via inland routes to the capital or head further along the southern coast. Just north of the town, the **Brockman Highway** leads inland east through the undulating countryside to the timber and farming town of **Nannup**. (The 'up' in many of the place-names in this region comes from an Aboriginal word meaning 'water'.) From here, two roads—one to **Bridgetown** and **Manjimup** and the other to **Pemberton**—head into the heart of Western Australia's 'tall timber country' and home to some of the tallest hardwood trees in the world, the Karri and the Jarrah. (Both belong to the eucalyptus family and grow to over 80 metres, or 260 feet, in height.) Although heavily timbered since the beginning of the century, vast forests remain and can easily be explored along scenic drives. Surrounded by Karri trees and flowering countryside, Pemberton is the region's loveliest town and offers bushwalks through the cathedral-like forests and along the banks of the nearby Warren River. (**Fine Woodcraft**, a gallery of high-quality woodwork from native timbers, is worth a visit.) **The Gloucester Tree**, just east of town, contains the world's highest fire-lookout tower and, for those with the energy to climb 60 metres (200 feet) to the top, the view is superb. The scenic **Pemberton–Northcliff Tramway**, a daily diesel-train trip through the forests to this town 30 kilometres (19 miles) to the south, is also recommended.

The main road east from Augusta runs inland for the first 300 kilometres (190 miles) or so. But several unpaved roads lead off to the coast, and those who take the time are rewarded with some of the most isolated and beautiful coastal scenery in Australia. The simplest such diversion is from **Northcliffe**, where a gravel road leads past the easy-to-climb **Mt Chudalup**, with its spectacular coastal views, and on to **Windy Harbour** and **Point D'Entrecasteaux**, some 30 kilometres (19 miles) to the south. At the point, named after the French explorer who passed by in 1792, limestone cliffs rise abruptly 150 metres (500 feet) above the sea. If you are sticking to the main road, known as the South Western Highway, the coast reappears dramatically at the dairy and beef-farming town of **Walpole**, overlooking **Nornalup Inlet** at the mouth of the **Frankland River**. From here to **Denmark**, 66 kilometres (41 miles) to the east, the unspoiled coastline is a rich mixture of rivers, inlets, beaches, rugged headlands and offshore islands, much of it protected as national parks. Inland, the gently rising hills are covered in Karri and other native trees, such as in the **Valley of the Giants** just east of Walpole. In spring, particularly from September to late October, the countryside is ablaze with the colour of wildflowers, creepers and trees, many of them—such as the carnivorous Pitcher Plant—unique to the area. With its relaxing atmosphere and many attractions, it is worth lingering a few hours, or even overnight, along this spectacular coastline.

Another 54 kilometres (33 miles) east of Denmark, or 400 kilometres (248 miles) southeast of Perth, is the historic port of **Albany**. The first settlement in Western Australia, it preceded the establishment of Perth by three years. Its magnificent physical setting on the Southern Ocean explains why the English grabbed Albany as their first strategic asset in Western Australia. Long before Major Edmund Lockyer and his band of soldiers and convicts came ashore on Christmas Day 1826, several Dutch, French and English explorers had passed through, and the area was popular with whalers and sealers, especially from France and the United States. Set on a saddle between two hills, Albany overlooks one of the best landlocked deepwater harbours in the world, circular-shaped **Princess Royal Harbour**, and the even larger adjacent **King George Sound**. Established originally as a military outpost of the New South Wales regiment, Albany grew into an important port and commercial centre as a coaling station for mail steamers from England to Australia's east coast. Bypassed in the early 1900s with the establishment of Fremantle Harbour, Albany began to decline although it did experience a brief revival during the First World War as a staging point for Australian troops heading to the Middle East. Surrounded by today's more modern suburbs, the atmosphere of those early days lives on among its fine collection of 19th-century buildings and streets.

With its rich history and natural beauty, Albany (population 20,000) is a relaxing place to spend a couple of days. (The town can also be reached easily by bus and air, and then seen by joining a local tour.) The three-storey lookout atop **Mt Melville**, with its panoramic views of the entire region, makes an ideal early stop. Another worthwhile visit

Moonlight Serenade

"Give us a toon on the peeany," said Mrs M'Swat after the meal, when the dishes had been cleared away by Lizer and Rose Jane. The tea and scraps, of which there was any amount, remained on the floor, to be picked up by the fowls in the morning.

The children lay on the old sofa and on the chairs, where they always slept at night until their parents retired, when there was an all-round bawl as they were wakened and bundled into bed, dirty as they were, and very often with their clothes on.

I acceded to Mrs M'Swat's request with alacrity, thinking that while forced to remain there I would have one comfort, and would spend all my spare time at the piano. I opened the instrument, brushed a little of the dust from the keys with my pocket-handkerchief, and struck the opening chords of Kowalski's "Marche Hongroise".

I have heard of pianos sounding like a tin dish, but this was not as pleasant as a tin dish by long chalks. Every note that I struck stayed down not to rise, and when I got them up the jarring, clanging, discordant clatter they produced beggars description. There was not the slightest possibility of distinguishing any tune on the thing. Worthless to begin with, it had stood in the dust, heat and wind so long that every sign that it had once made music had deserted it.

I closed it with a feeling of such keen disappointment that I had difficulty in suppressing tears.

"Won't it play?" inquired Mr M'Swat.

"No; the keys stay down."

"Then, Rose Jane, go ye an' pick 'em up while she tries again."

I tried again, Rose Jane fishing up the keys as I went along. I perceived instantly that not one had the least ear for music or idea what it was; so I beat on the demented piano with both hands, and often with all fingers at once, and the bigger row I made the better they liked it.

Miles Franklin, My Brilliant Career, 1901

is to one or more of Albany's historic buildings, such as **The Old Farm**
at Strawberry Hill, dating from 1831, the beautifully restored English
coach house-style **Old Post Office** and the grim solitary confinement
cells of the **Old Gaol**. Across from the latter and closer to the
waterfront is the **Residency Museum**. Used as a magistrate's residence,
convict hiring depot and barracks during the colonial period, the
restored building is now a branch of the WA Museum, the first outside
Perth. (Nearby is a replica of the brig *Amity*, which brought the first
settlers to Albany, and an obelisk to Major Lockyer.)

But perhaps the town's most unusual attraction is the **Albany
Whaling Station** located around the southern side of the harbour near
the tip of the windswept **Flinders Peninsula**. Now a museum, the
station was used until 1978 and sombrely recalls the days when
hundreds of whales were hunted down and killed annually in the
waters off the coast. The museum's centrepiece is the *Cheynes IV*, the
station's last whaling vessel, which now sits on dry land. (If you catch
the lingering odours from the grim whale-processing, you may agree
that 'whale memorial' would be a more appropriate name for the place
than museum.) Nearby **Torndirrup National Park**, with its spectacular
granite cliffs fronting on to the Southern Ocean, is the place to restore
one's spirits. When a heavy swell is running and the spray is flying, **The
Gap** with its sheer 24-metre (80-foot) drop and **The Natural Bridge** are
a spectacular sight. Closer to town, Marine Drive leading northeast out
of Albany provides beautiful views of King George Sound with its
collection of rocky islands and headlands. Further along are **Middleton
Beach**, **Emu Point** and **Oyster Harbour**, all providing excellent
swimming and fishing. About 20 kilometres (12 miles) east of Albany
is **Two People's Bay**, home to the Noisy Scrub Bird which was once
nearly extinct.

From Albany, there is a choice between heading back to Perth or
continuing east to Esperance and the gold-fields. En route back to the
capital, the town of **Mt Barker** (50 kilometres, or 31 miles, north) and
the nearby **Porongurup** and **Stirling ranges** make an interesting stop.
While only 1,000 metres (3,282 feet) high, the ranges rise abruptly
above the rolling farmlands. The Porongurup Range is the oldest in
the world. Rising between lush forests and valleys, its granite domes
have been weathered into strange shapes. This pattern continues, but
on an even grander scale, in the Stirling Ranges to the north. The
region also contains several vineyards which welcome visitors.
Continuing back to Perth, the road passes through the heart of
Western Australia's wheat-belt—a land of wide open spaces dotted
with quaint little settlements which always make a pleasant stop to
refuel, stretch your legs and have a cup of coffee.

Although **Wave Rock** is frequently described as a leading tourist attraction, the unusual 15-metre- (50-foot-) high rock formation near **Hyden** is actually quite difficult to reach, unless you are a resident 'sandgroper' with a whole year's worth of weekends. Located 340 kilometres (211 miles) east of Perth in the so-called Central South region, it can be reached—in a roundabout fashion—en route back from Albany or Kalgoorlie. (Or give it a miss and settle for a postcard instead.)

East to the Gold-fields

Located about 600 kilometres (372 miles) east of Perth, the Gold-fields region presents a dramatically different face to Western Australia. In contrast to the lush and temperate southern coastline, the red-coloured landscape is flat, desolate and hot. Without the discovery of gold late last century, the region would have remained as just another part of the vast Australian Outback. That man has settled here, survived and thrived is indeed remarkable.

From Albany, the trip to the twin towns of **Kalgoorlie–Boulder** at the heart of the Gold-fields takes roughly two days with a stop at Esperance, 476 kilometres (295 miles) to the east. Include a visit to the **Fitzgerald River National Park**, located on an undulating sand plain and dissected by river valleys with sharp cliffs and narrow gorges. Remote **Esperance** evokes a feeling of being at the edge of the earth, dramatized by its stark landscape of salt lakes, including its famous **Pink Lake**. (The town, and several others to the northeast, enjoyed brief world fame in 1979 when the American spaceship *Skylab* crashed to earth; pieces of debris are now on exhibit at the local museum.) From this coastal town, it is another 370 kilometres (230 miles) north through farming and grazing country and the gold-mining town of **Norseman** to Kalgoorlie. There are also regular air, rail and bus connections to the Gold-fields from Perth.

With a population of 20,000, **Kalgoorlie** and its sister city of **Boulder** are the home of the Golden Mile which, following its discovery in 1892, proved to be the richest square mile of gold-bearing ore in the world. The prosperity the mineral brought is obvious in the town's many grand buildings, such as the imposing **Town Hall**, and its many pubs along **Hannan Street**, named after the prospector who first discovered gold here. (Another local hero is Herbert Hoover, who worked in the town for several years before returning to the United States where he later became president.) Even the main street—wide enough to turn a bullock cart—is an impressive sight. The **Golden Mile Museum** provides much detail on the town's colourful history, and the

Hainault Tourist Gold Mine, open daily, gives visitors an insider's view of the underground mining process. A ride on the **Boulder Loopline Train**, which operates between the two towns, is also a pleasant experience. From Kalgoorlie, several tours operate out to ghost towns and old diggings in the surrounding countryside. **Coolgardie**, 40 kilometres (25 miles) to the west, preceded Kalgoorlie's discovery of gold and also offers a rich collection of historic buildings.

North to the Kimberleys

The countryside north of Perth is not nearly as spectacular as down south. Dry and harsh, the beauty of the land is more subtle and its scenic highlights tend to be far apart. For the visitor, seeing these requires time, energy and a fair bit of patience. Plus, there is always the risk of travelling half a day only to be disappointed. A frequently promoted attraction, for example, is the extraordinary **Pinnacles** in the **Nambung National Park**. Located inland from the coast in a painted desert, this vast collection of oddly shaped rocks eroded by the wind is particularly lovely at sunset. But to visit this remarkable sight some 250 kilometres (155 miles) north of Perth takes most of a day or even an overnight trip, with precious little in between. So, unless you are driving on through to the Pilbara and the Kimberleys, such sights are best left off your itinerary. Regretfully, the same goes for those lovely dolphins at Monkey Mia, which is even further away.

Located in the far tropical north of the state, the **Kimberleys** region begins at the romantic pearling town of **Broome**, some 2,020 kilometres (1,255 miles) by air from Perth. (For visitors, the best access into the area is by air from either the capital or Darwin in the neighbouring Northern Territory.) With its intense turquoise-blue sea, wide white sandy beaches and reddish rocks, Broome has a magical quality unmatched anywhere else in Australia. This quality is embellished by the town's quaint wood and corrugated-tin buildings, lush tropical vegetation and colourful residents, the most multicultural in Australia. Long isolated from the rest of the country and difficult to reach, Broome has only recently started coming out of its shell to become a tourist attraction. Much of that has come from the efforts of a British aristocrat and long-time Conservative politician, Lord Alistair McAlpine, who came and fell in love with the place. When important buildings were threatened with demolition, he bought and relocated them in other parts of the town. Today, the expatriate Englishman and local residents have joined to preserve Broome's unique atmosphere. All new buildings, for example, must blend in with the existing architecture.

Broome has a fascinating history. And even before William Dampier visited in 1699 and named **Roebuck Bay** after his ship, Malays had already discovered the region's rich underwater bounty of turtles, dugongs and oyster shells. But the town's future was sealed with the discovery in the 1880s of large quantities of pearl shell; by the early 20th century, Broome, named after the colony's then-governor, was supplying three-quarters of the world's need for mother-of-pearl, used mostly for making buttons. At the boom's peak, more than 400 pearlers were based in the town, attracting divers from around the South Pacific and Asia, with the best and most successful coming from Japan. Eventually, the introduction of plastic buttons after the First World War ended the town's boom days; it was only saved from total extinction by the development of a profitable cultured pearl industry. Broome fell into an easy slumber that, except for several Japanese bombing raids during the Second World War, continues to this day.

Located at the tip of a peninsula and blessed by gentle sea breezes, Broome—with a population of about 6,000—has a milder tropical climate than the rest of the Kimberleys region. (The best time to visit is during the dry season from April to October, especially for the colourful **Shinju Matsuri Pearl Festival** held every year in late August or early September.) Everything in the town is within easy walking distance, even the airport, and visitors are quickly absorbed by its charming atmosphere, especially around **Chinatown** with its old pearling sheds, shops and the nearby **Streeter's Jetty**. Along Carnarvon Street, the quarter's main street, **Sun Pictures** is the world's oldest—and still operating—open-air movie theatre, where the patrons sit in canvas seats under the stars. The **Court House** and **Anglican Church** are both fine examples of the local architecture. The **Historical Museum**, located in the Old Customs House a few blocks away, provides an excellent display on the development of Broome's pearling industry. The **Japanese Cemetery** is an impressive and fitting memorial to the hundreds of divers who died searching for the precious pearls. Out of town, nearby **Cable Beach**, named for the cable that once linked Broome with Java, is one of the town's most famous attractions. Its white sand beach stretches for 22 kilometres (14 miles) along the edge of the Indian Ocean. Lord McAlpine's recently opened **Cable Beach Resort**, built in traditional Broome-style architecture, and his **Pearl Coast Zoological Gardens**, with a large collection of Australian parrots and other fauna, are both just inland from the beach. Another nearby attraction is the **Broome Crocodile Park**, established by popular Australian travel documentary-maker Malcolm Douglas, which features over 70 salt- and freshwater crocodiles. The star of the park is 'Three Legs', a five-metre- (17-foot-) long monster caught in the Ord River near Kununurra.

Several tours operate out of Broome into the Kimberleys region. The easiest, especially for those with only a limited amount of time, is a scenic flight along the rugged and deeply indented coastline over vast **King Sound, Walcott Inlet** and the **Regent River**. The latter is famous for its tidal waters that swirl out to sea through a narrow gorge in torrential waterfalls. Cruises lasting up to two weeks explore the coast along the coral reefs of the **Buccaneer Archipelago** and as far north as isolated **Kalumburu** and the **King George River**. (As in the neighbouring Northern Territory, saltwater crocodiles are quite a hazard in these waters.) On land, safari tours of several days' duration head into the heart of the Kimberleys. (Aerial and ground tours also operate out of Derby, Hall's Creek, Kununurra and Wyndham. Because of the difficulty in moving around alone, ground tours are strongly recommended.)

Derby, 220 kilometres (136 miles) to the east at the head of King Sound, has a very different atmosphere from Broome and, as the oldest town in the Kimberleys, has more of a pastoral orientation. The area's large Aboriginal population has a proud history of resisting European settlement during the 1880s and, more recently, of establishing their own independent communities. The landscape changes noticeably and becomes the typical savannah that characterizes the region. Visitors will also spot their first Australian boabs—unusual trees with large bulbous trunks, sometimes centuries old, which appear to have their roots sticking up into the air. (Similar to the African baobab, they are found only in the Kimberleys and the Northern Territory.) They are also part of the local history, such as the huge **Prison Boab Tree** just south of town whose hollow interior once served as a lockup for a famous Aboriginal outlaw named 'Pigeon'. Derby is the gateway to the Kimberleys' Gorge Country, 150 kilometres (93 miles) further east, with the **Windjana** and **Geikie** the most accessible to visitors. Cut through an ancient limestone reef by rivers that flood every rainy season, the sheer cliffs and natural vegetation of the gorges are quite impressive, though perhaps not as striking as Katherine Gorge in the Northern Territory. Between these two gorges is the unusual **Tunnel Creek**, where a 750-metre- (2,460-foot-) long tunnel has been carved out of the Napier Range. (If you have a flashlight, you can walk through to the other end and enjoy a cold dip in the creek in the process.)

Elsewhere in this vast region, a trip into its northern section along the **Gibb River** and **Kalumburu Roads** (an alternative to the main highway) is quite rewarding for those with extra time and a sense of adventure. Passing through the **King Leopold Range**, the roads lead through one of the most remote parts of Australia, past gorges and waterfalls and isolated cattle stations. About 130 kilometres (80 miles) south of **Hall's Creek**, the **Wolfe Creek Meteorite Crater** is the second-largest in the world and can be reached easily by car.

At the eastern end of the Kimberleys, **Kununurra**, from an Aboriginal word meaning 'big water', is located just inside the Northern Territory border and best known as the home of Australia's greatest 'white elephant', the gigantic **Ord River Dam**. Built at tremendous cost in the 1960s, the dam created **Lake Argyle** which contains nine times as much water as Sydney Harbour. The idea was to use irrigation to turn this remote part of Australia into one of its most productive agricultural areas. But finding suitable crops that would not be consumed immediately by the area's voracious wildlife has proved endlessly frustrating. Birds ate the first cotton crops, and since then agricultural research scientists and farmers have tried alternative crops with only limited success. But the lake has proved quite a drawcard for tourists; a cruise and a swim on the vast artificial lake can be quite pleasant, especially on a hot day. A more recent development in the region has been the discovery of the world's largest deposits of diamonds and the establishment of the giant **Argyle mine** south of the town.

The countryside surrounding the town is stunning, with flat-topped ridges, vast grasslands and meandering creeks. But surely the region's most fascinating sight is the **Bungle Bungles**, three hours' drive south of Kununurra. Still accessible only by four-wheel drive, this vast collection of striped black and orange conical-shaped sandstone formations resembles at first glance a medieval city. Among the vegetation is the unique Bungle Bungle Fan Palm which, in many places, clings to the almost-vertical cliff faces. Until the mid-1980s, their existence was the Kimberleys' best-kept secret. Now protected as a vast national park, they are without question one of Australia's greatest natural wonders.

Queensland

Tropical Australia

Big, brash and beautiful, Queensland is the place other Australians love to hate—but cannot wait to visit on their next holiday. There is a lot of good old-fashioned jealousy involved, and the sentiment is not unlike that traditionally felt by many Americans about Texas. Indeed, American visitors are constantly reminded that Queensland is more than twice the size of Texas, and like Texans, Queenslanders are proud, boastful and terribly parochial, but also very friendly and hospitable. Blessed by an unmatched combination of natural beauty, climate and resources, Queenslanders love to stress how different they are from other Australians. No one in the rest of the country seriously disagrees, and other Australians reciprocate by dismissing Queenslanders as, among other nicknames, a bunch of 'banana benders'.

Located in the mostly tropical northeastern corner of the continent, Queensland is actually Australia's second-largest state, after Western Australia. The state occupies 1.7 million square kilometres (0.6 million square miles), or roughly one-quarter of the continent. Queensland's climate is unequalled in the rest of Australia, and its car licence plates proudly boast 'The Sunshine State'. The Tropic of Capricorn cuts through the centre of the state, giving it a wonderful mixture of tropical and subtropical climates.

In addition to its pleasant climate, Queensland offers a spectacular variety of scenery. Along its eastern waters is one of the world's greatest natural wonders, the 2,000-kilometre- (1,250-mile-) long Great Barrier Reef. The narrow coastal plain is characterized by rivers which flow through rich agricultural land into lovely harbours, lagoons and inlets flanked by beaches of golden sand. Further inland rises the rugged Great Dividing Range, and then stretch the vast dry plains of the Outback. In the northwest of the state, meandering streams flow through coastal marshes into the southern reaches of the Gulf of Carpentaria. In the far north lies the wild Cape York Peninsula, a remote area still accessible only by aircraft or four-wheel-drive vehicle. During the 'Wet', or rainy season, between December and March, huge areas of this vast tropical region are cut off completely from the rest of Australia. Despite man's intrusions upon the landscape, Queensland's natural beauty is stunning.

Queensland's climate, geography and history have also created a unique type of Australian. With a population of 2.4 million, the state is frequently described as the world's only successful European settlement in a tropical climate. But, in contrast to other states, more

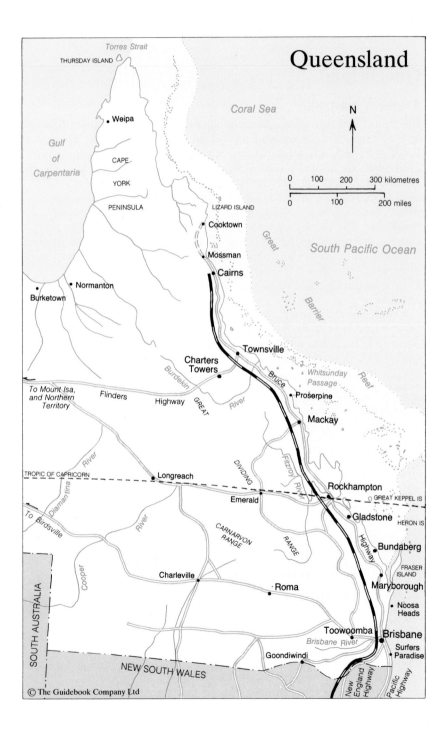

than half the population lives outside the capital of Brisbane, making Queenslanders the most widely dispersed population in the country. This resulted mainly from the pattern of European settlement which spread inland from fairly sizeable coastal communities such as Rockhampton, Mackay, Townsville and Cairns. At the same time, this decentralized development has reinforced strong regional feelings and moulded a tough and uncompromising conservatism among many Queenslanders.

This conservative streak is best illustrated by the state's politics. Queensland produced one of the country's most reactionary politicians in the colourful Sir Johannes Bjelke-Petersen, whose 19-year hold on the state's premiership ended only in 1987. Known universally as 'Joh', he stayed in power through clever manipulation of electoral boundaries, which enabled him to win elections with less than half the vote. His hard line on censorship, street demonstrations and Aboriginal rights earned Queensland the reputation of being Australia's 'Deep North', a play of words on America's Deep South. His push for economic 'progress' frequently put him at odds with the rest of the country, especially over its effect on the environment. In the late 1960s, for example, the Bjelke-Petersen government angered many Australians when it announced plans to drill for oil on the Great Barrier Reef. The public outcry forced a backdown. In more recent years, the saving of Queensland's few remaining tropical rain forests, such as the Daintree, north of Cairns, touched off further bitter and emotional battles. Shortly after his retirement, investigations unravelled a sordid web of political and police corruption extending throughout the state. Queenslanders today are still recovering from the shock.

On a more cheerful note, Queensland has created some of Australia's most enduring national institutions. The country's unofficial national anthem, *Waltzing Matilda*, came from a true incident which took place near the Outback settlement of Winton during the famous sheep shearers' strike of 1891. Australia's international flag-carrier, Qantas, began as a regional airmail and passenger carrier, known as the Queensland and Northern Territory Aerial Services Ltd, from the Outback town of Longreach. The country's famous Flying Doctor Service, an aerial ambulance service for the Outback, began at Cloncurry in 1928, and the School of the Air, a radio school for children in remote areas, was established about the same time.

Queenslanders have always counted on another bonanza to keep their development ethos alive. The latest is tourism, and today the state is Australia's favourite destination for both local and overseas visitors. (It is also the country's fastest-growing state, with many

Australians moving there from other states, either to work or retire.)
With the same energy devoted earlier to developing the state's
agricultural and mineral resources, billions of dollars have poured into
Queensland in recent years to build new tourist facilities. And, as with
those earlier booms, these have generated controversy, especially over
their effect on the environment. Once-idyllic spots, such as Cairns and
the Whitsundays, are already being overwhelmed by tourist
developments. But many locals argue that as long as the tourists
continue to arrive, such 'progress' is inevitable.

History

Although Spanish, Portuguese and Dutch explorers were familiar with
some of Queensland's coastline, modern history—as far as today's
Queenslanders are concerned—began in 1770 with Captain James
Cook. Sailing up the east coast of the continent after his stopover at
Botany Bay near Sydney, the English explorer liked the place so much
that he stopped a total of nine times along the coast. He charted many
features along the Queensland coast, slapping on nametags that
continue to be in use today. In commemoration of Cook's stop at one
particularly lovely beach near Mackay, the tiny settlement is now
called Seventeen Seventy.

Cook also made a quite unexpected stop when he experienced at
first hand the hazards of sailing the deceptively calm waters inside the
Great Barrier Reef. On 11 June 1770, his ship *Endeavour* was severely
damaged when it struck a submerged coral reef north of present-day
Cairns. He was fortunate to survive. Only by dumping all heavy
objects, including six cannons, overboard and patching the gaping hole
with canvas was Cook able to struggle ashore. Cook beached his vessel
at the mouth of what he named the Endeavour River, site of today's
Cooktown. After six weeks, the longest stay until then of Europeans
on the continent, the ship was finally repaired. After climbing atop
Lizard Island's highest peak, Cook spotted a narrow passage out
through the Reef and resumed his hazardous northern voyage. He
came ashore one last time at Possession Island, part of the Thursday
Island group just off the northern tip of the Cape York Peninsula.
Cook claimed the entire east coast of Australia for England's King
George III and named it New South Wales.

When the European settlement of the continent began around
Sydney in 1788, there were no immediate moves to exploit Cook's
northern discoveries. But by the early 1820s, officials were looking for
far-away locations to exile 'the worst class of offender', or criminals
convicted while in the colony. (Newcastle and Port Macquarie, in

today's New South Wales, were early such dumping grounds for incorrigible convicts.) Acting on orders from London, 30 hard-core convicts and their guards arrived at Moreton Bay in early 1824 to establish a penal colony. After six months on the coast at Redcliffe, the settlement was moved inland up the Brisbane River. The small community of Brisbane began to grow.

Meanwhile, after the crossing of the Blue Mountains west of Sydney in 1813, 'squatters', or illegal settlers on government land, and their flocks of sheep were moving up the colony's lush interior on the western side of the Great Dividing Range. Although strictly excluded from Moreton Bay because of its dangerous convicts, these settlers' proximity—and their need for a port—finally brought enough pressure on officials to close down the penal colony. In 1839, the area was opened up for free settlement.

From the beginning, the settlers of the Moreton Bay district developed a strong resentment towards 'southerners'—an attitude that continues to this day. Remote from Sydney, they felt neglected and misunderstood. With most ships heading into Sydney and Melbourne, few new migrants ventured north to settle, and locals blamed officials for not promoting their community. (They have certainly made up for that now.) Anxious for convict labour to develop their grazing lands, the settlers were particularly upset when, after much public pressure, the transportation of convicts to New South Wales ended in 1840. The result was a movement to agitate for the creation of a separate colony where such labour could continue. Transportation did briefly resume to Moreton Bay but had ended by the time the vast colony was formally separated from New South Wales in 1859 and given the name Queensland.

It was a brave move by the settlers of Queensland. In those early days, the colony had no industry and no money to pay its bills. But land was certainly plentiful, and its people were enthused with the challenge of bringing it under control. With more intensity than any other colony, Queenslanders were imbued early with a 'development at any cost' mentality that remains deeply entrenched today. The casualties have been the native Aborigines—and even the environment itself. In a particularly vicious campaign of settlement, hundreds of Aborigines were literally hunted down and killed. Their survivors became 'fringe dwellers' on the edge of white communities or were forced on to closed-off reserves. That development, and subsequent ones involving Chinese and Pacific Islanders, ingrained deep racist attitudes that still persist among many Queenslanders. (Liberal-minded locals frequently use the term 'redneck' to describe the more extreme racists among them.)

But from the European perspective, the settlement and development of Queensland has been one endless 'El Dorado'. Every time the colony—and, later, the state—appeared to be sinking, something new always came to the rescue. The first settlers were attracted by the grazing potential of the great grasslands of the colony's interior. Despite droughts, they soon prospered from sheep and cattle ranching. By the 1880s, the fear of drought diminished when farmers tapped Australia's Great Artesian Basin, a vast underground reservoir of water covering the southwestern third of Queensland. The discovery of extensive gold deposits was another fortuitous early development, setting off gold-rushes that continue today using modern technology. When gold was discovered on the Palmer River in the 1870s, thousands of Europeans and Chinese prospectors descended on northern Queensland. As in the southern colonies, resentment of the hard-working Chinese touched off much animosity from whites and sparked the 'White Australia' movement that eventually saw Asians virtually banned from Australia until the early 1970s.

The bonanza continued with the settlers' early success in growing sugar cane. From the 1860s onward, more and more of Queensland's lush tropical coastline was turned over to sugar, earning the colony a healthy income from exports to the other Australian colonies and England. But the successful development of this tropical crop came at quite a high human price. Because of the widespread belief that Europeans were physically incapable of working in the tropics, a virtual slave trade with the islands of the nearby South Pacific was soon established. Between 1863 and the turn of the century, 50,000 'Kanakas', or Melanesians, were brought into northern Queensland as indentured workers by unscrupulous island traders. Frequently, they simply kidnapped the Kanakas in a practice known as 'blackbirding'. Eventually, public pressure from the south brought an end to the trade, but the islanders' treatment is another sordid chapter in the racial history of Queensland. In the end, they also became victims of the 'White Australia' policy, and nearly all the surviving Kanakas were expelled by 1904. (This history is not forgotten even today by many South Pacific Islanders.) But the nation's burgeoning sugar industry was underway and the islanders' cheap labour was soon replaced by highly mechanized techniques. It is impossible to miss sugar's intrusion on the tropical landscape, ranking top of the list in its importance to the state's economy.

In more modern times, there have been other bonanzas from the exploitation of Queensland's incredibly rich natural environment. Keeping the locals' boom mentality alive, the state has produced discoveries of oil and gas, minerals and gems. And there is enough

"Clancy of the Overflow"

I

had written him a letter which I had, for want of better
    Knowledge, sent to where I met him down the Lachlan, years ago,
He was shearing when I knew him, so I sent the letter to him,
    Just "on spec", addressed as follows: "Clancy, of The Overflow".

And an answer came directed in a writing unexpected,
    (And I think the same was written with a thumbnail dipped in tar)
'Twas his shearing mate who wrote it, and verbatim I will quote it:
    "Clancy's gone to Queensland droving, and we don't know where he are."

In my wild erratic fancy visions come to me of Clancy
    Gone a-droving "down the Cooper" where the western drovers go;
As the stock are slowly stringing, Clancy rides behind them singing,
    For the drover's life has pleasures that the townsfolk never know.

And the bush hath friends to meet him, and their kindly voices greet him
    In the murmur of the breezes and the river on its bars,
And he sees the vision splendid of the sunlit plains extended,
    And at night the wondrous glory of the everlasting stars.

I am sitting in my dingy little office, where a stingy
    Ray of sunlight struggles feebly down between the houses tall,
And the foetid air and gritty of the dusty, dirty city
    Through the open window floating, spreads its foulness over all.

And in place of lowing cattle, I can hear the fiendish rattle
    Of the tramways and the buses making hurry down the street,
And the language uninviting of the gutter children fighting,
    Comes fitfully and faintly through the ceaseless tramp of feet.

And the hurrying people daunt me, and their pallid faces haunt me
    As they shoulder one another in their rush and nervous haste,
With their eager eyes and greedy, and their stunted forms and weedy,
    For townsfolk have no time to grow, they have no time to waste.

And I somehow rather fancy that I'd like to change with Clancy,
    Like to take a turn at droving where the seasons come and go,
While he faced the round eternal of the cashbook and the journal—
    But I doubt he'd suit the office, Clancy, of "The Overflow".

A B 'Banjo' Paterson, Singer of The Bush, *1889*

coal to supply the world for hundreds of years. Heading inland from
Mackay along the state's central coast, kilometre-long trains haul
coking coal for export from vast open-cut pits. (The giant 'draglines'
used to scrape off shallow dirt cover are part of any sightseeing
itinerary to Emerald.) Inland from Townsville is the giant Outback
silver–lead–zinc underground mine at Mt Isa, the world's largest such
deposit. Elsewhere, there are uranium, gold and copper mines. Weipa,
near the tip of the Cape York Peninsula, has the world's largest
reserves of bauxite. Australia's best timber comes from Queensland's
tropical rain forests. In recent years, tourism has been the state's latest
bonanza.

Getting Around

Queensland is particularly well served by overseas flights and boasts
three international airports—at Brisbane, Cairns and Townsville.
Although flights are less frequent than into Sydney and Melbourne,
one advantage is that it is a lot easier to clear immigration and
customs. (These gateways also give travellers the extra option of
arriving, for example, in Sydney and departing from Cairns or vice
versa.) In addition, there are regular air, rail and bus connections to
Brisbane from other parts of Australia. For self-drivers, the
Queensland capital is about a 12-hour drive from Sydney on either the
coastal Pacific Highway or the inland New England Highway.

Because of its vast size, the best way to get around Queensland is by
air, and then to hire a car or join a tour to explore the area. (Aerial
tours, especially in the far north and Outback, are also a great way to
see the sights.) The Brisbane area is ideal for the self-driver, but an
extensive range of tours is also available. Bus companies provide
regularly scheduled services around the state, including special tours.
Another, more relaxing, alternative is to catch a train. The *Sunlander*
and *Queenslander* provide a regular service between Brisbane and
Cairns, together with the recently introduced 'Daylight Rail Tour',
which stops nightly at first-class hotels and restaurants along the coast.
(For those wanting a taste of the Outback, regular train services run
far inland from Brisbane, Rockhampton and Townsville.) All trains
come with airconditioning, a dining car and sleeping berths.

For the more adventurous, the drive from Brisbane to Cairns—a
road distance of nearly 2,100 kilometres (1,300 miles)— takes at least
three days but is a most rewarding experience.

The Queensland Government and Travel Corporation runs travel
centres in all Australian capitals, except Darwin and Hobart, as well as
in Brisbane. The centres can also put visitors in touch with regional-

based tourist associations. (Overseas, the corporation has offices in New York, Los Angeles, Vancouver, London, Munich, Tokyo, Singapore and Auckland.) As in other states, the centres arrange accommodation, travel and tours throughout the state. (Compared to other states, Queensland also has the richest collection of detailed guides to various regions, including local histories and suggested itineraries and operators.)

Queensland is famous for its rich variety of tropical seafood and fruits. The succulent Queensland mud crab, which is exported to the rest of Australia and overseas, is a must for visitors, as well as coral trout, barramundi and other fish unique to the tropics. Crocodile, grown commercially, also features on many menus. With a well-established tourist industry, the state has a wide variety of first-class restaurants but fewer ethnic-style restaurants than in the southern states. Wines are grown in the cooler southeastern region of the state and are definitely worth a sip. The local beer is XXXX, pronounced four-ex, a bitter which really hits the spot on a hot day. (Other Australians say the name comes from Queenslanders' inability to spell—another nasty barb for the locals.) In North Queensland, NQ Lager enjoys wide popularity around Cairns. The state's Bundaberg Rum, manufactured in the city of the same name in central Queensland, is the country's most popular rum. (Truckies mix the drink with coke and call it 'Queensland Diesel'.) The state's country pubs are particularly colourful and always make a pleasant stop and a good way to meet the local characters. Typically, the beer comes in a 'stubbie', a short-necked bottle, and is served with its own styrofoam holder. (Popular souvenirs around the state, these are called 'stubbie holders'.)

Brisbane

Located in the southeastern corner of Queensland, the state capital, Brisbane was long just a quaint backwater along the banks of the muddy Brisbane River. Many Australians dismissed the city as simply an overgrown cattle town. Its biggest claim to fame was serving as General Douglas MacArthur's headquarters during the Second World War. But that image began to change with the state's mining boom in the 1960s when scores of Australian and foreign companies set up headquarters in the city. Soon, a frenetic building boom was under way that radically changed the city's skyline into a Down Under version of Dallas, Texas. In a burst of self-confidence, Brisbane also began to boost its international image by successfully hosting the Commonwealth Games in 1982 and, more recently, World Expo '88. Not content with that, the city even put in a strong—but

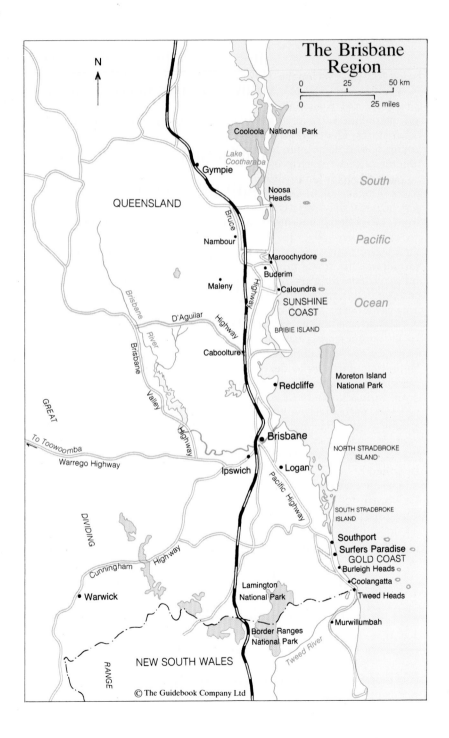

unsuccessful—bid for the 1992 Olympic Games.

Today, with a population of 1.1 million, Brisbane is a cosmopolitan city with its own special lifestyle and charm. Much of that comes from the city's location and climate. Some 32 kilometres (20 miles) downstream from Brisbane are the 1,000-square-kilometre (386-square-mile) bright blue waters of **Moreton Bay**, site of the original convict settlement, with its collection of over 300, mostly deserted, islands. Brisbane is surrounded by hills, the closer ones occupied by wooden Queensland-style homes built on stilts to keep cool. Adding to Brisbane's atmosphere is the city's lush tropical vegetation, especially its giant Moreton Bay figs, jacarandas and mango trees. Despite some sweltering days in summer, the climate is generally mild all year round. Compared to other Australian cities such as Sydney and Melbourne, life moves along at a much slower pace.

With its wide range of accommodation, from first-class hotels to backpacker inns, the city is a convenient base for day-trips to the **Gold and Sunshine Coasts**, **Moreton Bay** and inland to the garden city of **Toowoomba** on the Great Dividing Range.

To the regret of many Brisbanites, many of the city's grand colonial-era buildings, including the famous Bellevue Hotel, were demolished to make way for its modern glass and concrete towers. But enough remains to provide the visitor with a taste of Brisbane's past. The compact downtown area is located inside a bend in the Brisbane River, opposite the sandstone cliffs of prestigious **Kangaroo Point**. A stroll through the city in the cool of the early morning or evening is a pleasant experience. (If you prefer to ride and catch a commentary at the same time, flag down one of the city's new yellow **pedicabs** operated by athletic bronzed Aussies, a Down Under-version of the Chinese rickshaw puller.)

The 40-storey **Riverside Centre** at the northeastern corner of the city is a good place to begin exploring Brisbane. Located on the banks of the busy **Brisbane River**, the centre includes a terminal for government ferries and private cruises along the river or out into Moreton Bay. The boats range from the ordinary ferries used by commuters to luxurious paddle-steamers offering meals, drinks and even live music. Although Brisbane has tended to turn its back on the meandering river, especially in the construction of freeways and expressways right along its banks, a cruise provides a unique insight into the city. One trip goes upriver to the **Lone Pine Sanctuary**, a popular tourist attraction with the world's largest collection of koalas. For this and other destinations, a boat is an excellent, and more relaxing, alternative to catching a bus through Brisbane's crowded streets.

The Great Barrier Reef

The eighth wonder of the world...The earth's largest living 'thing'...
Visible by astronauts on the moon. The descriptions of Australia's Great
Barrier Reef go on and on.

Stretching for 2,000 kilometres (1,250 miles) along the northeastern
coastline of the continent, the reef is indeed one of nature's true
wonders. The structure *is* a bit misnamed, however, as it is neither 'a
reef' nor a 'barrier'. It is actually much more.

The Great Barrier Reef consists of literally thousands of individual
reefs, shoals, atolls, coral cays and islands stretching over a tropical area
of 267,000 square kilometres (103,000 square miles). Much of the actual
reef, which ranges between 15 and 150 kilometres (ten to 100 miles)
offshore, is a maze of vastly different-sized reefs separated by narrow,
and sometimes treacherous, channels leading to the deep and dark blue
waters offshore. Inside this so-called 'barrier', the distinctively turquoise-
blue waters are calm and shallow—an excellent spawning ground for
coral colonies to form 'fringe reefs' around coastal islands and the
mainland itself. The Great Barrier Reef as a whole is the largest
formation of coral reefs in the world.

Coral reefs are the world's only major geological feature built of
plants and animals. Australia's enormous collection has taken 25 million
years of construction work by that tiniest of animals, the coral polyp.
The skeletons of these flower-like polyps, their associated coralline algae
and hydrocorals, plus other plant and animal waste matter, have literally
built mountains on the sea floor. With at least 350 species—and in as
many sizes, shapes and colours—the corals attract a vivid collection of
other sea creatures and wildlife into a complex and beautiful
environment. There are 1,500 species of tropical fish alone, plus a
diverse sea life of sharks, turtles, rays, clams and other shellfish.
Dolphins, dugongs and whales migrate through the reefs. The water is
crystal clear, with visibility ranging up to 60 metres (200 feet). The reef
is a phenomenon that can only happen in the tropics. The skies above
are a brilliant blue, while the land abounds in bright-green tropical
vegetation and dazzling flowers. Blessed by a sea breeze, the
temperatures are ideal.

The reef, much of which is protected as the Great Barrier Reef
Marine Park, is definitely worth a visit. But the problem is deciding
which part of the reef to see. Much depends on your own itinerary, and
this chapter points to several possible destinations along its enormous
length. But everyone has a favourite, and mine is around Lizard Island,
90 kilometres (60 miles) northeast of Cooktown near the northern tip of
the Great Barrier Reef.

The best way to fully appreciate the sheer enormity of the reef is to
catch a low-level scenic flight from a Queensland coastal city such as
Mackay, Townsville or Cairns. For a closer look, some seaplanes and

helicopters actually land, but it is easier and cheaper to catch a high-speed catamaran to specially selected reefs or cays. (For those seeking a more leisurely pace, many centres offer yachts and motorized cruises, some lasting up to a week.) Once at their destination, many operators offer glass-bottomed boats, semi-submersibles or underwater observatories to view the reefs. Reef-walking at low tide in an old pair of sneakers opens up a rich and colourful world. Visitors are cautioned to 'admire, but don't touch'.

Snorkelling offers vivid water views, but the best view of the reef goes to the scuba diving enthusiast. Plunging below the surface, the diver is immediately surrounded by an incomparable underwater world that soon becomes a total addiction. While sharks can be a hazard, attacks are extremely rare.

In recent years, the reef has come under pressure from two predators—the Crown of Thorns starfish and massive tourism. Since 1981, much of the central third of the reef has been decimated by the starfish, touching off an intense scientific battle over its causes. Some experts argue that the infestations are a natural phenomenon, while others blame the growing intrusion of man. A special committee under the Great Barrier Marine Park Authority, based in Townsville, is still looking for answers.

So far, the growth of tourism has not seriously affected the reef itself, although some visitors might be a bit perturbed by the size of some tours. There are plenty of ways to see the reef, however, and it pays to explore around before signing up for a look. But whichever way you choose, you should approach the Great Barrier Reef with a sense of wonder.

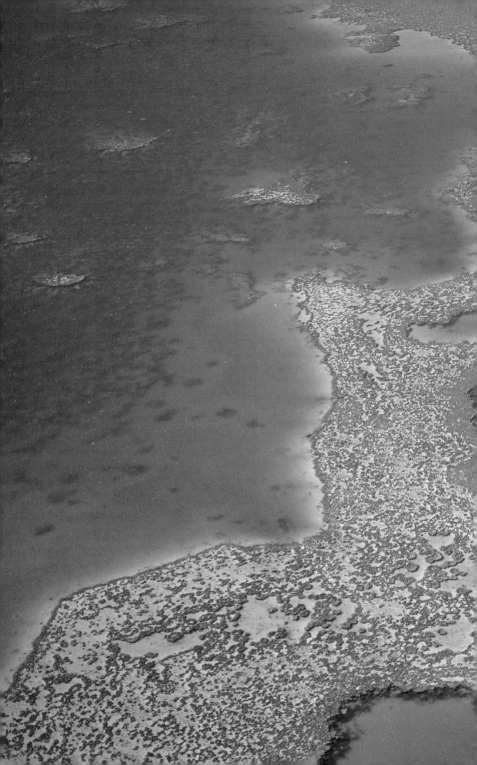

Further down the riverbank from the ferry landing and past some old colonial buildings is Brisbane's **Botanic Gardens**, a lush 20-hectare (50-acre) island of greenery in the shadow of the high-rise office blocks. Originally used by the convict settlement to grow vegetables, the park today offers a lush collection of tropical trees and other vegetation. Further on, near the tip of the point of the riverbend, is Queensland's **Parliament House**, an ornate high-domed French Renaissance-style structure opened in 1868 and recently restored. (The tall building next door is an extravagant parliamentary office block constructed during Joh's long reign as premier.) Back towards the city is **Queen Street**, turned into a tasteful mall as part of extensive renovation work for World Expo '88. Nearby, on one side of palm-fringed **King George Square**, is **Brisbane City Hall**, completed in 1930 and once the city's tallest structure. Further along Adelaide Street is the city's memorial to its war dead, **ANZAC Park** and the **Shrine of Remembrance**. Adding to the sombre atmosphere of the landscaped square is its collection of bulbous-shaped boab trees. Also for the historically minded is **MacArthur Chambers**, at the corner of Queen Street and Edward Street, which served as US General MacArthur's headquarters during the Second World War.

The downtown area contains numerous boutiques, department stores and souvenir shops. There is also a wide variety of restaurants and even the odd surviving old-fashioned Queensland pub. At night, Brisbane offers a range of entertainment from movies and theatre through to discos and cabarets. Brisbanites, who have never had much of a national reputation for culture, are especially proud of their newly opened **Queensland Cultural Centre**. Located on the south bank of the Brisbane River across the **Victoria Bridge**, the centre includes an art gallery, museum and performing arts complex. (The complex adjoins the site used for Brisbane's World Expo '88, now slated for redevelopment.)

There are several other attractions within a short taxi or bus trip from the city centre. To the northeast, **Fortitude Valley** is Brisbane's **Chinatown** district, with its oriental-style mall and numerous restaurants. (The 'valley' is also the city's sleazy district, although Queensland's strict morality laws keep the establishments fairly low-key.) On the road to the airport, the **Breakfast Creek Hotel**, an ornate 19th-century pub and a favourite hang-out for union bosses, is worth a visit. The **Mt Coot-Tha Botanic Gardens**, five kilometres (three miles) from the city, offers Australia's largest subtropical garden. Its **Planetarium Tea Rooms** provide delicious and refreshing Devonshire Teas—scones, or muffins, covered with strawberry jam and cream. Further up the road is the **Mt Coot-Tha Reserve and Lookout**, one of the city's major recreation areas, offering breathtaking views of the entire Brisbane region. Another popular attraction is the **Australian Woolshed**, 14 kilometres (eight miles) west of the city, where visitors can get a quick taste of the Outback by watching live displays of sheep mustering and shearing. (Public transport, taxis and tours operate to these three locations.)

If you have an extra day and want to see something still relatively unspoiled, head off to **Moreton Bay**. Compared to the heavily built-up Gold and Sunshine Coasts, the large circular-shaped bay is a natural wonder. (With the constantly blowing wind and sand, it is also easy to see why the penal colony quickly moved inland.) The larger islands of **Bribie**, **Moreton** and **North Stradbroke** are actually giant sandhills, or vegetation-covered sand dunes. In between these are freshwater lakes, surrounded by heaths of wildflowers and fragile forests. There is also excellent surfing, fishing and snorkelling. All are accessible by air or sea, with **Bribie** connected by road to the Bruce Highway. Five-day smooth-water cruises wander down out of Brisbane, through the Bay and then south to the Gold Coast. Many of the 300 or so Moreton Bay islands allow camping, and the larger ones offer less rustic accommodation, from caravans, or trailers, to the comfortable **Tangalooma Resort**. For history buffs, the tiny island of **St Helena** was once a prison settlement, and the original convict settlement was near present-day **Redcliffe**.

Heading inland from Brisbane on the Warrego Highway to Darwin, 3,700 kilometres (2,300 miles) away, a couple of hours' drive brings you to **Toowoomba**, known as 'The Garden City of Queensland'. Located atop the Great Dividing Range, the city of 80,000 offers a cool break from the more humid coastal plains below. At the heart of the rich **Darling Downs**, the city is an important agricultural centre for the vast Outback beyond. Its spacious parks, gardens and streets are lined with jacarandas, camphor laurels and liquidambars, all a true joy to see in spring when they are in bloom. Although less spectacular than the Blue Mountains west of Sydney, the surrounding hills provide bush walks and vistas of sandstone escarpments and thick forests. Toowoomba's natural beauty has also attracted a thriving arts-and-crafts community. The city's best restaurants are located in gracious colonial homes.

Southeast of Brisbane, on the New England Highway to Sydney, there is more natural beauty around the agricultural town of **Warwick**, founded in 1847. The winding highway crawls over **Cunninghams Gap** through a national park full of birdlife, including the distinctive bellbirds. (A triangular-shaped itinerary can easily take in both Toowoomba and the Warwick region. There are also regular bus and train services, plus bus tours from Brisbane.)

South to the Gold Coast

Much has been written and said about the **Gold Coast**, Australia's equivalent of America's Miami Beach. This is how Geoff Muntz, Queensland's own Minister for Tourism, National Parks and Sport, describes the area in a recently published tourist brochure:

'The Gold Coast blends highrise with superb surfing beaches, glittering nightclubs and cosmopolitan restaurants with quiet waterways, exclusive boutiques with crowded theme parks, family entertainment centres with untouched rainforest, and budget holidays with the ultimate in luxury.'

That sentence takes some beating as an exercise in superlatives! After all, something must be drawing the crowds that make the Gold Coast the country's most popular holiday destination. It is a place you either love or hate.

Located between Brisbane and the New South Wales border, the Gold Coast is a back-to-back collection of 20 resort towns along a 42-kilometre (26-mile) stretch of golden sand. The region stands as a monument to resort development gone slightly mad. This is Queensland progress in action. At the heart of the coast, in **Surfers Paradise**, the sky is filled with giant condominiums, apartment blocks and high-rise hotels. Their inhabitants feed the garish network of shops, restaurants and amusement parlours below. Amazingly, the beach—at least until the buildings block out the sun at about 3 pm—is absolutely wonderful. Before the tourists crowded ashore, the place was indeed a surfer's paradise. But the atavistic atmosphere of surf and sun breeds its own intoxication. It is easy to see why urbanized Australians love to spend their holidays on the Gold Coast. They feel comfortable in crowds, and everyone works hard at what the Aussies do best—having a good time. There are no inhibitions about foreign visitors joining the fun.

Away from 'Surfers', as it is popularly abbreviated, the pace is less frenetic, without the intrusion of high-rises and traffic jams. The Gold Coast area is a permanent home to more than 230,000 people, many of them retired 'southerners' who live in typical suburban homes. Others are young professionals or tourist industry workers. Certainly, the climate is nearly perfect, with almost 300 sunny days a year. A friend who works as a television cameraman on the Coast is really just a 'mad surfie' who spends his days surfing, his portable phone and camera close at hand. For these Australians, the Gold Coast offers an enviable lifestyle. For the visitor, rather than staying in a first-class hotel in Surfers, a more enjoyable alternative is to book into a smaller hotel or apartment in a coastal community, shop with the locals and generally set your own pace.

There is a lot more to the Gold Coast. Not all the beaches are crowded with tourists, and it is still possible to find one of your own and appreciate the coast's natural beauty. At **Currumbin**, near Coolangatta airport, the long beach's northern headland is a nature reserve and park containing a lovely bird sanctuary. Nearby, a creek flows through a lagoon into the South Pacific. To the north, there is a string of relaxed coastal towns such as **Burleigh Heads**, **Miami**, **Nobby's Beach**, **Mermaid Beach** and **Broadbeach** which front on to one long surfing beach.

Not surprisingly, as Australia's most popular holiday spot, the Gold Coast offers several family-oriented theme parks such as **Dream World**, **Sea World** and even a **Fisherman's Wharf**. Everything is on a grand scale. **Wet 'n' Wild**, inland on the road to Brisbane, is Australia's biggest water park. For the inveterate gambler, the Gold Coast offers the giant **Jupiter's Casino**, open 24 hours a day and including a luxurious first-class hotel. In addition, just about anything for water or land is available for hire, often with a few lessons included. Many visitors hire open-air Mini-Mokes and head off to find their own beach or head up into the hinterland.

Inland from the Gold Coast and stretching along the New South Wales border, the hinterland is a mountainous region covered in rain forest and dripping with waterfalls; it makes a lovely contrast to the coastal strip. Much of the area is natural parkland and home to numerous sanctuaries and small arts-and-crafts communities. One of the loveliest spots is the **Natural Arch** in **Numinbah Valley**, where a short walking track leads through rain forest and past a natural archway created by a waterfall. (On a warm day, a swim in the cold mountain water quickly refreshes.) Nearby is the **Lamington National Park**, created early this century, with some 160 kilometres (100 miles) of walking tracks that pass through several temperate zones. Lookouts in the region provide views into the lush **Tweed River** valley and a volcanic range topped by **Mt Warning**, both on the other side of the border. Northeast and inland from the Gold Coast is **Tambourine Mountain**, a collection of national parks that feature prehistoric Macrozamias, a palm that is more than 15,000 years old.

North to the Sunshine Coast

Located an hour's drive north of Brisbane, Queensland's **Sunshine Coast** has been largely spared the overdevelopment of its southern counterpart, although it also ranks as one of the state's leading resorts. Its 150 kilometres (93 miles) of sometimes rugged coastline offer a more relaxing and less crowded alternative to the Gold Coast. Inland, the coast's mountainous hinterland is dotted with lush rain forest and waterfalls. The rich volcanic soil provides fertile ground for a wide range of tropical fruit, including the soft-textured and delicious macadamia nut. Originally a native of Australia, the macadamia was transplanted to Hawaii where it has gained worldwide popularity. In recent years, Queensland has reclaimed the nut as its own.

Heading north out of Brisbane, the Bruce Highway—a four-lane high-speed expressway at this stage—first passes through flat dairy farming and pineapple country. The gateway to the Sunshine Coast comes at the **Glasshouse Mountains**, 100 kilometres (62 miles) north of the capital, a spectacular collection of nine extinct volcanoes named by Captain Cook back in 1770 because of their resemblance to glass kilns in his native Yorkshire. A turn inland at **Landsborough** leads up a steep ridge to the quaint farming community of **Maleny**, with its spectacular views of the Glasshouse Mountains and the coast, and then through to the rugged **Blackall Range**.

Continuing inland on its way to the farming and gold-mining town of **Gympie**, 170 kilometres (100 miles) north of Brisbane, the highway passes a host of man-made tourist attractions, such as the honey farm at **Super Bee**, the **Tanawha World** amusement park and the **Forest Glen Deer Sanctuary**. The best stop is at the **Sunshine Plantation**, also known as 'The Big Pineapple' after its star attraction, just south of Nambour. A cane train takes visitors through a tropical fruit plantation, and the Polynesian-style pavilion features a restaurant and a shop selling souvenirs and an extensive range of fruit. (The plantation's tropical fruit jams make excellent souvenirs.) Nearby **Nambour** is tucked into a picturesque valley and is the region's main agricultural and commercial centre. During the harvesting season between July and December, colourful narrow-gauge cane trains on their way to the town's sugar mill frequently halt traffic along the busy highway. At **Yandina**, a further seven kilometres (four miles) to the north, the **Ginger Factory** is the world's largest processor of the tasty root and a popular attraction. **Eumindi**, renowned for its arts-and-crafts community, has a colourful Saturday market offering porcelain ware, wooden carvings and a range of tropical fruit.

Several roads turn off the Bruce Highway to the coast, allowing travellers to take in both the beaches and the hinterland without backtracking (all in one day, if you are in a hurry). The coastal communities are more widely dispersed than on the Gold Coast and are separated by bushland and hills. Fearful of repeating the experience of its southern counterpart, the Sunshine Coast has imposed regulations that restrict buildings to only three storeys. (This has not prevented developers from scoring a few scandalous victories, especially around **Maroochydore**.) As a result, man's presence along the coast is less intrusive than on the Gold Coast.

Caloundra, just north of **Bribie Island**, is the Sunshine Coast's most southerly community and offers several surfing and swimming beaches. Heading north, the harbour of **Mooloolaba** is one of the east coast's safest anchorages and a finishing point for an annual yacht race from Sydney. A large prawning and fishing fleet is based in the town, and sports fishermen can join trips to offshore reefs. **Maroochydore**, a long-established beach resort at the mouth of the wide **Maroochy River**, is the coast's largest town and site of the region's airport. (Direct flights link the coast with Sydney and Melbourne.)

Past the upriver sugar town of **Bli Bli** and then the volcanic outcrop of **Mt Collum**, the narrow hilltop coastal road leads through several quiet coastal resorts set alongside beaches and rocky headlands. From **Peregian**, a long stretch of sandy beach ends at **Noosa National Park**, a 380-hectare (900-acre) forested headland overlooking the resort town of Noosa.

When Australians talk of visiting Queensland's Sunshine Coast, **Noosa** is where they like friends and relatives to think they are going. Located on the southern bank of the **Noosa River**, the coastal resort town has worked hard at developing a classy image. Noosa is now a favourite vacation spot for well-heeled executives and their families from Sydney and Melbourne. Not surprisingly, the boutiques and restaurants along **Hastings Street** have prices to match those cities' most exclusive suburbs. High-rise buildings are banned and, with a minimum of disruption to the natural environment, accommodation is mostly in modern two-storey apartment blocks and a handful of motels. Compared to the brashness of Surfers Paradise, Noosa has a quiet—if slightly over-priced—charm. And, just to make certain that the country's much-vaunted egalitarianism does not suffer too much from the intrusion of Mercedes-Benz and Volvos, a typical Aussie caravan park continues to hold on to one of Noosa's most expensive pieces of real estate at one end of Hastings Street.

So far, the popularity of Noosa as a tourist resort has not intruded too drastically upon the region's superb physical environment, although one well-connected politician has lobbied for years to open up the river's pristine northern bank to massive development. The Noosa National Park, preserved only after heavy lobbying by the town's old-timers, provides extensive walking tracks leading to rugged headlands and small isolated beaches. And although heavy storms constantly endanger the town's main beach, a small undeveloped peninsula extending out to the mouth of the Noosa River provides an excellent surfing beach on one side and a quiet and protected lagoon on the other.

Upstream, past the long-established towns of **Noosaville** and **Tewantin**, a unique collection of lakes and covered sand dunes forms part of the **Cooloola National Park**, an ideal spot for fishing or just relaxing. Houseboats can be hired, and water cruises and four-wheel-drive tours operate from Noosa into the park and along the northern beaches to the **Teewah Coloured Sands** and other points.

Although there is no direct road from Noosa, **Rainbow Beach** marks the northern end of the Sunshine Coast. (The best access is through **Gympie**.) The beach, accessible only by four-wheel-drive vehicles at low tide, receives its name from the towering cliffs of multi-coloured sandstone which line its length. The coastal town is also one of the main entry points to **Fraser Island**, the world's largest sand island. (The other is through **Maryborough** and **Hervey Bay** further to the north.) Once known as Great Sandy, the 120-kilometre- (74-mile-) long island was renamed in 1836 after Eliza Fraser, the sole survivor from passengers shipwrecked and then attacked by Aborigines. In the early 1970s, conservationists backed by the federal government successfully prevented the island's destruction by sand-mining. Today, its unique mixture of rain forests, wildflower heaths, coloured sands and freshwater lakes and streams are preserved as a national park. For the four-wheel-drive enthusiast, a camping holiday on the island is an unforgettable experience. **Orchid Beach**, also accessible by aircraft which land on the beach, is the island's only resort.

Central Queensland

Stretching 600 kilometres (370 miles) between the Sunshine Coast and Mackay, Central Queensland is a rich agricultural and mining region, providing mostly sugar and coal. Tourism is not as heavily developed here as in other parts of Queensland. For the visitor with a bit of time, the region offers an unspoiled look at 'the real Australia'. Most of the towns are inland farming communities linked by road to small and peaceful coastal resort towns. The land is basically flat with occasional hills, and the vegetation is somewhat sparse.

In fact, one notable feature of the Queensland coast is that there are relatively few areas of naturally occurring rain forest. Such lush vegetation, normally associated with tropical and subtropical climates, is only found in small pockets where the mountains are close to the coast, such as around Mackay and Cairns.

Heading north from the Sunshine Coast, the 'Sugar Coast' centres on lovely **Maryborough**, founded in 1843 as a river port for the sugar industry and the arrival of Kanaka workers. As one of Queensland's oldest settlements, the town has a well-preserved collection of colonial buildings and mansions, tree-lined streets and parks. **Hervey Bay**, 34 kilometres (21 miles) to the east, is a quiet resort and fishing town that is also a major gateway to nearby **Fraser Island**. (The waters off Hervey Bay, a popular spot for whales who come north from Antarctic waters for the Australian winter, are now a marine reserve.) The hinterland, known as the **Burnett** after its major river, offers a mixture of farming, including the state's leading citrus orchards, gemstone-mining and the **Bunya Mountains**, part of the Great Dividing Range.

Bundaberg, 374 kilometres (232 miles) north of Brisbane, boasts a climate similar to Hawaii and is best known as the home of Australia's potent Bundaberg Rum, or 'Bundy' as it is affectionately known. Located east of the Bruce Highway, Bundaberg (population 33,000) is also the southern gateway to the **Great Barrier Reef**, with water and air links to some 13 islands and 22 reefs. Part of the Capricorn Section of the **Great Barrier Reef Marine Park**, the unique coral cays of **Lady Elliot** and **Lady Musgrave** are the best-known destinations. (The trip by fast catamaran takes about two and half hours or between 35 and 40 minutes by seaplane.) Uninhabited Lady Musgrave Island is home to thousands of seabirds and a nesting ground for giant turtles. Combined with the clear waters of the lagoon and surrounding reef, the island offers incomparable diving, snorkelling, swimming and walks. (Lady Elliot has a small resort.) Back along the coast, there are at least seven beaches near Bundaberg, including **Mon Repos Environmental Park**, where hundreds of turtles come ashore between November and February to lay their eggs.

Another 130 kilometres (80 miles) north of Bundaberg are the quiet resort towns of **Agnes Waters** and **Seventeen Seventy**, where Captain Cook landed briefly in 1770. **Gladstone**, with its beautiful natural harbour, is a heavily industrialized town of 22,000, boasting the world's largest aluminium refinery and a smelter that produces 25 percent of the country's aluminium. Its port is also the busiest in Queensland, exporting millions of tonnes of coal from inland open-cut mines.

Rockhampton, with a population of 56,000, is the state's first tropical city: a distinctive 14-metre- (50-foot-) high spire in the centre of the city's **Curtis Park** marks the Tropic of Capricorn. Located on the banks of the **Fitzroy River** some 40 kilometres (25 miles) from the coast, Rockhampton is the capital of Australia's largest beef-producing area. One of its most charming features is that the railway from Brisbane runs right down the middle of the main street. The nearby **Capricorn Coast** offers several low-key resort towns, including the controversial Japanese-owned **Iwasaki Resort** set on 8,500 hectares (20,000 acres) of prime coastal land at **Yeppoon**. Offshore, and inside the calm waters of the **Great Barrier Reef**, there are dozens of tropical islands, including the popular resorts of **Great Keppel** and **Heron**.

West of Rockhampton, the Capricorn Highway leads 263 kilometres (163 miles) to the farming and coal town of **Emerald**. It is also the gateway to the largest sapphire-producing fields in the world, and visitors are encouraged to fossick. To the southwest is the **Carnarvon Gorge National Park**, one of Australia's most beautiful inland parks, with its Aboriginal rock paintings, sandstone cliffs, wildlife and rare ferns and palms.

Known as the 'Sugar Capital of Australia', the coastal city of **Mackay** (population 48,000) is one of the loveliest towns along the long Queensland coast. Set at the foot of a steep mountain range and surrounded by endless fields of sugar cane, the city's eight sugar mills process one-third of Australia's crop. Within driving distance of Mackay, a pleasant city of flowering tropical trees and restored colonial buildings, there are at least 30 beaches, many set in national parks featuring tame wallabies, kangaroos, koalas and scrub turkeys. Some 80 kilometres (50 miles) inland is **Eungella National Park**, 49,000 hectares (120,000 acres) of tropical rain forest and mountain streams inhabited by the illusive platypus.

Mackay and the sugar town of **Proserpine**, 124 kilometres (77 miles) to the north, are also important entry points to the **Whitsunday Islands**, easily one of the most beautiful places in Australia. Named by Captain Cook, the Whitsundays are a collection of 74 tropical islands scattered across calm azure-blue waters between the jungle-covered

Australia's Aborigines

Before the arrival of Europeans over 200 years ago, Australia belonged to the Aborigines. For at least 40,000 years, this racially distinct people, divided into roughly 500 tribes, roamed the continent as hunter-gatherers. The Aborigines held deep spiritual links with the land and treated it as sacred. And while they had no written language, their legends about its creation—known as the Dreamtime—were handed down from generation to generation through ritual ceremony and paintings.

The Aborigines' long and cosy isolation from the rest of the world was rudely shattered when the first English settlers arrived in 1788. To these newcomers, Australia was 'terra nulius', or an empty land, and ripe for occupation. But it quickly turned into a titanic clash of cultures in which the Aborigines were nearly wiped out by massacre, disease and starvation. Only in recent years have ordinary Australians started to come to terms with this tragic side of their history.

From an estimated 300,000 at the beginning of white settlement, Aborigines today number about 160,000 or about one percent of the population. Many live in cities or as 'fringe-dwellers' on the edge of white settlements. Others live on isolated 'reserves' or on their own land, especially in the Northern Territory. Despite their small numbers, however, these original Australians are at the bottom of the heap, both economically and socially. They have a lower life expectancy by 18 years than the rest of Australians, and their infant mortality rate is more than triple the national average. Only a handful have finished university or occupy professional positions and few even finish high school. Their unemployment rate is 50 percent, and on many reserves it is much higher. They also suffer from high alcohol abuse and many drift into crime. Aborigines also make up a disproportionate percentage (11 percent) of the nation's prison population. The most tangible sign of the despair felt by many of today's Aborigines is the 100 plus who have died in police custody or prison in the past ten years. Many are suicides.

The treatment of the Aborigines has left a sad legacy and, not surprisingly, it is a frequent source of international embarrassment to the Australian government. But to be fair, Canberra has done much to improve the lot of the Aborigines over the past 20 years, spending billions of dollars in improving housing, health and educational facilities. The federal government has also pushed for the granting back of vast tracts of land to the Aborigines. The catchword these days is 'self-management', or allowing the Aborigines to manage their own affairs rather than have policies imposed from Canberra. The strategy appears to be working. One of the most successful programmes, for example, is the Aboriginal-run radio and television network in central Australia, which is seen as a model for Third World countries. A more ambitious— but highly controversial—government goal is to sign a belated 'treaty' with the Aborigines, an act never undertaken by Australia's colonizers.

In many ways, it is amazing that the Aborigines have survived at all. Despite their deprivations, recent years have seen a strong renaissance in Aboriginal culture, particularly in the arts. Paintings from the so-called Papunya School, which use modern acrylics on canvas to portray ancient legends, are in high demand around the world. Plays, novels and black histories also enjoy a wide following. Further impetus has come from the 'out-station movement' in which Aborigines have moved out of Western-style settlements to pursue a traditional lifestyle. (But they do make some compromises and are not shy about holding on to 'mod cons', or modern conveniences, such as four-wheel-drive vehicles, water pumps and hunting rifles.) In many Aboriginal communities, alcohol is now banned.

Another sign of improvement is the growing willingness of Aborigines to share their culture and lifestyle with outsiders. Especially in the Northern Territory, Aborigines now run several tours on to their lands to explain their traditional lifestyle and legends. When the first European explorers ventured into the hostile environment of the Australian Outback, many faced starvation, thirst and even death. But as today's visitors quickly discover, the desert is full of 'bush-tucker' that would have made their trips a lot easier.

While public attitudes towards Aborigines have changed markedly in recent years, there is still a surprising amount of prejudice against them, especially in country towns and the Outback regions of Australia. The most frequently heard complaint is that the Aborigines receive unemployment and other social security benefits and simply do not want to work 'like normal people'. There is also some bitterness, from companies and state governments, that Aboriginal communities can veto mineral exploration and mining on their lands. Much is also heard of how 'militant Aborigines', usually city-dwelling and well-educated blacks, allegedly manipulate others into disrupting the status quo. For these Australians, the only decent Aborigine is one who has totally renounced his or her own culture. But looking back on the legacy of the past 200 years, that is one option that many Aborigines have clearly rejected.

coastline and the Great Barrier Reef. Most of the islands are uninhabited national parks, covered in dense rain forest and surrounded by unspoiled beaches. Resort development has been restricted to only six islands. For the more adventurous, camping is permitted on most of the islands, while those looking for something more comfortable can choose resorts ranging in price from the reasonable to the absolutely outrageous. **Hayman Island**, the most luxurious, has spent millions of dollars upgrading to five-star status and is clearly the place for anyone with lots of spare cash. With a touch of the Gold Coast, **Hamilton Island** has its own jet airstrip, and houses its 1,400 guests in accommodation ranging from Polynesian-style 'bures' and beachfront suites to penthouses and isolated villas. Less spoiled— and more downmarket—are resorts on **Lindeman**, **South Molle**, **Daydream** and **Long** islands. Other islands have camping facilities.

Airlie and **Shute Harbour** are the Whitsundays' two main coastal communities and provide a wide range of accommodation and transport to the islands and the reef. Seaplanes and helicopters fly passengers on aerial tours of the region, with many landing passengers to reef-walk, snorkel and view the coral reefs. Boats run regular services and tours to the islands. Renting your own yacht, or 'bare-boating', and then cruising the tranquil waters of the Whitsundays has become popular in recent years, allowing visitors the luxury of anchoring off their own island for the night. Several companies provide diving trips to the Great Barrier Reef, 70 kilometres (43 miles) away, with many providing courses as well.

North Queensland

Beginning at the picturesque coastal town of **Bowen**, about 60 kilometres (37 miles) north of Proserpine, North Queensland stretches all the way to the tip of the Cape York Peninsula. The vast region's unequalled and varied tropical beauty, including the Great Barrier Reef, has long made it one of Australia's most popular tourist destinations. Both Townsville and Cairns have international airports, the only such facilities outside any Australian state capital. (A recommended option is for travellers to fly into Townsville, hire a car and then explore the way north to Cairns. It is one of the loveliest drives in Australia.)

With a population of over 105,000, **Townsville** is Australia's largest tropical city. With a year-round average temperature of 28°C (82°F), Townsville boasts more hours of sunshine than any other city in Australia and has a relaxing lifestyle to match. Founded in 1864 as a port for the cattle industry, the city is now the region's most important business and commercial centre, exporting 1.5 million tonnes of sugar, minerals and beef a year. A sophisticated city with a lively arts scene and its own university, Townsville is also a leading centre for tropical and marine research and the headquarters of the Great Barrier Reef Marine Park Authority. One of the city's best tourist attractions is the **Great Barrier Reef Wonderland**, the world's largest live coral reef aquarium which opened in 1987. (The city also has Queensland's second casino, the **Sheraton Breakwater Casino**.)

Castle Hill, with an elevation of 290 metres (950 feet), makes an ideal vantage point from which to view the city's environs, including **Magnetic Island**, a large hilly and bush-covered island in **Cleveland Bay**, named by Captain Cook after his ship's compass went slightly haywire. Reached by regular ferries from the Wonderland complex, the island—most of which is national park—is a popular suburb and resort. Townsville also offers water and air access to the **Great Barrier Reef**, including the resort islands of **Orpheus**, **Hinchinbrook**, **Dunk** and **Bedarra**.

Inland from Townsville, historic **Charters Towers** is well worth visiting. Located 130 kilometres (80 miles), or about an hour's drive, to the southwest, it was a thriving gold-mining town of over 20,000 people in the 1870s and was once the largest settlement in north Queensland. Today, with a population of about 7,000, its surviving buildings make up one of the finest collections of early Australian architecture in the country. During the Second World War, because of its inland position and higher elevation, Charters Towers was an important American base for aircraft making bombing raids into New Guinea and other South Pacific battle zones. The nearby ghost town of **Ravenswood** has a rich nostalgic atmosphere from the gold-boom days.

Heading north from Townsville up the Bruce Highway, the vegetation changes rapidly from 'dry' to 'wet' tropical, as volcanic mountain ranges encroach on the coastline. Northwest of **Ingham**, a sugar town along the attractive **Herbert River**, an unpaved road leads to a series of spectacular waterfalls which tumble into deep gorges. Halfway between Townsville and Cairns, **Cardwell** is one of the region's oldest and most beautiful towns, and sits between the rain forest of the rugged coastal range and the calm waters of the Coral Sea. Just offshore is **Hinchinbrook Island**, Australia's largest island national park, which offers a wide variety of tropical vegetation along with fringing coral reefs. (There is a small resort on the island's northeastern tip.)

Tully, a busy sugar and banana town at the foot of **Mt Tyson** (674 metres, or 2,200 feet), boasts the highest rainfall in the country and, to celebrate, holds a **Rain Festival** every August. The nearby **Tully River**

offers excellent white-water rafting and canoeing. At **Mission Beach**, 25 kilometres (16 miles) east of the town, lush rain forest comes right down to white sand beaches, providing a pleasant gateway to **Dunk** and **Bedarra** islands, two of the Barrier Reef's most attractive resort-islands. The area is famous for the cassowary, one of Australia's rarest birds, and the irridescent-blue Ulysses butterfly, the world's largest. Cruises to the **Great Barrier Reef** and the islands depart from **Clump Point** at the northern end of Mission Beach. Further north, between the sugar towns of **Innisfail** and **Babinda**, the **Bellenden-Ker National Park** west of the highway features Queensland's highest mountain, **Mt Bartle-Frere** (1,657 metres, or 5,440 feet).

   Cairns (population 49,000) is Queensland's most northerly city and the 'capital' of what the locals proudly call '**Far North Queensland**', or simply **FNQ**. Although rapid tourist development in recent years has destroyed much of its small-town charm, Cairns (pronounced 'cans') remains one of the most beautiful cities in Australia. Located on the shores of **Trinity Bay**, the city is set against a magnificent backdrop of jungle-covered mountains. Their peaks are often shrouded in clouds, giving visitors the feeling of being on a tropical island. The streets and parks are lined with tropical plants and flowers, including the fragrant frangipani and multicoloured bougainvillaeas. Away from the modern hotels and restaurants along the palm-fringed **Esplanade**, many of the homes are elegant 'North Queenslanders', large wooden homes on stilts with yards full of giant mango and other fruit trees.

As the best-known gateway to the **Great Barrier Reef**, Cairns has built up a huge infrastructure to cater to the growing number of Australian and overseas tourists. Cruises operating from the busy **Cairns Marina** make regular runs to resort islands such as **Green**, **Fitzroy** and **Lizard** as well as to the reef itself. Aircraft and helicopters take visitors over—and on to—the reef and up to **Cooktown** and the **Cape York Peninsula**, and, with an incredibly rich hinterland and coastline, there are numerous road tours available as well. (In downtown Cairns, visitors can simply shop around for the most suitable package tour.) Accommodation ranges from backpackers' hostels to high-priced luxury resorts.

The beauty of Cairns is that there is a lot more to see than just the Great Barrier Reef. Just west of the city, a drive through sugar cane fields leads to **Crystal Cascades** at the foot of the sharply rising **Kuranda Range**. Walking trails follow the swiftly flowing **Freshwater Creek** and, on a hot day, it is difficult to resist jumping into the deep crystal-clear pools to cool off. Nearby is **Lake Placid**, a wildlife and fish sanctuary formed by the damming of the **Barron River Gorge**. Further west are the **Atherton Tablelands**, originally settled by gold-miners but now a rich agricultural district offering virgin rain forest, extinct volcanoes, lakes, waterfalls and gorges. The most exciting way to visit the tablelands is on the **Kuranda Scenic Railway**. Departing from downtown Cairns, the train winds its way up the steep walls of the spectacular Barron River Gorge and is the highlight of many people's visit to the region.

Another pleasant destination is north of Cairns where, after passing the beachside suburbs of **Trinity Bay** and **Palm Cove**, the highway winds between steep hills and the golden beaches of the **Marlin Coast**. (Because of 'stingers', or poisonous jellyfish, swimming is not possible between December and March; the safest place to swim is at a hotel swimming pool or in the inland creeks.) **Port Douglas**, 75 kilometres (46 miles) north of Cairns, is one of the north's oldest towns and was once a busy port with a population of 12,000. Close to the Reef, the town (population 2,000) is experiencing a tourist boom and, like Cairns, much of its sleepy charm has disappeared. From atop **Flagstaff Hill**, there are spectacular views of the **Low Isles** and **Four Mile Beach**. (The recent construction of the exclusive **Sheraton Mirage** resort just inshore from the beach has clearly changed the town dramatically.)

Mossman, 14 kilometres (eight miles) to the north, is Queensland's most northerly sugar town and has changed little over the years. Inland, past the towering hulk of **Mt Demi** (1,160 metres, or 3,800 feet), the **Mossman Gorge National Park** is a tropical delight of rain forests, cascades and waterfalls. Just to the north is palm-fringed **Newell Beach** with its spectacular views down the coast. Ferries at the small township of **Daintree**, 36 kilometres (22 miles) north of Mossman on the banks of the crocodile-infested Daintree River, provide four-wheel-drive access into the **Cape Tribulation National Park**, a wilderness area of tropical forest and isolated beaches flanked by the northernmost extension of the Great Dividing Range. A public outcry over plans for massive tourist development in the region has led to the preservation of much of the area, including the nearby **Daintree National Park**, as a permanent wilderness.

Isolated at the end of an uncomfortable dirt road 330 kilometres (200 miles) north of Cairns, **Cooktown** has until recently been spared massive tourist development. (Plans are now afoot to build a large tourist resort in the town.) Famous as the site where Captain Cook beached the *Endeavour* after it was holed on a nearby reef in 1770, the town boomed during the Palmer River gold-rush of the 1870s and was once Queensland's second-largest city. Today, with a population of only 1,200, Cooktown's historic buildings and atmosphere make it one of the most pleasant towns in Australia. Parking their beat-up four-wheel-drive vehicles outside, rustic local characters in shorts, boots and cowboy hats pass the day guzzling beer in styrofoam 'stubbie-holders', stirring occasionally for a game of darts or pool. The pace in the steamy tropical climate is intoxicatingly slow. (Several aerial tours stop in Cooktown for two or three hours before heading out over the Reef.)

From Cooktown or the Atherton Tablelands, another dirt road heads another 700 kilometres (430 miles) through the wilderness of the **Cape York Peninsula**. For the adventurous, safari tours operate during the dry season (May to November). Aircraft also link Cairns with the **Wilderness Lodge** at the tip of the peninsula and the nearby **Thursday Island** and **Torres Strait Islands**.

Outback Queensland

Queensland offers plenty of wide open spaces beyond its narrow coastal strip and the Great Dividing Range. Outback Queensland makes up about two-thirds of the state and is divided into three regions, all equally vast.

The **Gulf Savannah**, located in the northwestern corner of the state, earns its name from the vast grasslands and meandering rivers along the southern rim of the **Gulf of Carpentaria**. The region was made famous by the explorers Burke and Wills, who arrived on the edge of the Gulf in 1861, only to die tragically on the 4,000-kilometre (2,500-mile) journey back to Melbourne. Their discovery did little to encourage settlement, and even today the Gulf region remains largely undeveloped and isolated from the rest of Australia. (Adding to the isolation, heavy monsoon rains between December and March cover the area in water, and most roads remain unpaved.) The discovery of gold in the early 1880s sparked some interest, but most of its handful of settlers today raise cattle, giving the region a frontier atmosphere. For the adventurous, a visit offers a fascinating and unique insight into Outback Australia.

With a population of only 1,100 and located on a gravel ridge, **Normanton** is the Gulf's largest settlement and home to one of the world's oddest railways, the fascinating *Gulflander*. Once a week, the 1922 railmotor and its two cars head out of the incongruous-looking corrugated tin-roofed Victorian Gothic railway station on the edge of town and rattle off through the grasslands for a four-hour journey to **Croydon**, a once-thriving gold-mining town 150 kilometres (90 miles) to the east. Surrounded by flat wetlands at the mouth of the **Norman River** 70 kilometres (43 miles) to the north, **Karumba** was once a refuelling stop for Sunderland flying boats connecting Sydney with England in the 1930s. Today, Karumba is the main port for the Gulf's rich prawning and barramundi industry, and the **Karumba Lodge Motel** offers some of the best seafood in Australia. (The region's wetlands and river estuaries are notorious for their crocodiles, and swimming is downright dangerous.)

Further west is tiny **Burketown** (population 235), the model for Neville Shute's famous novel *A Town Like Alice*, about life in a small Outback town. Nearby **Escott Lodge** on the **Nicholson River** is a cattle station. It is open to tourists and holds the annual Barramundi Championships. To the southwest is the **Riversleigh Fossil Field**, a large and scientifically important fossil find dating back 15 million years and discovered only in 1984. It contains the predecessors of today's kangaroos and platypus.

The next Outback region to the south is centred on the mining town of **Mt Isa** (population 24,000) which contains one of the world's largest deposits of copper, silver, lead and zinc. (Located on the major route from Queensland into the Northern Territory and with regular air connections, a stopover can be easily arranged and provides a most rewarding look into the Outback.) Known as the **Central West**, the region is characterized by rolling plains of spinifex and rugged ranges which are home to troops of kangaroos and wild camels, left-overs from the gold-mining days. The area also features some of Australia's largest cattle and sheep stations, or ranches. The region has a rich history, and the countryside is dotted with many old, and even modern, ghost towns.

The **Combo Waterhole**, located a few kilometres southeast of tiny **Kynuna**, was the inspiration for Australia's most famous ballad *Waltzing Matilda*. (In nearby **Winton**, a statue of a 'swagman' honours 'Banjo' Paterson's ballad.) The ballad itself was based on a true incident which took place during a great economic depression in the 1890s when hundreds of swagmen, or tramps, wandered the countryside looking for work. After stealing and slaughtering a sheep on a nearby property, a 'swaggie' was sitting down to his meal when the property owner and police arrived. Rather than be captured, he jumped into the waterhole and drowned.

A more modern legend comes from **McKinlay**, south of **Julia Creek**, which was turned into the fictitious town of 'Walkabout Creek' for the movie *Crocodile Dundee*. (After the worldwide success of the film, the **Federal Hotel** became so busy that the publican finally sold up and moved on to somewhere more peaceful!)

East of Mt Isa, **Cloncurry** was once a thriving gold and copper town and is now a thriving pastoral centre. Surrounding the town are the remains of old copper and gold mines and, from more recent times, the remains of the **Mary Kathleen**, once a thriving uranium mine. Cloncurry is also well known as the place where the **Flying Doctor Service** was established in 1928, and where the idea—and the overdraft —for **Qantas** originated in 1921. Known as the Queensland and Northern Territory Aerial Services, the airline was originally established to carry passengers and mail in this Outback region and later expanded to Brisbane. When tenders were called in 1934 for a company to manage Australia's fledgeling overseas airline, Qantas won the contract—and then kept its name. But controversy continues in the region over the airline's home town, with **Winton**, where the first board meeting took place, and **Longreach**, where the airline was based after 1922, also claiming credit as its birthplace. (Qantas itself leans towards the latter and has named its latest range of aircraft after the town.)

Another side to the area's history is remembered at the tiny settlement of **Kajjabi**, where a memorial honours the hundreds of Kalkadoon Aborigines who were killed resisting the region's settlement by Europeans. The confrontation ended in their defeat at **Battle Mountain** in 1884.

In Queensland's **South West**, the last Outback region, **Boulia** is the home of the **Min Min lights**, mysterious lights which appear to hover and move about. After nearly 100 years, no one has yet explained the phenomenon, first spotted at the local graveyard. Interestingly, the local Aborigines have no legends surrounding the lights. Some say the lights are caused by volatile gases released into the atmosphere by artesian wells.

Boulia is also the self-proclaimed capital of the **Channel Country**, a reference to the region's normally dry rivers which overflow with water during the annual rainy season, reviving the landscape and providing luxurious feed for cattle and sheep.

Further south, near the border with South Australia and the Northern Territory, is one of Australia's most famous Outback towns, **Birdsville**. During the colonial period, the town was a customs collection point and is now best known for its annual country race meeting. Every September, thousands of tourists descend on the tiny town by road and air, including many in their own planes. Overnight, the population mushrooms from 30 to several thousand, who then indulge in a wild weekend of horse-racing and heavy drinking around its only hotel, the rustic **Birdsville Hotel**. (From here, the unpaved **Birdsville Track** heads down into South Australia.) To the west is the **Simpson Desert**, a true desert of reddish sandhills and spinifex which stretches far into the neighbouring Northern Territory.

Heading east, **Charleville** is Outback Queensland's second-largest town and lies at the heart of 'mulga country'. (Mulgas are pine-like trees that provide fodder for cattle and sheep during droughts.) **Longreach**, along the Capricorn Highway between the coast and Mt Isa, is the home of the **Australian Stockman's Hall of Fame**, an outstanding museum to Australia's Outback pioneers opened by the Queen in 1988. Built out of corrugated roofing-iron, the large complex is a living monument which houses the Outback's folklore, writings, art and history and is well worth seeing. The town was also the headquarters of Qantas between 1922 and 1934. The hangar used to assemble and store its first aircraft is still in use.

Northern Territory

The Last Frontier

The Aussies like to think of the Northern Territory as the real
Australia. It does not really matter that most of them—or about 70
percent of the nation's 16 million people—live comfortably in the
coastal cities of southeastern Australia. They only rarely venture into
the Outback, although that is starting to change. But in the Australian
psyche, the Northern Territory fulfils much the same purpose as the
Wild West once did for the Americans. With its vast horizons, rugged
beauty and sparse population, the Northern Territory is Australia's
Last Frontier.

For Australians, and many foreign visitors, the Northern Territory
evokes a less complicated era when larger-than-life characters squared
off against one of the earth's toughest environments. Most of the time,
the battle between European Man and Nature ended in a toughly-
fought draw. The cocky survivors retreated to the nearest pub to spin a
few yarns or brawl with their mates. (The region's native Aborigines,

who had traditionally lived in total harmony with this harsh land, also paid a heavy price, most sadly visible among the alcoholic 'fringe-dwellers' who inhabit the edges of today's white settlements.) This romantic image of a place full of wild characters also sells, such as in the internationally popular film, *Crocodile Dundee*. The wise-cracking Mick Dundee, played by Paul Hogan, was a crocodile poacher who saw his chance to play tour guide for a lovely visiting American woman reporter. Although he was a mere caricature, every Aussie likes to believe there is something of that swaggering and colourful man in each of them.

While it is hard to find a real 'Crocodile Dundee', the Northern Territory is indeed a very special place. Shaped like a large rectangle with a ragged fringe at the top, the Territory sprawls over 1.3 million square kilometres (502,000 square miles) of central and northern Australia. This is about 20 percent of the continent's surface, or equal to the combined areas of France, Spain and Italy. The Tropic of Capricorn runs just north of Alice Springs, placing two-thirds of the Territory inside the tropics. Covering 50,000 square kilometres (19,300 square miles) in the Territory's southeast, the Simpson Desert is regarded as one of the most forbidding places on earth. (The Tanami, northwest of Alice Springs, is slightly less so.)

Because of its tropical position, there are only two seasons in the Northern Territory—a wet and a dry season. And while temperatures do go to extremes, such as the Centre's chilly nights in August or blazing 44°C (112°F) days in January, the climate is agreeable. Even the air feels more pure, especially in the dry desert areas. Combined with its incomparable scenery and wildlife—including the human variety—the Territory has a truly unique character that has long made it a personal favourite. Adding to the Territory's enchantment are its two distinct faces—the green and tropical Top End and the red-brown deserts of the Centre. Both are worth seeing.

In the Territory's northern quarter, or Top End, the mostly flat terrain is characterized by rivers and 'billabongs', or lakes, which boast a rich collection of wildlife, including the Territory's famous crocodiles and barramundi fish. The landscape is typical savannah, or lightly wooded grasslands, which provides a rich home for the Territory's famous ant hills, some rising to 15 metres (50 feet), and kangaroos. Here and there are pockets of lush tropical rain forest. The region's most dominant physical feature is the two billion year-old Arnhem Land plateau, seen most dramatically in the Kakadu National Park east of Darwin. Over millions of years, cascading waterfalls along its magnificent escarpment have hauled away the material that forms the wide flood plains below. The flat coastline harbours vast mangrove swamps, broken occasionally by low-lying headlands, while offshore the waters are dotted with islands, some of which—such as Bathurst and Groote Eylandt—are quite large.

The Top End's primitive beauty fluctuates dramatically with its two seasons—known by locals simply as 'The Dry' and 'The Wet'. During the six month-long dry season from May to October, the blazing sun bakes the landscape and its inhabitants into a stupor, drying out the flood plains and turning the grasslands a golden brown. The cloudless skies take on a whitish tinge from the swirling dust and smoke from bushfires and then turn a bright orange-red during the brief tropical sunsets. It's also when Territorians go a bit 'troppo', or slightly crazy. Just as everyone's nerves are at breaking point, the monsoon rains finally arrive. In one of nature's most awesome sights, huge banks of clouds roll in from the Timor Sea. Then, in a ground-shaking blaze of thunder and lightning, the rains start and the land springs back to life. For the next six months, the Top End turns into one vast lake teeming with unmatched wildlife. By the end of The Wet, everyone is going troppo from *too much* rain.

By contrast, the Centre is classic Australian Outback. This vast and stunning land of deserts and semi-arid plains offers a mixture of light and colour seen nowhere else on earth. The sky is a bright blue, and the clear air gives the sun a sparkling quality. The colour of the landscape, including the soil itself, is a distinctive reddish-brown touched with yellow, earning it the name 'the Red Centre'. But these colours are mixed with the dark purple of ancient mountain ranges, the bleached sandstone of the region's many gaps, or chasms, and the blinding white sands of dry river beds. Filling out this scene are the Centre's majestic ghost gums, a ubiquitous white-bark eucalypt whose roots reach far down to tap subterranean watercourses and are found in the most unlikely places.

Unlike the lively Top End, the Centre—a truly ancient landscape where the mountain ranges appear like the bones of long-extinct dinosaurs—exudes a feeling of timelessness. Here, it is easy to understand the strong spiritual bond that the Aborigines have with the land. Their vivid tales from the prehistoric Dreamtime, when giant creatures roamed and then formed the landscape, are even easier to understand. This comes home most dramatically in a visit to Ayers Rock, Australia's best-known natural landmark, southwest of Alice Springs. Only the most jaded traveller walks away unmoved from this giant red monolith rising over 300 metres (1,000 feet) above the desert floor. For the Aborigines, this majestic rock and the nearby Olgas are at the heart of their spirituality. Outsiders should approach with a sense of reverence.

The mood and appearance of the Centre can change as dramatically, and as quickly, as in the Top End. Even the lightest rain turns the desert into a vast ocean of flowers, and the trees sprout new leaves. And when those heavy monsoon clouds from the Top End sneak through occasionally to the Centre, such as in early 1989, the resulting torrents of water are powerful enough to wash away even the most modern roads, railways and bridges. It took a full emergency operation with helicopters and fixed-wing aircraft to rescue the hundreds of travellers stranded in isolated settlements which, not surprisingly, soon ran out of beer. (This event, which followed a lesser flood the previous year, now has scientists speculating that the Greenhouse Effect could result in a permanently green central Australia.)

But the Northern Territory's beauty would not be nearly so enticing if it was not so underpopulated. The place is virtually empty, making it easily the least-populated part of Australia. Its entire population is only 145,000, or more than ten square kilometres (four square miles) per inhabitant. (With the recent boom in tourism, however, there are

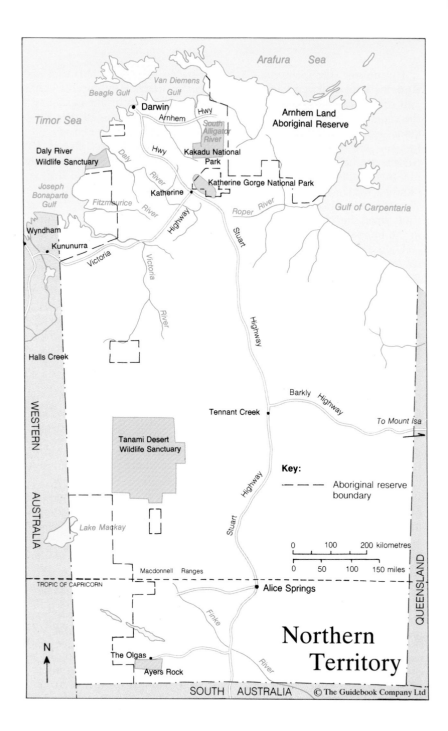

now ten tourists for every resident!) Roughly 25 percent of the Territorians are Aborigines. Many are still tribal, but now use modern ways to preserve their ancient culture. They have their own radio and television stations, and run specialist guided tours using gutsy 'roo bar-equipped four-wheel-drive Landcruisers. The Aborigines now have control over their own land, or roughly half the Territory, thanks to progressive—but highly controversial—Land Rights legislation in the 1970s.

The non-Aboriginal population, as elsewhere in Australia, sticks mostly to the Territory's two largest towns, Darwin and Alice Springs, and a handful of smaller towns. They are a real hodgepodge of people, including civil servants from Canberra and many young Australians looking to the territory as the place to 'have a go'. But it is the locals, the Crocodile Dundee-style characters, who make the Territory such a refreshing change from the rest of Australia.

History

Unlike the rest of Australia, the Northern Territory owes much of its history, character and orientation to its proximity to Southeast Asia. (Darwin is closer to Hong Kong than Sydney, and Jakarta and Singapore are only a couple of hours away.) Many anthropologists believe that the Aborigines first arrived on the Australian continent in today's Northern Territory. During the last Ice Age, or roughly 40,000 years ago, lower seas provided a land bridge between the continent and Southeast Asia that allowed migration to take place. When the seas rose, these newcomers were cut off from the rest of the world and evolved their own unique culture. With an entire continent to explore, they showed no interest in building boats and heading back.

There was a further flow from Southeast Asia in relatively more recent times, around 500 years ago. By the 15th century, Macassar traders in present-day Indonesia regularly visited the Northern Territory coast to collect sea-slug (*bêche-de-mer*) and sandalwood. Such goods ended up as far away as China, then a naval power in its own right, doubtless touching off the early tales of a mythical Southland. Relations with the Macassars were good. In return for iron knives, fish hooks and glass bottles, the Aborigines helped them with their annual harvest. Some even married and returned home with these visitors, while other contacts brought new words into the Aborigines' vocabulary. Among the more fascinating rock paintings discovered at Kakadu, east of Darwin, are several showing the Macassars in their distinctive sailing vessels. More importantly for their eventual survival, such external contacts also made the Top End's Aborigines the most resistant to European settlement.

When the Dutch colonized the East Indies in the early 17th century, this trade was closed down. As elsewhere in what they had labelled New Holland, their explorations along the continent's northern coast between 1606 and 1656 found little of immediate economic value. The Dutch did not settle, but their legacy lives on today in several place names, such as Arnhemland, Groote Eylandt and Van Diemen Gulf.

The Dutch were followed by the British who, after setting up the penal colony of New South Wales in 1788, began to explore the continent. As part of his epic circumnavigation of Australia between 1802 and 1804 (see page 44), Captain Matthew Flinders charted the Territory's coastline. (His old nemesis from South Australia's Encounter Bay, the French explorer Nicholas Baudin, see page 157, also passed by in 1803, naming several features.) But no attempt to settle the region was made until 1824 when, fearful of French annexation and growing Dutch trade, the British took formal possession and built a settlement at Port Essington on the Coburg Peninsula, northeast of present-day Darwin. Their ambition was to build a city to rival Singapore and serve as an entrepôt in the lucrative Far East trade. But this, and three other attempts between 1824 and 1868 to establish a permanent settlement on Australia's northern coast, were all dismal failures. They were the first Europeans to learn at first-hand the unforgiving nature of this harsh and isolated region.

These early settlers left behind a curious legacy, the Asian water buffalo. Turned loose by the departing settlers, these animals proliferated in their new—and predator-free—surroundings, taking over vast tracts of the Top End. Today, the animal is the unofficial symbol of the Northern Territory, featuring in a wide range of souvenirs—and the odd meal—for visitors. But because their large numbers have severely damaged the natural landscape, and to prevent the spread of brucellosis and tuberculosis, the wild herds are gradually being wiped out, domesticated, or exported back to Asia. Certainly, in a land of 'macho' characters, none have quite the swagger, or glamour, of the Territory's famous buffalo-catchers, who use high-powered four-wheel-drive vehicles to chase down and then physically grapple the buffaloes to the ground.

Attempts by European explorers to reach Australia's northern coast by an overland route were also full of frustrations. After an epic 5,000-kilometre (3,100-mile) journey that took 14 months, the German-born explorer Ludwig Leichhardt reached Port Essington from Brisbane in 1845 by skirting the rugged western edge of the Gulf of Carpentaria. But the opening up of the Northern Territory to European settlement was due primarily to the South Australian-based explorer John McDouall Stuart, who, after two earlier attempts, successfully crossed the continent for the first time in 1862 (see page 159). In his four and a half years of exploration, Stuart covered vast areas of the Territory and faced the constant threat of attacks by Aborigines. Largely on the basis of his exploration, the colony of South Australia took over the administration of the Territory from the British in 1863.

The new administrators were able to establish a permanent settlement in the Territory with the creation of Palmerston, later renamed Darwin, in 1869. Another early success was the construction of the Overland Telegraph along Stuart's trail from Adelaide to Darwin between 1870 and 1872. (As noted elsewhere, the project introduced camels to the Outback; they too were turned loose and proliferate throughout the Centre.)

But South Australian officials had considerable difficulty in attracting serious settlers to the Northern Territory. Land sales, the key to the earlier successful settlement of South Australia, never took off, and initial attempts to raise sheep on the vast stretches of grassland failed miserably. Cattle proved more successful, although always at the whim of drought, flood, fire and disease. But then, as now, there was always a handful who came seeking adventure—and fortune. The population, including thousands of Chinese, surged briefly when gold was discovered around Pine Creek in the early 1870s but dwindled quickly when the fields were exhausted. Only the hardiest stayed on, either on vast stations—some as large as 12,000 square kilometres (4,600 square miles)—or in small towns. Even Darwin barely grew in its first 100 years.

Unlike other parts of Australia, the land-hungry settlers also met strong resistance from the native Aborigines, thousands of whom were killed in massacres. In the most notorious case in August 1928, now known as the Coniston Massacre, some 70 Aborigines were hunted down and killed by police 260 kilometres (160 miles) northwest of Alice Springs after they had slaughtered several cattle during a severe drought. (The public outcry finally forced such expeditions to end, but it is still possible to find elderly Aborigines who recall the massacre.) More Aborigines starved to death when deprived of their traditional hunting grounds or died from diseases introduced by the newcomers. By the 1930s, most of the surviving Aborigines were settled on to Christian-run missions, often on the least valuable land. Today, nearly half of the Territory is back in Aboriginal hands, mostly reserves, and their population is gradually recovering.

Despite the best efforts of the South Australian government, the Northern Territory remained largely undeveloped—and underpopulated. When the Federal government took over the Territory's administration in 1911, its non-Aboriginal population was less than 3,500. But the politicians in far-away Melbourne, then the national capital, had no better luck. The Northern Territory continued to be an enormous drain on national budgetary resources—as it is even today. (This remains the largest inhibitor against full statehood for the Territory.) For four years in the late 1920s, they even tried to split the place in two, with the 20th parallel forming a division between the administrative units of Central and North Australia. But there was halting progress, such as the completion of the old *Ghan* railway into Alice Springs and the extension of the Darwin line south to Katherine. Roads were rudimentary at best.

The Second World War changed all that. And, once again, it was the Territory's promixity to Southeast Asia that came into play. After bombing Pearl Harbor in December 1941, the Japanese moved quickly to expand their position in Asia, moving rapidly south into the Indonesian archipelago. Darwin was wide open to attack. On 19 February 1942, Japanese aircraft launched a devastating bombing raid on the port, township and nearby airbase. Hundreds of people, including soldiers, fled south in panic. Over the next 18 months, Darwin was attacked another 63 times, leaving nearly 250 dead. But once calm was restored, Darwin and the Northern Territory assumed a strategic importance that continues to this day. (Guam-based US B-52s regularly transit through Darwin en route to Diego Garcia in the Indian Ocean.) At the same time, new roads and airstrips were built, and the large presence of troops provided a ready market for locally produced vegetables and beef. When the war ended, new settlers moved in.

In 1978, Territorians were granted self-government, but making a viable economic proposition out of the Northern Territory remains an illusion. Heavy federal subsidies keep the place afloat. Cattle is a big industry but there is no widespread agriculture. The Territory is rich in minerals, such as the manganese of Groote Eylandt and the copper of Tennant Creek. But much controversy—from Aborigines, politicians and environmentalists—has dogged the development of the Territory's large reserves of uranium. (Visitors to Kakadu National Park east of Darwin, for example, travel on a road built to service the huge Ranger uranium mine further along the road.) But in recent years, the pressure for economic development for its own sake has become less important because of the Territory's tourism boom. With two million domestic and foreign tourists now visiting the Territory every year, the danger is that its richest resource—its incredible natural beauty—will be destroyed.

Getting Around

The Northern Territory is divided roughly into two sections, the Top End and the Centre. (There are also three other smaller but distinctive areas: the Barkly Tableland and the Gulf Country to the east, and the Victoria River Basin on the west, plus the Simpson and Tanami deserts.) To cover such a vast area is not easy. For a week or ten-day look at the Territory, the best approach is to fly into either Darwin or Alice Springs, explore around by car and then fly on to the next city. With tourism becoming highly organized—and slightly crowded—in the Northern Territory, having a car gives you independence. But there are also some well-run bus tours and, for those with extra time, four-wheel-drive adventures into otherwise inaccessible areas.

One early word of warning: The Territory has lots of flies, especially in summer. T-shirts decorated with big blowflies are a top-selling tourist souvenir. Plus, in the Top End, there are mosquitoes. So, stock up on Aeroguard—the Aussie-made insect repellent.

All major highways into and around the Territory are now bitumized, or paved, and stretch like long black ribbons over the countryside. This is road train country, a land where powerful trucks, complete with 'roo bars and floodlights, barrel down the road pulling up to three trailers behind. (At night, you can see the UFO-like glow of these monsters from 20 kilometres, or 12 miles, away.) These 50-metre- (150-foot-) long giants—hauling petroleum, frozen food and groceries—are the lifeblood of the Territory and need to be treated with extreme caution. When you pass, make sure you have a couple of free kilometres ahead, take a deep breath—and then floor it! (The driver is always ready with an encouraging wave when you finally pass him.)

Animals require further caution, especially at night. (The ubiquitous 'roo bars on all the vehicles are not just for show.) Few stations, or ranches, are fenced, and stray cattle do wander out on to the roads. Then there are kangaroos, camels, donkeys and the occasional herd of 'brumbies', or wild horses. (Road trains have a difficult time stopping, resulting in regular casualties.) Watch your speed and, especially on the very long, straight stretches, concentrate.

The Northern Territory Tourist Commission is an excellent contact point for arranging itineraries, including accommodation. (They have offices in Europe and the United States, as well as in all of Australia's capital cities.) Affiliated tour operators in all major settlements offer everything from day trips through to two- to three-week adventure holidays. (The Territory's famous camel safaris operate out of Alice Springs.) You are not permitted to enter Aboriginal tribal lands without permission, but several operators now specialize in showing these areas to outsiders. They are frequently the most beautiful and pristine in Australia and well worth seeing. (Tours range in duration from half a day to two weeks.) The self-driver has a wide choice from sedans and campers through to four-wheel-drive vehicles. But do buy some reliable maps, make sure you are well equipped, and leave behind any inhibitions about asking people for directions. Most travel is by road, although there is a rail link from the southern states into Alice Springs. There are also aerial tours using light aircraft or helicopters, and numerous river and ocean cruises.

With its tourism boom of recent years, the Territory now offers a wide variety of new or renovated accommodation ranging from five-star to less pricey roadside motels and roadhouses. (The latter are also where you fuel up and meet the 'truckies'.) Plus, especially in the Centre, there is nothing wrong with just camping out under the incomparable southern skies, although it can get a bit chilly in the winter months.

The Territory offers a wide choice of culinary delights, although visitors should avoid eating seafood in the Centre. It is one of the few places in Australia where kangaroo meat can be eaten legally, and restaurants have put a lot of imagination into presentation. (One of the most interesting meals I have tried was a kangaroo 'shepherd's pie' baked in a deep dish.) Buffalo steaks are also tasty, and the Top End's seafood is legendary, especially the succulent barramundi fish and giant prawns, or shrimp. The Territory manufactures its own beer, including the famous two-litre 'Darwin Stubby', and a stop at a rustic pub is always an adventure. ('Dress Code' signs at the door, often quite imaginative, are always worth a souvenir picture.) Wearing cowboy hats and grasping styrofoam 'stubby holders', the locals size up visitors before beginning a conversation. Tea and coffee are not so easy to find, although the roadhouses—which are similar to American truck stops—always have a full pot brewing. (They also serve hardy meals of steak, sausages and chips—usually topped with a couple of fried eggs.) A really unusual attraction is the Hornsby Winery on the outskirts of Alice Springs, the only one in the Territory.

Speaking of food (or 'tucker'), be warned about becoming a meal for the Territory's famous crocodiles. Protected since the mid-1970s, these saltwater creatures have now proliferated into a serious tourist hazard. Colourful signs warn of the danger, but visitors should avoid swimming in shallow creeks. (Reproductions of the universally tagged sign are a popular and readily available tourist souvenir, so do not tear down the signs.) The best way to see crocodiles is from a boat or at a crocodile farm, such as the 7,000-strong Crocodile Farm 20 minutes south of Darwin on the Stuart Highway.

And, if that monster is not enough, those venturing into the ocean during the rainy season need to be careful of 'stingers'. These giant box jellyfish can really ruin a nice day, and their stings can be fatal to children.

Darwin and the Top End

With a population of 75,000, Darwin is the capital and administrative centre of the Northern Territory. Located in the heart of Australia's tropics, this city of broad streets and shady parks sits on a cliff-sided peninsula overlooking a vast harbour and, beyond that, the Timor Sea. Darwin is the Territory's largest city and, as Australia's most northern, it plays a key role in the nation's links with Southeast Asia. (Strategically, Darwin is also extremely important, especially as many Australians see any potential enemy arriving from the north.)

Unlike any other Australian city, Darwin has a close affinity with Asia and even a touch of its atmosphere. This is reflected most obviously in its ethnic mix of Chinese, Indonesians, Malays and Filipinos, many of whom trace their families back to the last century. (The long-serving mayor of Darwin, for example, is a Chinese-Australian, and the weekend open-air markets always feature lots of good Asian tucker.) Casually-dressed businessmen dining at the city's upmarket restaurants talk about sewing up deals in Singapore and Jakarta — not in far-away Sydney and Melbourne. Most locals also prefer nearby Asia to the rest of Australia for their annual holidays. Down at the city's docks, freighters and barges head off to exotic destinations such as Brunei, Ambon and Kota Kinabalu. And coming from the other direction in recent years are the modern descendants of the old Macassar traders — this time under arrest for fishing illegally in Australian waters.

The city's present location was discovered in 1839 by the captain of the *Beagle*, J.C. Wickham, who named it Port Darwin after his former shipmate, the famous naturalist Charles Darwin. But it took another 30 years, and four failed settlements elsewhere in the region, before a town was finally established on the site. Officially known as Palmerston, the locals rebelliously preferred Darwin and the name was finally officially adopted in 1911. Through the Territory's often troubled history, including the Japanese bombings of World War II, Darwin has proved a tough survivor. As recently as 1974, a Christmas Day cyclone destroyed most of the city. With that tempest went a lot of Darwin's tropical colonial charm, especially its older buildings. After Cyclone Tracy, Darwin was totally redesigned and rebuilt. Today, with its skyline of squat airconditioned buildings, Darwin looks like a place just daring the next cyclone to strike.

But behind this slightly impersonal modern façade, Darwin is still charming. Except at the extremes of the two seasons, the climate is warm and pleasant, averaging 32°C (90°F) throughout the year. The atmosphere is relaxed, and the sights and smells are lush and tropical. The streets are lined with palms, flowering acacias and bougainvilleas, while the turquoise-blue Port Darwin is fringed with musky mangrove swamps. The sunsets—short and brilliant—are always worth pausing for, even if it is only to raise your glass on Hotel Darwin's famous patio. The city's accommodation (airconditioned, of course) is comfortable and, with its multicultural face, there is a large variety of restaurants. There is even a casino, the **Diamond Beach Hotel-Casino**, one of two in the Territory.

Not all of the city was destroyed by Cyclone Tracy and a walk around **Historic Darwin** evokes some of the old atmosphere. Located in the southeast of the city, this precinct centres around the **Smith Street Mall**. Its best-known feature is the **Victoria Hotel**, or 'The Vic', which was built in 1894 and last restored in 1978. The pub is a good place to pause for a quick meal or a drink between exploring the nearby souvenir shops and galleries. Walking towards the port, the Mall ends beside the white-colonnaded **Commercial Bank**, another hardy survivor dating from 1884.

Further down Smith Street, **Browns Mart**, now a theatre, has a colourful history as a mining exchange, market, police station and brothel, while across the street the **Old Town Hall** reflects the brief prosperity of the Territory's gold boom in the 1880s. Nearby, the **Tree of Knowledge**, behind the modern **Civic Centre**, is an ancient banyan tree whose spreading leaves and branches have been witness to all that has befallen Darwin. Then, rejoining Smith Street, a short stroll leads past **Christ Church Cathedral**, rebuilt after Cyclone Tracy, and the **Police Station and Old Court House**. From along the **Esplanade**, there are views from the park down to Darwin's wharf—badly bombed during the Second World War—before reaching the city's finest example of colonial architecture, **Government House**. Known as the 'Seven Gables', it was one of Darwin's first buildings, with construction beginning in 1870. Despite its exposed position at the end of the peninsula, the building has survived and is now the residence of the Territory's Administrator, the equivalent of a state governor-general. (The **Hotel Darwin**, another refurbished survivor with its own elegant grounds, is around the Esplanade back towards the city.)

Away from downtown and only a few minutes' drive away, Darwin offers several worthwhile attractions. The most unusual, but certainly the most popular, is the daily 'fish feeding' at **Doctor's Gully** on the northwestern edge of the city. At high tide, thousands of fish congregate and then go into a feeding frenzy as visitors toss bread into the waters. (You are not allowed to catch them, but it provides a unique view of the local fishlife.) Further along, the **Botanical Gardens**—established in 1891 and covering 34 hectares (84 acres)—boast the world's largest collection of palm trees and 400 other species of tropical and subtropical plants. (The Gardens are open seven days a week and a good restaurant serves lunch and dinner.) Nearby, the **Museum of Arts and Natural Sciences**, a modern structure overlooking Fannie Bay, provides an insight into Aboriginal history and arts, plus more modern developments. (Open daily, the museum also has a first-class restaurant.) At **East Point**, a lush tropical reserve about five kilometres (three miles) north of the city, there are numerous reminders of the Japanese bombing of Darwin in 1942 and 1943, including concrete blockhouses, command and observation posts, and the **Artillery Museum**. For history buffs, the museum offers a large and fascinating collection of artifacts, photographs and newspaper clippings from the Second World War period.

To fully appreciate the charms and beauty of the Top End, however, head out of Darwin. Most attractions take a day or less to see. But unless you find the nightlife of Darwin enticing, which takes some doing, it is much more rewarding to leave the place behind for a few days and 'go bush'. There are numerous extended tours out of Darwin (and Alice Springs) to the following destinations, but for the self-driver it is easy to plan your own itinerary without backtracking.

The highlight of any trip to the Top End—and Australia for that matter—is **Kakadu National Park**. Located a leisurely two hours' drive (220 kilometres, or 137 miles) east of Darwin, the Arnhem Highway first passes through the vast flood plains of the Adelaide River with its feral water buffaloes and other wildlife. Then, after a stop at the famous **Bark Hut Inn**, a typical old-style Territorian pub, the entrance to the park is only another 20 minutes away. At 20,000 square kilometres (7,800 square miles), Kakadu is Australia's largest national park and is so unique that when the government applied for its registration on UNESCO's list of World Heritage properties in the late 1970s it qualified on both natural and cultural grounds. In more recent years, the park has become world-famous as the 'Home of Crocodile Dundee'.

Derived from the Gagadju, one of several Aboriginal groups who have occupied the area for at least 25,000 years, the massive park preserves one of the world's most stunning—and varied—tropical environments. Inland, the park's landscape is dominated by the spectacular sandstone escarpment of the **Arnhem Land Plateau**, with its plunging waterfalls and deep gorges surrounded by mini-rain

In The Beginning...

*I*n the beginning the Earth was an infinite and murky plain, separated
from the sky and from the grey salt sea and smothered in a shadowy
twilight. There were neither Sun nor Moon nor Stars. Yet, far away,
lived the Sky-Dwellers: youthfully indifferent beings, human in form but
with the feet of emus, their golden hair glittering like spiders' webs in the
sunset, ageless and unageing, having existed for ever in their green, well-
watered Paradise beyond the Western Clouds.

On the surface of the Earth, the only features were certain hollows
which would, one day, be waterholes. There were no animals and no
plants, yet clustered round the waterholes there were pulpy masses of
matter: lumps of primordial soup—soundless, sightless, unbreathing,
unawake and unsleeping—each containing the essence of life, or the
possibility of becoming human.

Beneath the Earth's crust, however, the constellations glimmered, the
Sun shone, the Moon waxed and waned, and all the forms of life lay
sleeping: the scarlet of a desert-pea, the iridescence on a butterfly's wing,
the twitching white whiskers of Old Man Kangaroo—dormant as seeds
in the des·rt that must wait for a wandering shower.

On the morning of the First Day, the Sun felt the urge to be born.
(That evening the Stars and Moon would follow). The Sun burst through
the surface, flooding the land with golden light, warming the hollows
under which each Ancestor lay sleeping.

Unlike the Sky-Dwellers, these Ancients had never been young. They
were lame, exhausted greybeards with knotted limbs, and they had slept
in isolation through the ages.

So it was, on this First Morning, that each drowsing Ancestor felt the
Sun's warmth pressing on his eyelids, and felt his body giving birth to
children. The Snake Man felt snakes slithering out of his navel. The
Cockatoo Man felt feathers. The Witchetty Grub Man felt a wriggling,
the Honey-ant a tickling, the Honeysuckle felt his leaves and flowers

unfurling. The Bandicoot Man felt baby bandicoots seething from under his armpits. Every one of the 'living things', each at its own separate birthplace, reached up for the light of day.

In the bottom of their hollows (now filling up with water), the Ancients shifted one leg, then another leg. They shook their shoulders and flexed their arms. They heaved their bodies upward through the mud. Their eyelids cracked open. They saw their children at play in the sunshine.

The mud fell from their thighs, like placenta from a baby. Then, like the baby's first cry, each Ancestor opened his mouth and called out, 'I AM!' 'I am - Snake... Cockatoo... Honey-ant... Honeysuckle...' And this first 'I am!', this primordial act of naming, was held, then and forever after, as the most secret and sacred couplet of the Ancestor's song.

Each of the Ancients (now basking in the sunlight) put his left foot forward and called out a second name. He put his right foot forward and called out a third name. He named the waterhole, the reedbeds, the gum trees—calling to right and left, calling all things into being and weaving their names into verses.

The Ancients sang their way all over the world. They sang the rivers and ranges, salt-pans and sand dunes. They hunted, ate, made love, danced, killed: wherever their tracks led they left a trail of music.

They wrapped the whole world in a web of song; and at last, when the Earth was sung, they felt tired. Again in their limbs they felt the frozen immobility of Ages. Some sank into the ground where they stood. Some crawled into caves. Some crept away to their 'Eternal Homes', to the ancestral waterholes that bore them.

All of them went 'back in'.

Bruce Chatwin, The Songlines, 1987

forests. Below, the low-lying hills are covered in grass and woodlands which give way to a network of billabongs and waterways bordered by Pandanus palms and paperbark trees. Finally, these join into a network of rivers—the misnomered **Alligator Rivers**—which meander northwards out into the **Van Diemen Gulf** through mud flats and mangrove swamps. Everywhere throughout the park, the land teams with unmatched plant and wildlife which scientists are still cataloguing. But there is nothing mysterious about the crocodiles. This is the home turf of Australia's famous estuarine or saltwater crocodiles, nicknamed 'saltie', who can be spotted sunning themselves along the riverbanks or cruising along the streams. Swimming is definitely not recommended.

Kakadu's personality changes dramatically with the seasons. During The Wet, from November to March, heavy run-offs from the plateau swell over the riverbanks and flood the wetlands, limiting vehicle access to some sites and raising temperatures to an uncomfortable and muggy 35°C (95°F). Most visitors prefer The Dry, from May to September, when temperatures and humidity drop to a more tolerable level.

With its wide variety of attractions, including its renowned Aboriginal rock art, visitors need more than just a quick one-day visit. (The **Park Information Centre**, near the township of **Jabiru**, makes a good first stop.) The park offers three hotels, including the crocodile-shaped **Four Seasons Kakadu**, and camping sights for overnight accommodation. From these, it is easy to link up with cruises on the **South Alligator River** and **Yellow Water**, or four-wheel-drive tours to spectacular **Jim Jim Falls** which tumbles off the escarpment into a huge waterhole. But no visit to Kakadu is complete without a look at its cultural side, and the park is one of the few places where the original inhabitants retain such strong spiritual links with their land. (Aborigines provide tours and commentaries for visitors.) Over 1,000 art sites have been identified in the park, some of which are believed to date back to when the Aborigines first arrived on the continent 40,000 years ago. The best collections—and most easily accessible—are at **Obiri (Ubirr)** and **Nourlangie Rock**, where painting styles cover thousands of years of Aboriginal history.

Further to the south, the **Katherine Region** offers a different—but almost as dramatic—aspect of the Top End. The region, 350 kilometres (217 miles) southeast of Darwin on the Stuart Highway, can be reached directly by road or air. But for the self-driver, especially after the last destination, a more scenic approach is over the Kakadu Highway. Now being paved, the gravel road runs through the southern end of the park, past the spectacular Arnhem escarpment and then through rolling pastoral country where buffalo, cattle, horses and donkeys graze by the roadside. A brief diversion to **UDP Falls**, also known as **Waterfall Creek Falls**, is well worthwhile and there is a camping ground for those wishing to stay overnight. After about 200 kilometres (124 miles), the highway ends at **Pine Creek**, a historic 1870s mining town where visitors can still pan for gold., Katherine is only another hour's drive away.

The landscape around this more elevated part of the Top End is typical savannah—open grasslands with scattered trees. Ant hills are scattered over the countryside. (The voracious termites' habit of eating the interior of tree branches provides the Aborigines with the finest didgeridoos in Australia.) In The Wet, the grass turns a bright green, dotted here and there with wild orchids and other flowering bushes. Then, in The Dry, everything turns a golden brown and bushfires roar through, enriching the soil for the next season and baring the land's natural features. Despite its flat appearance, there is a hidden mixture of canyons, caves, waterfalls—and even a tropical oasis. The area has a feeling of extreme remoteness, yet intimacy, that has given it the bittersweet nickname of the Never Never Country.

The modern town of **Katherine,** the Territory's third-largest (population 6,000) and site of the vital Tindal Royal Australian Air Force (RAAF) Base, is an excellent spot from which to explore the surrounding region. (The main industry in these parts is cattle, plus some vegetable and fruit farming, although tourism has now become big business.) There is plenty of accommodation, service stations and supermarkets.

Katherine Gorge National Park, 30 kilometres (19 miles) to the northeast, is the region's most famous landmark. Actually a collection of 13 gorges cut through the sandstone plateau, visitors board flat-bottomed boats to explore the first two sections, hiking a short distance between them. From the cool waters of the **Katherine River**, the canyon walls rise steeply up to 60 metres (200 feet), a glowing mix of red and brown against the green of the struggling vegetation. The Johnstone, or freshwater, crocodile—smaller and less dangerous than the 'saltie'—can often be seen lazing in the water or on the riverbank. Ancient Aboriginal rock carvings can also be spotted at several places. Following a ten-year controversy which angered many Territory whites, the Aborigines gained control of the park in 1985 and now help in its management. Closer to Katherine, don't miss the **Springvale Homestead**, the area's oldest building and a pleasant overnight stop, and the oddly named **Katherine Low Level Nature Park**, with its swimming holes and tree-lined riverbanks. In the town itself, the **MiMi Aboriginal Arts and Crafts Centre** is worth a browse.

(At Katherine, the Victoria Highway, part of Australia's Route

One, heads off to the Kimberley region of Western Australia. A popular holiday destination for many Top Enders is the tiny settlement of **Kununurra**, 500 kilometres, or 310 miles, from Katherine. See page 228.)

On the other side of Katherine, 30 kilometres (19 miles) to the south, are the **Cutta Cutta Caves**, a spectacular labyrinth of limestone formations; rangers conduct guided tours twice daily (10.30 am and 1.30 pm). **Mataranka**, 100 kilometres (62 miles) south of Katherine, provides another contrasting side to the Top End. Within easy walking distance of this historic homestead, which now provides meals and accommodation, are the famous **Mataranka Thermal Pools**. In the middle of a hot day in the tropics, a dip in the warm waters surrounded by a lush rain forest might sound a bit silly, but you will climb out feeling years younger and ready for some more exploring. Immortalized by the Australian classic, *We of the Never Never* by Jeannie Gunn, the first European woman to live here, the area has a rich pioneering history that is best reflected at the **Old Elsey Cemetery**. Only 15 minutes from Mataranka, the dusty graveyard says much about those tough early days of European settlement. (Gunn's highly readable book is available at souvenir shops throughout the region.)

Heading back up the Stuart Highway, **Umbrawarra Gorge**, west of Pine Creek, and the **Butterfly Gorge Nature Park** make good picnic spots on the return to Darwin. **Adelaide River** has a dramatic and moving tribute to the region's devastation during the Second World War in its well-groomed **Memorial Cemetery**, the final resting place for civilians and soldiers killed in the Darwin bombings. Nearby **Batchelor**, just off the highway, was a wartime American training centre and is now the gateway to scenic **Litchfield Park**—a mini-Kakadu—further to the west. (Still relatively unknown, the park is worth a look, even if you are just popping down from Darwin for the day.) Then, back near the junction of the Stuart and Arnhem highways, drop in at the **Crocodile Park**, some 40 kilometres (25 miles) out of Darwin. The management boasts an incredible 7,000 of the reptiles in residence. After that, you will know you are almost back in Darwin when you spot the **World's Largest Buffalo**—a popular tourist stop for water buffalo-related souvenir products.

In Between

There is very much of a transition zone between the Top End and the Centre. The Territorians bill this as **the Tablelands**. This region starts not far south of Mataranka and the topography is that of a rising plateau. Vegetation is sparse and the rugged landscape is littered with huge rocks—most dramatically at the **Devils Marbles** near **Wauchope**. There is little to break the monotony of the countryside. But for the adventurous self-driver who wants to drive between Darwin and The Alice, there are some memorable stops along the way, such as **Daly Water's** two pubs and the memorials to white explorers. The largest settlement, roughly halfway, is **Tennant Creek** (population 3,000), a still-functioning gold and copper town. (From here, the Barkly Highway heads off east through the desolation to Queensland.) Eventually—after a good day's drive—the dark ridges of the Macdonnell Ranges appear on the horizon and the traveller enters Australia's magic centre.

Alice Springs and the Centre

Forced to choose my one favourite place in Australia, I would have to pick the Centre. There is a mixture of light and colour here which is seen nowhere else—making the place and the people uniquely Australian. This special atmosphere is easily absorbed by the visitor and it is rare that one leaves without some very pleasant memories. The secret to exploring the Centre is to have plenty of time and to go for more than just the standard tourist circuit of Alice Springs, Ayers Rock and the Olgas. There are hidden pockets of beauty all over the vast landscape. Especially for the self-driver, there are many opportunities to revel in one's own insignificance.

Located near the geographical centre of the continent, Alice Springs is the Territory's second-largest settlement, with a population of 23,000. 'The Alice' is also Australia's most famous—or at least most romantic—town, as immortalized in Neville Shute's post-war novel, *A Town Like Alice*, later made into a successful television mini-series. Set just north of a gorge which cuts through the magnificent **Macdonnell Ranges**, the town is an oasis with broad tree-lined streets, grassy parks and comfortable homes. (Perversely, Alice Springs is also Australia's number one nuclear target because of the 'spy base' at nearby **Pine Gap**—a top-secret American-run installation tapped into a host of spy satellites. You will certainly hear about it and even run into the odd close-mouthed Yank. They are easily identified by their American-built left-hand-drive vehicles.)

Physically, Alice Springs is laid out on a simple grid and has a small hill at each end of town, **Billy Goat Hill** and **Anzac Hill**. (The latter offers a particularly nice view of the town's setting.) To one side of downtown runs the dry bed of the **Todd River** with its distinctive ghost gums, often with clusters of Aborigines sheltering in the shade. With the imposing red- and orange-coloured ramparts of the Macdonnell

Ranges as a backdrop, and surrounded by rolling sparsely wooded countryside, there is a comfortable—even cosy feeling—about The Alice.

The Alice owes its existence to the Overland Telegraph (see pages 159 and 227) which linked Australia to the world for the first time in the 1870s. Because of a small spring and waterhole about three kilometres (1.8 miles) north of the present town, the region was chosen as the site of an important repeater station for the transcontinental telegraph line. Now a historic reserve, the **Old Telegraph Station** is well worth a look. The original sandstone buildings have been restored, and there is a small museum. (Alice, by the way, was the wife of the South Australian Superintendent of Telegraphs, Charles Todd, after whom the river was named.) The flatter land around the present town was surveyed out as a railhead and, as the terminus of camel caravans from Oodnadatta (see page 191), it turned into a Wild West sort of place known as Stuart, after the famous explorer. When the trains finally arrived in 1929, it began to grow, and when the nearby telegraph station was closed down three years later, the locals officially changed the name to Alice Springs.

Today, with a wide range of accommodation and eateries, Alice Springs makes an excellent base from which to venture out into the surrounding vastness. The town also has several attractions of its own, including a heritage walk through its oldest part. As such things go, the **Todd Street Mall** is quite tasteful and, once the visitor slows to the local pace, there are many quality museums, galleries and boutiques in which to browse. (Also, of course, there are a couple of giant airconditioned shopping centres and supermarkets—great for stocking up before a trip.) In addition to the historic buildings, such as the **Old Stuart Gaol**, **Adelaide House** and the **Flynn Memorial Church**, many visitors enjoy dropping by the **Panorama Gurth** in Hartley Street, a 360-degree painted landscape of the Centre. Otherwise, there are some passable restaurants and, slightly out of town, the local **casino**. Alice Springs is famous for some of Australia's most colourful festivals—such as the annual camel-racing carnival in May and the Henley-On-Todd Regatta and Beerfest in October. The latter features races with bottomless boats along the dry Todd River bed and, of course, much laughter.

A notable feature of Alice Springs, especially compared to other Australian cities, is the large number of Aborigines—probably about half the local population—walking in the streets, shopping or just hanging out. Most depressing are the alcoholic Aborigines who drink themselves into a stupor and then fall asleep in the open. (Interestingly, most whites deliberately ignore their presence, and there is

very little obvious public socializing between the two races.) At the same time, however, the town is at the heart of the Aborigines' cultural renaissance. Galleries are full of Papunya School paintings and wooden carvings, and the local commercial television station is owned and operated by Aborigines. They also run an extensive multi-language radio, video and cassette network into distant black out-stations. If you are sincerely interested in visiting Aboriginal settlements, it is relatively easy to link up with the right people, including getting the necessary permits. Certainly, my best trip to the Centre was to the Aboriginal settlement at **Haasts Bluff**, a slightly gruelling six-hour drive—the last half through dirt and sand—west of Alice Springs, returning by way of Hermannsburg. When the hired four-wheel drive acted up, there was a tough bush mechanic out there to fix it. And the Aborigines warmly welcomed me as their guest.

Near Alice Springs, there are a couple of attractions. Just outside town, do not miss the **Frontier Camel Farm** which offers rides and cuddles with these lovely-eyelashed animals. There is also **Chateau Hornsby**, the Centre's only winery, which offers wine tastings and barbecued meals. (Hardly a wine connoisseur, I found the drop quite marvellous, although it could have been just the amazing desert atmosphere!) The **Araluen Arts Centre**, **Diarama Village** and the **Pitchi Richi Sanctuary** are also worth seeing, plus there is even a *Ghan railway museum*.

The ultimate scenic prize of this region is, of course, **Ayers Rock** and the **Olgas**, or—as they are starting to become known in their original names—**Uluru** and **Katatjuta**. But you should save that for last, and first spend a few days exploring other places. There is a wide choice.

If you are in the Centre in early August, do take the three- to four-hour drive northwest of Alice Springs (270 kilometres, or 168 miles) to the **Yuendumu Festival** when more than 2,000 tribal Aborigines hold an annual cultural and sports festival. The traditional chanting and dancing goes on for several days. Since April 1988, the Aboriginal-owned cattle station offers the world's most remote museum and art gallery where 'Men Only' are allowed to gaze upon a traditional sand painting preserved indoors. (Papunya paintings, modern acrylic renditions of this art form, are now a big hit in London and New York.)

But the more popular touring spots are east and west of Alice Springs, along the back of the Macdonnell Ranges with its mixture of gaps or chasms, nature parks, and old homesteads and mines. These make excellent day trips and, for those who venture out to the end of the road, there is always rustic but comfortable accommodation.

(Ordinary two-wheel-drive vehicles are fine, although some areas can be accessed only by four-wheel drives.) Of the two directions, however, **Namatjira Drive** to the west of town certainly offers more attractions. **Simpson's Gap**, located in a national park, is only 15 minutes away, but there is a richer collection further along, such as at **Standley Chasm** and the **Serpentine Gorge Nature Park**. The landscape includes wide meadows that blossom with flowers after a drop of rain. At the end of the paved road, **Glen Helen Tourist Resort** overlooking the **Finke River**—the world's oldest river—makes a nice overnight stop. To the west, the land opens up and looming **Mt Zeil**, the Territory's highest peak at 1,510 metres (5,000 feet), lies another 40 kilometres (25 miles) away. (Haasts Bluff and Papunya are inside the adjoining Aboriginal reserve.)

Due south of Glen Helen on the other side of the Ranges, but requiring a drive most of the way back to Alice Springs, is **Hermannsburg**, a once spartan and strict mission station established by German Lutherans in 1877. Located 120 kilometres (75 miles) southwest of Alice Springs, it is today an Aboriginal-run settlement, and many old residents have moved away to out-stations on their traditional lands. With its squat whitewashed buildings and church, it is worth a brief stop before heading into the **Finke Gorge National Park**, 20 kilometres (12 miles) to the south. Preserved as a wilderness area, the rough four-wheel-drive track follows the dry riverbed which is lined with the ubiquitous ghost gum plus other vegetation. After bouncing over a rocky, almost back-wrenching, track you arrive at mysterious **Palm Valley**, an oasis of unique cabbage palms that have remained unchanged for the past 10,000 years. (They reflect an era when central Australia was once a tropical paradise; only 3,000 or so survive in a 60-kilometre, or 37-mile, radius.) Nearby, the landscape is dominated by a huge and breathtaking amphitheatre of red sandstone cliffs and rocky outcrops, such as **Shield Rock**, an ancient Aboriginal initiation site. A thorough look around takes a couple of hours. (It is also possible to do a one-day four-wheel-drive tour to the valley for about A$50.)

Finally, on the road to Ayers Rock and the Olgas, roughly 450 kilometres (280 miles) southwest of Alice Springs, a number of attractions break up the monotony of what can be a five-hour drive. About 100 kilometres (62 miles) to the south on the Stuart Highway, the **Virginia Camel Farm** is the home of the legendary Noel Fullerton, who has caught and domesticated a large herd of camels for safaris into the Outback. The safaris last from several hours to a couple of weeks, with the longest heading as far away as Palm Valley. A shorter run— by camel or four-wheel drive—goes to spectacular **Rainbow Valley**,

with its multi-coloured sandstone ridges jutting out of the flat landscape. It is particularly beautiful at sunset. Another 30 kilometres (19 miles) further south, the **Henbury Meteorites National Reserve**— comprising 12 craters, the largest being twice the size of a football field—also marks the turn-off for a dirt and gravel road leading due west to **King's Canyon**, a back-road way to 'The Rock'. A three-hour drive away, this impressive canyon cuts a mighty swath through solid sandstone, leaving behind huge multi-coloured walls and gigantic boulders. Back towards the highway, **Wallara Ranch** provides comfortable accommodation and marks the junction of a dirt road leading south to Ayers Rock.

The Lasseter Highway, about 80 kilometres (50 miles) south of the Henbury Meteorites, is the more commonly used route into the **Uluru National Park**—home of **Ayers Rock** and the **Olgas**. (Regular flights also operate into the park from Alice Springs airport and other state capitals.) Finally paved in the mid-1980s, the road—and improved accommodation in the park—has done much to improve access to what are clearly Australia's most famous landmarks. From the turn-off at **Erldunda,** the 235-kilometre- (146-mile-) long highway passes through a desert countryside that varies widely from dense scrub to bare red dirt, with the pincushion-like spinifex and dark green desert oaks providing the most dramatic vegetation. There are two roadhouses along the way—at **Mt Ebenezer** and **Curtin Springs**—just in case you get stranded or Uluru is full. Also, visitors are warned not to get too excited when they see **Mt Connor** to the south of the highway. Many mistake this crusty mountain for Ayers Rock itself.

Whether you are arriving by air or by road, Ayers Rock is surely one of the most majestic sights in the world. Either way, the brooding rock can be spotted from miles away across the flat landscape. With its sheer sides rising dramatically above the surrounding plain, the rock is actually the tip of a giant monolith—the world's largest—formed about 500 million years ago and now almost entirely covered by debris and sand. Composed mostly of aggregated sand, gravel and rocks, Ayers Rock rises to a height of 348 metres (1,142 feet) above the surrounding plains and is nearly nine kilometres (six miles) in circumference.

About 30 kilometres (19 miles) to the west rise another collection of monoliths known as the Olgas. Dominated by the even higher **Mt Olga** at 546 metres (1,792 feet), the rock formation is 22 kilometres (14 miles) in circumference. Appropriately, the Aborigines call these *Katatjura*, or 'Many Heads'. The colours and moods of these great natural wonders change throughout the day and are especially dramatic at sunrise and sunset. It is easy to understand the Aborigines' strong spiritual attachment to this landscape.

The first European to pass through the region was the South Australian-based explorer Ernest Giles in 1872, who named Mt Olga after the Queen of Spain. The next year, explorer William Gosse led an expedition to the Rock and named it after the colony's premier, Sir Henry Ayers. These explorers were soon followed by miners, dingo hunters and missionaries, and eventually large cattle and sheep stations were established in the region. Not surprisingly, there were frequent clashes with the local Aborigines, many of whom were forced into missions as droughts and grazing depleted resources. Despite such treatment, their culture and traditions survived and, when mass tourism began to develop in the early 1970s, they launched a long legal battle to protect this sacred region. In a landmark move in 1985 that was bitterly resented by many Territory whites, the Aborigines were formally given title to what is now called the Uluru National Park. At the same time, Ayers Rock and the Olgas were formally renamed to Uluru and Katatjuta, their traditional names. The park was immediately leased back to the government and is now run as a joint enterprise.

The arrangement has worked well, despite occasional reports that the Aborigines are not getting enough royalties, and today has developed into one of Australia's best-run tourist complexes. When I first visited the Rock in 1982, accommodation—clustered around its base—was rudimentary at best, and most visitors simply camped out for the night. But after the Rock was turned over to the Aborigines in 1985, all these tourist facilities were destroyed and replaced with the **Yulara Tourist Village**, a discreet 20 kilometres (12 miles) from Uluru. The ultra-modern complex, with its own solar-powered heating and desalination system, is tastefully tucked away behind low sandhills and offers everything from first-class hotels through to serviced camping sites. (It is also the only place visitors are allowed to stay near the park.)

Many visitors make the mistake of trying to see Ayers Rock and the Olgas all in one day. But, like Kakadu National Park, they really need at least two full days—and preferably up to four—to be appreciated fully. It is easy to become totally relaxed in this magnificent desert setting and there is much to see.

Before venturing out into the park, drop by the **Visitors Centre** inside the Yulara Resort which offers a wealth of displays and information on the park, including its wildlife, landscape and Aboriginal culture. The Centre also provides several Ranger Tours by the Conservation Commission of the Northern Territory, such as 'The Edible Desert' tour, pointing out traditional foods and medicines used by Aborigines, and 'Down Under the Southern Stars', an

(Right) Noel Fullerton runs camel safaris out of Alice Springs
(Below) A ghost gum grows out of the sandstone
of Palm Valley, central Australia

incomparable look at the constellations and Aboriginal legends of the southern skies. Closer to the Rock, the Liru Tour—a two-hour tour conducted by Aboriginal and non-Aboriginal rangers—is highly recommended. Behind the Entry Station to the park, the Aboriginal-run **Maruku Arts and Crafts Complex** provides not only an exhibition of traditional crafts but also an opportunity to visit with the artisans themselves. A film show tells the story of the Aborigines' deep attachment to this land, including explanations of their legends. The visitor also soon finds that the surrounding desert is hardly barren, supporting a rich variety of plant and animal life. For example, there are over 400 species of flowers, shrubs and trees—with new ones recorded all the time—which provide a lush home for reptiles, birds and mammals. Of particular fascination are several aquatic crustaceans—for example, the Shield Shrimp, often found in rock pools atop Ayers Rock after rain. These creatures have remained unchanged for over 150 million years.

Visitors to Ayers Rock and the Olgas do need to take a few precautions. Take along plenty of drinking water, and wear protective clothing, including a hat, to ward off the blazing sun. A light jacket, especially in the winter months, is also sensible. You are also warned that sacred sites are of particular importance to the Aborigines and are off-limits to outsiders. Elsewhere, be careful about touching Aboriginal art sites and venturing off the marked tracks.

The vegetation is so sensitive that it takes years, even decades, to recover from trampling feet.

The Aborigines have always been baffled—if not a little insulted—by visitors' fascination with climbing Uluru, but it is something that many rush off to do as soon as they arrive. Assuming you are reasonably fit and healthy, the one-hour climb to the top is an extremely rewarding—even spiritual—experience. (The worst part is right at the beginning as climbers struggle up the steep side of the Rock along a safety chain, but caution needs to be exercised throughout the climb.) Once on the top, many visitors are surprised that it is not flat. Instead, the path to the cairn, where climbers can sign the guest book, undulates through a collection of shallow ravines. Near the cairn, there is even a tiny cave and several hardy trees. The view out over the surrounding countryside stretches for more than 150 kilometres (90 miles), taking in the Olgas and a host of other lonely peaks and mountain ranges. For the less energetic, there are several marked walking tracks around the base of the Rock.

The Olgas, located about an hour's drive to the west over a rough unpaved road, offer a fascinating contrast to Ayers Rock. (In fact, old Outback veterans frequently disagree over which is more attractive, so you will simply have to see both!) Dating from the same geological era and once a gigantic rock many times the size of Ayers Rock, the Olgas—or Katatjuta—are a collection of 36 individual domes rising from the flat desert floor. When a fascinated Giles first explored the Olgas in 1873, he recorded in his journal that they appeared like 'rounded minarets, giant cupolas and monstrous domes'. Dominated by Mt Olga, the sharply rising domes are dissected by shaded gorges that shelter unique plant life, while trees and shrubs flourish along crevices where water and soil have collected.

There are several marked tracks, including a two-hour walk to the **Katatjuta Lookout**, with spectacular views of Ayers Rock, the dry saltpans of Lake Amadeus and far-away mountain ranges. Although shorter, the trail through **Olga Gorge** is difficult and slow but is also well worthwhile. But with no local accommodation available, it is important to keep track of time and not become stranded.

To round off your visit, a **scenic flight** by fixed-wing plane or helicopter over Ayers Rock and the Olgas is highly recommended, especially in the late afternoon or at sunset. At last count, four companies provide this service from the Yulara airstrip—and at a most reasonable price.

Useful Addresses

Outside Australia

The Australian Tourist Commission, or ATC, a federally-funded body, actively promotes tourism to the country and has 11 offices overseas. The Commission is an excellent first-stop contact for intending visitors. In addition to handling queries, the offices will mail out the *Destination Australia Book*, a comprehensive 130-page booklet printed in six languages. As a joint publishing venture with tourist-related companies, the guide includes up-to-date details on accommodation and tours throughout Australia.

In addition, several Australian state governments operate their own travel information offices in several countries. They are useful for more detailed information about each state. While most are not in a position to make reservations, their officers can suggest itineraries, tours and accommodation before your departure. They can also put you in touch with their head offices in Australia, or you can write to them direct at the addresses provided below under the separate state and territory listings.

Australian Tourist Commission and state tourist body offices are listed immediately below:

Australian Tourist Commission

Sydney (Head Office)
Level 3, 80 William Street, Woolloomooloo, NSW 2011. Tel. (02) 360-1111.

North America
Los Angeles
Suite 1200, 2121 Avenue of the Stars, Los Angeles, CA 90067. Tel. (213) 552-1988.

New York
31st Floor, 489 Fifth Avenue, New York, NY 10017. Tel. (212) 687-6300.

Chicago
Suite 2130, 150 North Michigan Avenue, Chicago, IL 60601. Tel. (312) 781-5159.

Toronto, Canada
Suite 1730, 2 Bloor Street West, Toronto, Ontario M4W 3E2. Tel. (416) 925-9575.

Asia
Hong Kong
Suite 604–5, Sun Plaza, Canton Road, Tsimshatsui, Kowloon. Tel. (3) 311-1555.

Singapore
Suite 1703, 17th Floor, United Square, 101 Thomson Road, Singapore, 1130.
Tel. (65) 255-4555.

Japan
8th Floor, Sankaido Building, 9–13 Akasaka 1-chome, Minato-ku, Tokyo 107.
Tel. (03) 582-2191.

4th Floor, Yuki Building, 4–56 Hirano-machi, Higashi-ku, Osaka 541. Tel.
(06) 229-3601.

New Zealand
15th Floor, Quay Tower, 29 Customs Street West, Auckland 1. Tel. (09) 79-
9594.

Europe
London
Gemini House, 10–18 Putney Hill, Putney, London SW15. Tel. (01) 780-2227.

Frankfurt
Neue Mainzerstrasse 22, D6000 Frankfurt/Main 1, Federal Republic of
Germany. Tel. (069) 23-5071.

Tourism Commission of New South Wales
Sydney (Head Office)
Shell House, 140 Phillip Street, Sydney, NSW 2000. Tel. (02) 231-7100.

Britain
NSW House, 66 The Strand, London WC2N 5LZ. Tel. (01) 839-6651.

United States
New South Wales Government Office, Suite 2250, 2049 Century Park East,
Los Angeles, CA 90067. Tel. (213) 552-9566.

New Zealand
15th Floor, Quay Tower, 29 Customs Street West, Auckland 1. Tel. (09) 79-9118.

Japan
Suite 525–6, 5th Floor, Fuji Building, 2–3 Marunouchi, 3-chome, Chiyoda-ku,
Tokyo. Tel. (03) 215-3969.

Victour, Victorian Tourism Commission

Melbourne (Head Office)
Building D, World Trade Centre, Cnr Flinders and Spencer Streets,
Melbourne, Vic. 3000. Tel. (03) 619-9444.

Britain and Europe
c/o Office of Agent-General for Victoria, Victoria House, Melbourne Place,
The Strand, London WC2B 4LG. Tel. (01) 836-2656.

United States
Suite 1270, 2121 Avenue of the Stars, Los Angeles, CA 90067. Tel. (213) 553-6352.

Canada
Suite 220, 120 Eglinton Avenue East, Toronto, Ontario M4P IE2. Tel. (416) 487-1151.

Japan
Suite 304, Tokyo Chamber of Commerce and Industry Building, 3-2-2
Marunouchi, Chiyoda-ku, Tokyo 100. Tel. (03) 213-3061.

Southeast Asia
Unit 17–03, Goldhill Square, 101 Thomson Road, Singapore, 1130. Tel. (65) 255-6888.

New Zealand
15th Floor, Quay Tower, 29 Customs Street West, Auckland 1. Tel. (09) 79-4566.

Tasbureau (Tasmanian Tourist Bureau)

Hobart (Head Office)
6th Floor, Marine Board Building, 1 Franklin Wharf, Hobart, Tas. 7000. Tel.
(002) 30-0211.

North America
Suite 1200T, 2121 Avenue of the Stars, Los Angeles, CA 90067. Tel. (213) 552-3010.

Japan
c/o Tourism Australia, 8th Floor, Sankaido Building, 9–13 Akasaka 1-chome, Minato-ku, Tokyo 107. Tel. (03) 582-2789.

New Zealand
15th Floor, Quay Tower, 29 Custom Street West, Auckland 1. Tel. (09) 79-5535.
ATC offices in London, New York, Frankfurt and Singapore also provide information on Tasmania.

Western Australian Tourism Commission
Perth (Head Office)
772 Hay Street, Perth, WA 6000. Tel. (09) 322-2999.

Britain and Europe
Western Australia House, 115 The Strand, London WC2R OAJ. Tel. (01) 240-6637.

North America
Suite 1210, 2121 Avenue of the Stars, Los Angeles, CA 90067. Tel. (213) 557-1987.

Japan
8th Floor, Sankaido Building, 9–13 Akasaka 1-chome, Minato-ku, Tokyo 107. Tel. (03) 582-2677.

Hong Kong
Room 615, Swire House, 11 Chater Road, Central, Hong Kong. Tel. (5) 21-0666.

Malaysia
6th Floor, UBN Building, Letterbox 51, 10 Jalan P. Ramlee, 50250, Kuala Lumpur. Tel. (03) 232-1248.

Singapore
Unit 03–03, Thong Sia Building, 30 Bideford Road, Singapore. Tel. (65) 732-8187.

New Zealand
P.O. Box 4515, Auckland 1. Tel. (09) 37-0268.

Queensland Tourist and Travel Corporation
Brisbane (Head Office)
123 Eagle Street, Brisbane, Qld 4000. Tel. (07) 833-5400.

Britain and Europe
Queensland House, 392–3 The Strand, London WC2N 5LZ. Tel. (01) 836-3224.

North America
611 North Larchmont Boulevard, Los Angeles, CA. Tel. (213) 465-8418.

Japan
Suite 1303, Yurakucho Denki Building, 7–1 Yurakucho 1-chome, Chiyoda-ku, Tokyo. Tel. (03) 201-7861.

New Zealand
9th Floor, Quay Tower, 29 Customs Street West, Auckland 1. Tel. (09) 39-6421.

In Australia

Within Australia, each state and territory has **travel centres** in its capital city. Most also operate such centres in other state and territory capitals. As noted throughout this guide, these centres are extremely helpful and will book tours, accommodation and transport. (The addresses of these centres are listed separately under each state and territory listing below.)

Australia offers visitors a wide range of accommodation, and the **hotels** listed below represent the top of the range. But, as hotels can be quite costly, more budget conscious visitors should consider other options, such as less-expensive hotels or motels. As the top-priced hotels are mostly in downtown areas, visitors can make considerable savings by staying in outer suburbs, such as Sydney's Manly or Bondi, and then travelling into the city during the day. Especially during the week and outside school holiday periods, visitors travelling around the country can often find hotel or motel accommodation without reservations. But just to be safe, do book ahead through a state travel centre or a motel chain, such as Flag Inns or Best Western Homestead Motor Inns, which offer nationwide booking services. Also, do not overlook pubs (also known as hotels) which often have rooms available for the night, even if the washroom facilities are often located down the hall. (After checking in, you can mix with the locals in the downstairs bar.) On-site vans offer an even cheaper option. These are caravans, or trailers, which can be hired for the night—or the week—with shared toilet facilities. (While cutlery is provided, you have to supply your own bed linen.)

The **restaurants** listed below also represent the top of the range and are recommended as much for their fantastic views as for their cuisine. Further recommendations can be found in the 'Good Food Guides' published in all major cities and available from local newsagencies or bookshops. Also, don't be shy about asking around or doing your own exploring. In many country towns, the best restaurants are often at local motels. Restaurants licensed BYO, for 'Bring Your Own', require patrons to bring their own liquor, usually available at a nearby 'bottle shop'.

Other information listed below includes major tour operators, airlines, and rail and bus operators in each state and territory.

New South Wales

Hotels

The Regent of Sydney, 199 George Street, Sydney, NSW 2000. Tel. (02) 238-0000.

Hotel Inter-Continental, 117 Macquarie Street, Sydney, NSW 2000. Tel. (02) 230-0200.

Sheraton-Wentworth Hotel, 61–101 Phillip Street, Sydney, NSW 2000. Tel. (02) 230-0700.

Ramada Renaissance Hotel, 30 Pitt Street, Sydney, NSW 2000. Tel. (02) 259-7000.

Restaurants

Doyles on the Beach, 11 Marine Parade, Watson's Bay, NSW 2030. Tel. (02) 337-1350.

Bennelong Restaurant, Sydney Opera House, Bennelong Point, Sydney, NSW 2000. Tel. (02) 241-1371.

The Manor House, 393 Darling Street, Balmain, NSW 2041. Tel. (02) 810-4914.

The Boulevard Restaurant, 25th Floor, 90 William Street, East Sydney, NSW 2000. Tel. (02) 357-2277.

Travel Centres

The Travel Centre of New South Wales (operated by Tourism Commission), Cnr Pitt and Spring streets, Sydney, NSW 2000. Tel. (02) 231-4444.

Tourist Information Service, Arrivals Level, Sydney International Airport, Mascot, NSW 2020. Tel. (02) 669-5111.

Canberra Tourist Bureau (Australian Capital Territory, ACT), 64 Castlereagh Street, Sydney, NSW 2000. Tel. (02) 233-3666.

Victour (Victorian Tourism Commission), 192 Pitt Street, Sydney, NSW 2000. Tel. (02) 233-5499.

Tasbureau (Tasmanian Tourism Commission), 129 King Street, Sydney, NSW 2000. Tel. (02) 233-2500.

South Australian Government Travel Centre, 143 King Street, Sydney, NSW 2000. Tel. (02) 323-8388.

Western Australian Tourist Centre, 92 Pitt Street, Sydney, NSW 2000. Tel. (02) 233-4379.

Queensland Government Travel Centre, 75 Castlereagh Street, Sydney, NSW 2000. Tel. (02) 232-1788.

Northern Territory Tourist Bureau, 89 King Street, Sydney, NSW 2000. Tel. (02) 235-2822.

Tours
Captain Cook (Harbour) Cruises, 106 Jetty, Circular Quay, Sydney, NSW 2131. Tel. (02) 27-4548.

Vagabond Cruises, 221 Clissold Street, Ashfield, NSW 2131. Tel. (02) 797-9666.

Thomas Cook (tours, plus agent for airship tours over city), 44 Market Street, Sydney, NSW 2000. Tel. (02) 234-4000.

The Tour Company, 168 Walker Street, North Sydney, NSW 2060. Tel. (02) 957-2700.

I.D. Tours, South Pacific, 30 Atchison Street, St Leonards, NSW 2065. Tel. (02) 965-4343.

ATS Pacific, 3–40 Miller Street, North Sydney, NSW 2060. Tel. (02) 957-3811.

Airlines
Australian Airlines, Cnr Hunter and Phillip streets, Chifley Square, Sydney, NSW 2000. Tel. (02) 669-9555.

Ansett Airlines, Cnr Oxford Square and Riley Street, Sydney, NSW 2000. Tel. (02) 268-1111.

East-West Airlines, 54 Carrington Street, Sydney, NSW 2000. Tel. (02) 268-1166.

Kendall Airlines, 43 Thompson Street, Wagga Wagga, NSW 2650. Tel. (069) 21-5011.

Eastern Australian Airlines, Tamworth Airport, Tamworth, NSW 2340. (P.O. Box 49, Westdale, NSW 2340.) Tel. (067) 67-7105.

Rebel Air (Charter). Tel. (02) 69-5018.

Rail

State Rail Authority of New South Wales, Passenger Sales, 509 Pitt Street, Sydney, NSW 2000. Tel. (02) 212-6314.

Bus

Urban Transport Authority of New South Wales, 1–31 York Street, Sydney, NSW 2000. Tel. (02) 29-6350.

Sydney Explorer, 11–31 York Street, Sydney, NSW 2000. Tel. (02) 224-4780.

Ansett Pioneer, Cnr Oxford and Riley streets, Sydney, NSW 2000. Tel. (02) 286-8666.

Deluxe Coachlines, Cnr Castlereagh and Hay streets, Sydney, NSW 2000. Tel. (02) 212-1599.

Clipper Tours, Alma Road, North Ryde, NSW 2113. Tel. (02) 888-3144.

Australian Capital Territory

Hotels

Hyatt Hotel Canberra, Commonwealth Avenue, Yarralumla, ACT 2600. Tel. (062) 70-1234.

The Capital Parkroyal, 1 Binarra Street, Civic, ACT 2600. Tel. (062) 47-8999.

The Pavilion Hotel, Cnr Canberra Avenue and National Circuit, Forrest, ACT 2603. Tel. (062) 95-3144.

The Diplomat International, Cnr Canberra Avenue and Hely Street, Griffith, ACT 2603. Tel. (062) 95-2277.

Canberra International Hotel, 242 Northbourne Avenue, Dickson, ACT 2602. Tel. (062) 47-6966.

Restaurants

Hill Station Restaurant, Shepherd Street, Hume, ACT 2602. Tel. (062) 60-1393.

The Oak Room, Hyatt Hotel Canberra, Commonwealth Avenue, Yarralumla, ACT 2600. Tel. (062) 73-1808.

Jean Pierre Carousel, Red Hill Lookout, Red Hill, ACT 2603. Tel. (062) 73-1818.

City of Canberra Cruising Restaurant (on Lake Burley-Griffin), Acton Ferry Terminal, Acton Park, Acton, ACT 2601. Tel. (062) 95-3544.

Travel Centres

Canberra Tourist Bureau, Jolimont Centre, Northbourne Avenue, Canberra City, ACT 2600. Tel. (062) 45-6464.

Canberra Visitors Information (on edge of the city), Northbourne Avenue, Dickson, ACT 2602. Tel. (062) 45-6450.

Victour (Victorian Tourism Commission), Jolimont Centre, Northbourne Avenue, Canberra City, ACT 2600. Tel. (062) 47-6355.

Tasbureau (Tasmanian Tourism Commission), 5 Canberra Savings Centre, City Walk, Canberra, ACT 2600. Tel. (062) 47-0070.

Queensland Government Travel Centre, 25 Garema Place, Canberra, ACT 2600. Tel. (062) 48-8411.

Northern Territory Tourist Bureau, 35 Ainslie Avenue, Canberra City, ACT 2600. Tel. (062) 57-1177.

Tours
Murrays Australia, P.O. Box 60, Red Hill, ACT 2603. Tel. (062) 95-3677.

Canberra City Scenic Tours. Tel. (062) 57-5375.

Airlines
Australian Airlines, Cnr Northbourne Avenue and Alinga Street, Canberra, ACT 2600. Tel. (062) 46-1811.

Ansett Airlines, 4 Mort Street, Canberra, ACT 2600. Tel. (062) 45-1111.

East-West Airlines, Shop 3, Cinema Centre, Bunda Street, Canberra, ACT 2600. Tel. (062) 45-6511, or 57-2411.

Rail
State Rail Authority of New South Wales, Cnr Wentworth and Kingston avenues, Kingston, ACT 2602. Tel. (062) 390-111.

Bus
ACTION (public bus, including tours). Tel. (062) 51-6566, or 46-2170.

Victoria

Hotels
Hyatt-on-Collins, 123 Collins Street, Melbourne, Vic. 3000. Tel. (03) 657-1234.

The Regent Melbourne, 25 Collins Street, Melbourne, Vic. 3000. Tel. (03) 653-0000.

Menzies at Rialto, 495 Collins Street, Melbourne, Vic. 3000. Tel. (03) 620-9111.

The Windsor, 103 Spring Street, Melbourne, Vic. 3000. Tel. (03) 653-1234.

Hotel Como, 630 Chapel Street, South Yarra, Vic. 3141. Tel. (03) 824-0400.

Restaurants

Jean Jaques By the Sea, 40 Jacka Boulevard, St Kilda, Vic. 3182. Tel. (03) 534-8221.

La Madraque, 171 Buckhurst Street, South Melbourne, Vic. 3205. Tel. (03) 699-9627.

Last Aussie Fish Caf, 256 Park Street, South Melbourne, Vic. 3205. Tel. (03) 699-1942.

Masani's Restaurant, 313–5 Drummond Street, Carlton, Vic. 3053. Tel. (03) 347-5610.

Travel Centres

Victour, 230 Collins Street, Melbourne, Vic. 3000. Tel. (03) 619-9444.

Travel Centre of New South Wales, 353 Little Collins Street, Melbourne, Vic. 3000. Tel. (03) 67-7461.

Canberra Tourist Bureau, 247 Collins Street, Melbourne, Vic. 3000. Tel. (03) 654-5088.

Tasbureau (Tasmanian Tourism Commission), 256 Collins Street, Melbourne, Vic. 3000. Tel. (03) 653-7999.

South Australian Government Travel Centre, 25 Elizabeth Street, Melbourne, Vic. 3000. Tel. (03) 614-6522.

Western Australian Tourist Centre, 35 Elizabeth Street, Melbourne, Vic. 3000. Tel. (03) 614-6833.

Queensland Government Travel Centre, 257 Collins Street, Melbourne, Vic. 3000. Tel. (03) 654-3866.

Northern Territory Tourist Bureau, 415 Bourke Street, Melbourne, Vic. 3000. Tel. (03) 67-6948.

Tours

AAT Kings, 181 Flinders Street, Melbourne, Vic. 3000. Tel. (03) 666-3363.

Ansett Pioneer, 465 Swanston Street, Melbourne, Vic. 3000. Tel. (03) 668-2422.

Australian Pacific, 181 Flinders Street, Melbourne, Vic. 3000. Tel. (03) 63-1511.

Melbourne Cruises (on Port Phillip Bay and Yarra River). Tel. (03) 63-2054.

Williamstown Bay and River Cruises. Tel. (03) 397-2255.

Airlines

Australian Airlines, 441 St Kilda Road, Melbourne, Vic. 3004. Tel. (03) 829-2211.

Ansett Airlines, 489 Swanston Street, Melbourne, Vic. 3000. Tel. (03) 668-2222.

East-West Airlines, 2nd Floor, 230 Collins Street, Melbourne, Vic. 3000. Tel. (03) 650-4726.

Kendell Airlines (intrastate flights), 431 Little Collins Street, Melbourne, Vic. 3000. Tel. (03) 67-2677.

Sunstate Airlines (intrastate flights). Tel. (03) 665-3333.

Rail
V/Line (public trains, including bus-rail tours). Tel. (03) 619-1500.

Metropolitan Transport Authority (city trains, buses and trams). Tel. (03) 617-0900.

Bus
Contact Metropolitan Transport Authority (see above).

Tasmania

Hotels
Sheraton Hobart, 1 Davey Street, Hobart, Tas. 7000. Tel. (002) 35-4355.

Wrest Point Federal Hotel Casino, 410 Sandy Bay Road, Hobart, Tas. 7000. Tel. (002) 25-0112.

Innkeepers Lenna of Hobart, 29 Runnymede Street, Hobart, Tas. 7000. Tel. (002) 23-2911.

Innkeepers Penny Royal Watermill, 145 Patterson Street, Launceston, Tas. 7250. Tel. (003) 31-6699.

Launceston Federal Country Club Hotel Casino, Country Club Avenue, Prospect Vale, Tas. 7250. Tel. (003) 44-8855.

Restaurants
Prospect House, Main Road, Richmond, Tas. 7025. Tel. (002) 62-2207.

Mures Upperdeck Restaurant, Victoria Dock, Hobart, Tas. 7000. Tel. (002) 31-1999.

Dear Friends, 8 Brooke Street, Hobart, Tas. 7000. Tel. (002) 23-2646.

Russel's Restaurant, 3 Russel Street, Evandale, Tas. 7256. Tel. (003) 91-8622.

Shrimps Restaurant, 72 George Street, Launceston, Tas. 7250. Tel. (003) 34-0584.

Travel Centres

Tasmania Travel Centre, 80 Elizabeth Street, Hobart, Tas. 7000. Tel. (002) 30-0211.

Victour (Victorian Tourism Commission), Trafalgar Centre, 126 Collins Street, Hobart, Tas. 7000. Tel. (002) 31-0499.

Northern Territory Tourist Bureau, 93 Liverpool Street, Hobart, Tas. 7000. Tel. (002) 34-4199.

Tours

The Cruise Company Ltd (Harbour and Derwent River cruises), Brooke Street Pier, Franklin Wharf, Hobart, Tas. 7000. Tel. (002) 34-9294, or 34-4032.

Par Avion (aerial tours of wilderness areas), Cambridge Airport, Hobart. (P.O. Box 100, Lindisfarne, Tas. 7015.) Tel. (002) 48-5117.

Airlines

Ansett Airlines, 178 Liverpool Street, Hobart, Tas. 7000. Tel. (002) 38-1111.

East-West Airlines, 138 Collins Street, Hobart, Tas. 7000. Tel. (002) 38-0200.

Airlines of Tasmania (intrastate flights), Hobart Airport. Tel. (002) 48-5030.

South Australia

Hotels

Hyatt Regency Adelaide, North Terrace, Adelaide, SA 5000. Tel. (08) 231-1234.

The Hilton International Adelaide, 233 Victoria Square, Adelaide, SA 5000. Tel. (08) 217-0711.

The Eden, 65 Hindley Street, Adelaide, SA 5000. Tel. (08) 239-0855.

The Terrace Adelaide, 150 North Terrace, Adelaide, SA 5000. Tel. (08) 217-7552.

Hotel Adelaide, 62 Brougham Place, North Adelaide, SA 5006. Tel. (08) 267-3444.

Restaurants

Mistress Augustines, 145 O'Connell Street, North Adelaide, SA 5006. Tel. (08) 267-4479.

Jolleys Boathouse, Jolleys Lane, Adelaide, SA 5000. Tel. (08) 223-2891.

Henry Ayers House Restaurant, 288 North Terrace, Adelaide, SA 5000. Tel. (08) 224-0666.

Duthys, 19 Duthys Street, Malvern, SA 5061. Tel. (08) 272-0465.

Mount Lofty House, 74 Summit Road, Adelaide Hills, Crafers, SA 5152. Tel. (08) 339-6777.

Travel Centres

Tourism South Australia (Head Office), 18 King William Street, Adelaide, SA 5000. Tel. (08) 212-1644.

South Australian Government Travel Centre, 18 King William Street, Adelaide, SA 5000. Tel. (08) 212-1644.

Travel Centre of New South Wales, 7th Floor, Australian Airlines Building, 144 North Terrace, Adelaide, SA 5000. Tel. (08) 51-3167.

Victour (Victorian Tourism Commission), 16 Grenfell Street, Adelaide, SA 5000. Tel. (08) 231-4129.

Tasbureau (Tasmanian Tourism Commission), 32 King William Street, Adelaide, SA 5000. Tel. (08) 212-7411.

Western Australian Tourist Centre, Cnr Grenfell and King William streets, Adelaide, SA 5000. Tel. (08) 212-1344.

Queensland Government Travel Centre, 10 Grenfell Street, Adelaide, SA 5000. Tel. (08) 212-2399.

Northern Territory Tourist Bureau, 9 Hindley Street, Adelaide, SA 5000. Tel. (08) 212-1133.

Tours

Adelaide Sightseeing, 101 Franklin Street, Adelaide, SA 5000. Tel. (08) 231-4144.

Premier Roadlines, 111 Franklin Street, Adelaide, SA 5000. Tel. (08) 217-0777.

Beyond Tours (for Outback safaris), Scout Outdoor Centre, 192 Rundle Street, Adelaide, SA 5000. Tel. (08) 223-4455.

Augusta Airways (for aerial tours), P.O. Box 1756, Port Augusta, SA 5700. Tel. (086) 42-3100.

Airlines

Australian Airlines, 144 North Terrace, Adelaide, SA 5000. Tel. (08) 216-1911.

Ansett Airlines, 142 North Terrace, Adelaide, SA 5000. Tel. (08) 233-3322.

Airlines of South Australia (intrastate flights). Tel. (08) 233-3322.

Rail and Bus

State Transport Authority, 136 North Terrace, Adelaide, SA 5000. Tel. (08) 210-1000.

Western Australia

Hotels

The Sheraton Perth Hotel, 207 Adelaide Terrace, Perth, WA 6000. Tel. (09) 325-0501.

The Hyatt Regency, 99 Adelaide Terrace, Perth, WA 6000. Tel. (09) 322-0121.

Burswood Island Resort and Casino, Great Eastern Highway, Victoria Park, WA 6100. Tel. (09) 362-7777.

Parmelia Hilton Hotel, Mill Street, Perth, WA 6000. Tel. (09) 322-3622.

Observation City Resort Hotel, The Esplanade, Scarborough, WA 6019. Tel. (09) 245-1000.

The Esplanade Plaza Hotel, Cnr Marine Terrace and Essex Street, Fremantle, WA 6160. Tel. (09) 430-4000.

Restaurants

San Lorenzo, 23 Victoria Avenue, Claremont, WA 6010. Tel. (09) 384-0870.

Tenelli's, Shop 24, Orchard Village, Perth, WA 6000. Tel. (09) 321-3068.

Pierre's Garden Restaurant, 8 Outran Street, West Perth, WA 6005. Tel. (09) 32-7648.

Prideau's, 176 Stirling Highway, Claremont, WA 6010. Tel. (09) 386-8933.

Bridges Seafood and Garden Restaurant, 22 Tydeman Road, North Fremantle, WA 6159. Tel. (09) 430-4433.

Travel Centres

Western Australian Tourism Commission, 11th Floor, St George's Terrace, Perth, WA 6000. Tel. (09) 220-1700.

Western Australia Tourist Centre, 772 Hay Street, Perth, WA 6000. Tel. (09) 322-2999.

Victour (Victorian Tourism Commission), 56 William Street, Perth, WA 6000. Tel. (09) 481-1484.

Tasbureau (Tasmanian Tourism Commission), 100 William Street, Perth, WA 6000. Tel. (09) 321-2633.

Queensland Government Travel Centre, 55 St George's Terrace, Perth, WA 6000. Tel. (09) 325-1600.

Northern Territory Tourist Bureau, 62 St George's Terrace, Perth, WA 6000. Tel. (09) 322-4255.

Tours

Boat Torque Cruises, Pier 4, Barrack Street Jetty, Perth, WA 6000. Tel. (09) 325-6033.

Feature Tours, 1 Cambridge Street, Leederville, WA 6007. Tel. (09) 381-4822.

Golden Swan Cruises, No. 2 Jetty, Barrack Street, Perth, WA 6000. Tel. (09) 325-9916.

Airlines

Australian Airlines, 55 St George's Terrace, Perth, WA 6000. Tel. (09) 323-8444.

Ansett Airlines, Cnr St George's Terrace and Irwin Street, Perth, WA 6000. Tel. (09) 323-1191.

Ansett WA (for intrastate flights). Tel. (09) 323-1191.

Skywest Airlines (for intrastate flights). Tel. (09) 478-9898.

Rail

Westrail Travel Centre, Cityrail Travel Centre, Wellington Street, Perth, WA 6000. Tel. (09) 326-2159.

Bus

Deluxe Coachlines, 762 Hay Street, Perth, WA 6000. Tel. (09) 322-7877.

Bus Australia, 77 Belmont Avenue, Belmont, WA 6104. Tel. (09) 478-3388.

Queensland

Hotels

Sheraton Brisbane Hotel and Towers, 249 Turbot Street, Brisbane, Qld 4000. Tel. (07) 835-3535.

Hilton International Brisbane, 190 Elizabeth Street, Brisbane, Qld 4000. Tel. (07) 231-3131.

Mayfair Crest International, King George Square, Brisbane, Qld 4000. Tel. (07) 229-9111.

Brisbane City Travelodge, Roma Street, Brisbane, Qld 4000. Tel. (07) 238-2222.

Restaurants

Roseville Restaurant, 56 Chester Street, Newstead, Qld 4006. Tel. (07) 358-1377.

Victoras, The Hilton International Brisbane, 190 Elizabeth Street, Brisbane, Qld 4000. Tel. (07) 231-3131.

Michaels at the Riverside Centre, 123 Eagle Street, Riverside Centre, Brisbane, Qld 4000. Tel. (07) 832-5522.

Fountain Room, The Cultural Centre, Stanley Street, Brisbane, Qld 4101. Tel. (07) 840-7111.

Travel Centres

Queensland Tourist and Travel Corporation, Level 36, Riverside Centre, 123 Eagle Street, Brisbane, Qld 4000. Tel. (07) 833-5400.

The Queensland Travel Centre, 196 Adelaide Street, Brisbane, Qld 4000. Tel. (07) 833-5255.

Travel Centre of New South Wales, Cnr Queen and Edward streets, Brisbane, Qld 4000. Tel. (07) 229-8833.

Victour (Victorian Tourism Commission), 221 Queen Street, Brisbane, Qld 4000. Tel. (07) 221-4300.

Tasbureau (Tasmanian Tourism Commission), 217 Queen Street, Brisbane, Qld 4000. Tel. (07) 221-2744.

Western Australian Tourist Centre, 243 Edward Street, Brisbane, Qld 4000. Tel. (07) 229-5794.

Northern Territory Tourist Bureau, 260 George Street, Brisbane, Qld 4000. Tel. (07) 229-5799.

Tours

Adai Cruises (river and Moreton Bay), BP Marina, Kingsford Smith Drive, Breakfast Creek, Qld 4446. Tel. (07) 262-6978.

Tag-A-Long Tours (four-wheel-drive tours to Moreton Bay), 139 Connaught Street, Sandgate, Qld 4017. Tel. (07) 269-0050.

Helijet (helicopter trips over Great Barrier Reef). Tel. (079) 46-9144 (Hamilton Island), or (070) 53-7366 (Cairns).

Quicksilver Connections (Great Barrier Reef cruises), Cairns Tour Service, 87 Lake Street, Cairns, Qld 4870. Tel. (070) 51-8311, or 98-5373.

Airlines

Australian Airlines, 247 Adelaide Street, Brisbane, Qld 4000. Tel. (07) 260-3311.

Ansett Airlines, Cnr Queen and George streets, Brisbane, Qld 4000. Tel. (07) 854-2222.

Rail
State Rail, 305 Edward Street, Brisbane, Qld 4001. Tel. (07) 235-2222.

Bus
City Council Bus Information, City Plaza Building, 69 Ann Street, Brisbane, Qld 4000. Tel. (07) 225-4444.

Greyhound Coaches, Roma Street, Brisbane Transit Centre, Brisbane, Qld 4000. Tel. (07) 844-3300.

Northern Territory
Hotels
The Beaufort Hotel, Esplanade, Darwin, NT 5790. Tel. (089) 82-9911.

Diamond Beach Hotel Casino, Gilruth Avenue, Darwin, NT 5790. Tel. (089) 46-2666.

Sheraton Darwin Hotel, 32 Mitchell Street, Darwin, NT 5790. Tel. (089) 82000.

Darwin Travelodge, 122 The Esplanade, Darwin, NT 5790. Tel. (089) 81-5388.

Sheraton Alice Springs, Barrett Drive, Alice Springs, NT 5750. Tel. (089) 52-8000.

Four Season Alice Springs, Stephens Road, Alice Springs, NT 5750. Tel. (089) 52-5066.

Lasseters Hotel Casino, Barrett Drive, Alice Springs, NT 5750. Tel. (089) 52-5066.

Travel Centres
Northern Territory Government Tourist Bureau, 31 Smith Street Mall, Darwin, NT 5790. Tel. (089) 81-6611.

Northern Territory Government Tourist Bureau, 51 Todd Street, Alice Springs, NT 5750. Tel. (089) 52-1299.

Tours
Australian Frontier Holidays, Cnr Daly and Mitchell streets, Darwin, NT 5790. Tel. (089) 81-5144.

AAT Kings Tours, 74 Todd Street, Alice Springs, NT 5751. Tel. (089) 52-1700.

Australian Pacific Tours, P.O. Box 3671, Alice Springs, NT 5751. Tel. (089) 52-6922.

Ayers Rock Touring Company, P.O. Box 142, Yulara, NT 5751. Tel. (089) 65-2066.

Aussie Balloons, P.O. Box 2055, Alice Springs, NT 5752. Tel. (089) 53-0544.

Airlines
Australian Airlines, 16 Bennett Street, Darwin, NT 5790. Tel. (089) 82-3311.
Ansett Airlines, Smith Street Mall, Casuarina Shopping Centre, Darwin, NT 5790. Tel. (089) 80-3333.
Ansett NT, 46 Smith Street Mall, Darwin, NT 5790. Tel. (089) 80-3333.
Air North, P.O. Box 381333, Winneville, NT 5789. Tel. (089) 81-7188.

Addresses and telephone numbers sometimes change. The author welcomes corrections and suggestions from guidebook users; please write to The Guidebook Company, 20 Hollywood Road, Hong Kong.

Recommended Reading

Because Australia is relatively less well known than other tourist destinations, it is worth taking the time to read up on the place before you arrive. But because of the difficulty in obtaining books on Australia overseas, an early visit to any large Australian book store will open up a wealth of reading matter, such as detailed histories, novels and even poetry. For those looking for readable souvenirs, there is a tremendous variety of large 'coffee-table books' on sale as well. (However, unless you want to lug them around the country, they are best purchased just prior to departure.) In this genre, the popular *A Day in the Life of Australia*, with contributions from over 150 overseas photographers, is widely available overseas.

For a dose of history, *A Short History of Australia* (Mentor, NAL Penguin, 1987) by Manning Clark, the country's most respected historian, investigates the nation's origins up to the present day. The best-selling *The Fatal Shore* (Knopf and Collins Harvill, 1987) by Australian-born Robert Hughes, takes a detailed look at the country's convict history up until the end of transportation in 1868. *Australia Since the Coming of Man* (Lansdowne Press, 1982), by Russel Ward, is a well-illustrated and informative volume with a self-admitted bias towards Australia's downtrodden classes.

Ross Terrill's *The Australians* (Simon & Shuster, 1987) is a personal voyage of discovery by a long-time expatriate academic from the United States who returns to his native land. He looks at Australia from a unique perspective.

While perhaps not as well known as his other books, Bruce Chatwin's *The Songlines* (Jonathan Cape, 1987) provides a fresh and exciting insight into the ancient culture of Australia's Aborigines. Chatwin uses the rich nomadic traditions of the Aborigines to take the reader on a personal voyage of psychic discovery. It is a rich and haunting book that lingers in the mind long after one has put it down.

Australia has produced many excellent modern novelists in recent years, and many of their works provide an insight into the country and its culture. Peter Carey is perhaps the best known outside Australia with his *Oscar and Lucinda* winning the 1989 Booker Prize in Britain. (His earlier works include *Illywacker* and *Bliss*.) Also worth reading is C.J. Koch's *The Doubleman*, about growing up in Tasmania in the 1950s.

Finally, keep an eye out for television documentaries on Australia. The best of recent years was the *Nature of Australia* series jointly produced by the BBC and the Australian Broadcasting Corporation in 1988.

Index